Sou Baroque Art

A Study of
Painting, Architecture and Music
in Italy and Spain of the
17th & 18th Centuries

By
Sacheverell Sitwell

New York
Alfred A. Knopf
mdccccxxiv

Printed in Great Britain
by The Riverside Press Limited
Edinburgh

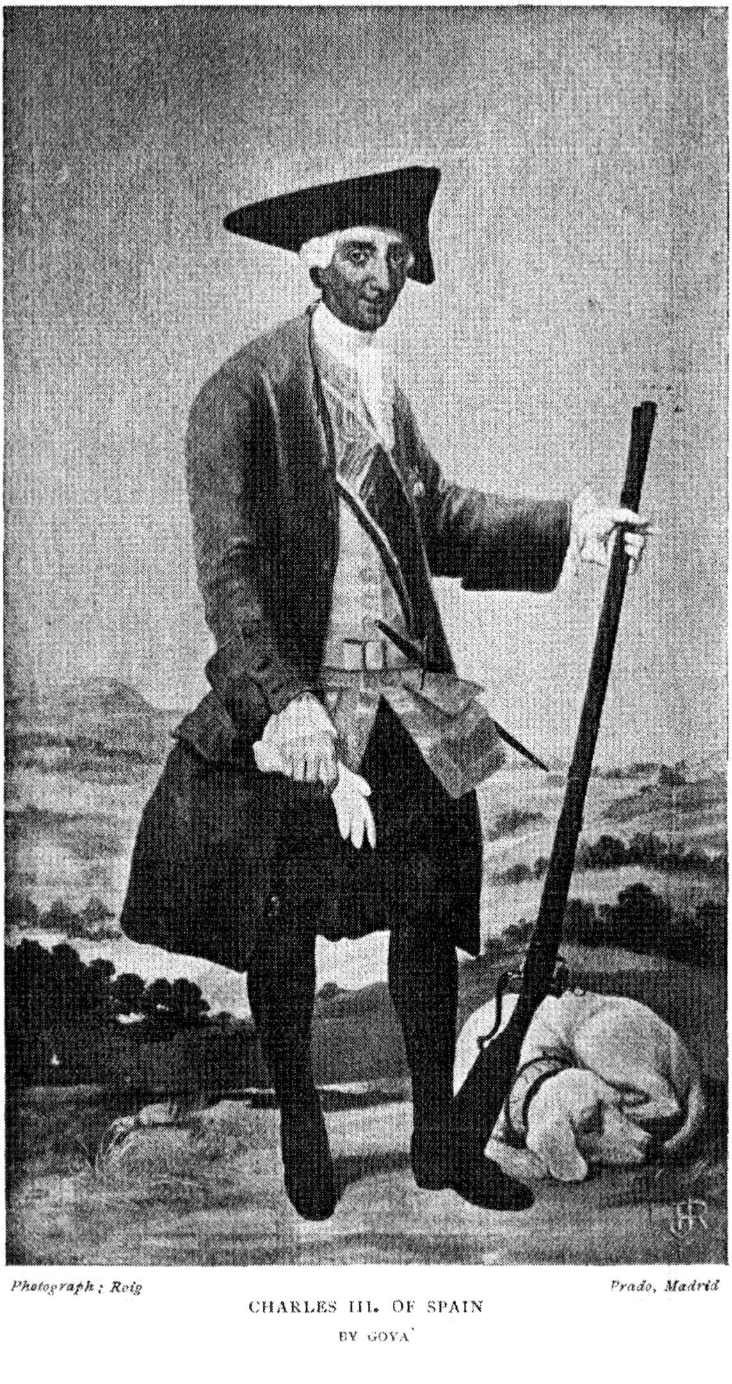

Photograph: Roig *Prado, Madrid*

CHARLES III. OF SPAIN

BY GOYA

Contents

opportunity of gratefully acknowledging the debt I owe to Mr Baxter.

I have incurred other obligations only less profound towards Mr Cunninghame Graham, Mr W. H. Koebel, and Mr Henry Baerlein, whose respective works I cite in my bibliography. My thanks are also due to Messrs Alinari of Florence, and to the Delphin Verlag of Munich, the Ernst Wasmuth Verlag of Berlin, and the Paul Neff Verlag of Esslingen for permission to reproduce various of the illustrations, and my thanks are particularised below each Plate. It is to my profound regret that it has been impossible to reproduce photographs of Mexican buildings, but interested persons may find no lack of these in the work of Mr Sylvester Baxter already mentioned, and in F. Dies Barroso's *El Arte en la Nueva España*, Campania de Artes Graficas, Mexico, 1922.

In this final paragraph I want to take the last opportunity that offers to defend my subject. Let no reader imagine that because this book deals with a particular period and school, the writer prefers the works of this date to those of any other. So far is this from being the case that a book on Venetian sixteenth-century art, that culmination of the civilisation of Europe, would have been the lightest labour to his enthusiasm. But such a work could hardly find a place, so huge is the plethora of facts, and so fierce and dogmatic are the critics. Thus the subject eventually chosen, concerning these painters and architects once famous and now considered obsolete, gave a free rein to the search into forgotten volumes through which it was undertaken. I know that the subjects of my choice are arraigned, in the earnest tones of the learned, because they possessed an entirely scenic conception of life, but the camera should have taught us by now how elusive a quarry is realism. Life, in its human aspect, is very ugly, and has always been so, it being the duty of Art to improve and select, transmuting for our own eyes that which we know to have been sordid into what we can be persuaded was beautiful. Let not our generation, then, who are painfully learning to distil once more these forgotten vapours, blame their near ancestors for the density of their smoke-cloud — there are many things still with us which would be better hidden! Baroque art needs no defence now: the victory has been won a long time. But although Bernini and Borromini are given at the least their due of praise, there are many excellent painters and architects on whom a strong light has not yet been flashed. This, then, is my own apologia, and I need no longer explain and defend my choice of subject.

25th July 1923.

Part i

The Serenade at Caserta

Part i

The Serenade at Caserta

Shall call the winds thro' long arcades to roar,
Proud to catch cold at a Venetian door.

ALEXANDER POPE.

Six o'clock in the morning, and already the heat of Naples was such that it required confidence to believe in any hours of darkness. Most of the houses were still latticing the light with their barred shutters. They were skimming a soft music off the stillness, and as, one by one, the windows were thrown back, so that the shutters threw their shadow on the wall, the very strings of this fluttering music were visible, lying there as plain as anything for skilled fingers. Opposite the Church of San Domenico, in the middle of the square, there sprang forth a foaming, bubbling geyser, blowing out its lava like fine glass. With marble and tufa it suggested equally and simultaneously a fountain playing with molten malleable stone, and a very quivering temporary trestle. The one was leaping desperately against the sky, which had lowered a cloud as cymbal for the fountain to beat upon, and the other was manifestly a hasty affair, a platform to preach from, or a pulpit high above the surging crowd. Nearer view strengthened the truth of these two guesses, as the fountain threw higher at every step you approached, and now, from close by, the saint could be seen standing, bold and balanced on his perch. The rapid alternation of these two ideas, thrown swiftly from one shuttle of the mind to the other, melted smoothly into what seemed a sure explanation. With a satisfying shock I remembered, in Marco Polo, the fountain that played with force enough to balance a metal ball three feet above its brim. So here was St Dominic standing like a lodestar between the hot heavens and the noisy populace, his only support the thin shaking petals of water.

Leaving the square, with its palaces of the nobles that gave on to this lawn of light, thus atoning for the want of gardens and shady trees, a walk down a narrow dark street tunnelled its way into a further square. Here again rose another "guglia," this time a tribute to the Virgin and the work of that sculptor Fansaga who had invented the deathless rocket with still wings to support St Dominic and keep him ever before the public eye without so much as a flash of feathers. Chief ornament of this square was the new Jesuit Church, with its rather childish façade of diamond rustication challenging an expert climber like the ladder bars on a telegraph pole. On coming nearer, the diamond points arranged themselves in formations of triangles and quincunxes that altered with every pace, and were as interesting as a walk through an orchard, where you move continually down fresh avenues, and where each step down a new alley looses the parabolas that play and flash among the fruit trees.

The two side doors were open. Pushing upon the heavy leather curtain you felt the unexpected sensation of a sudden marooning, not on a lonely island, but as if a stronger hand dragged you on to the stage of a theatre and left you to fill this desert as best you could. Far ahead on the left was a bandstand draped with red brocade and loaded with music-stands. Looking to each side the walls seemed alike hung with silk, for the marbles were so arranged with their strong patterns that brocade was revealed as their cheap and evident imitation. And marble was as much the truer as crystal to glass.

Up above an invisible hand suddenly pulled the curtain of a distant window with a creaking string that only slowly lay still again. Then the voice of a small moulting bird squeaked over a scaffolding, and before its words could be pieced together I had forgotten to listen to them. A dangerous affair of ropes and planks jutted out from over the great

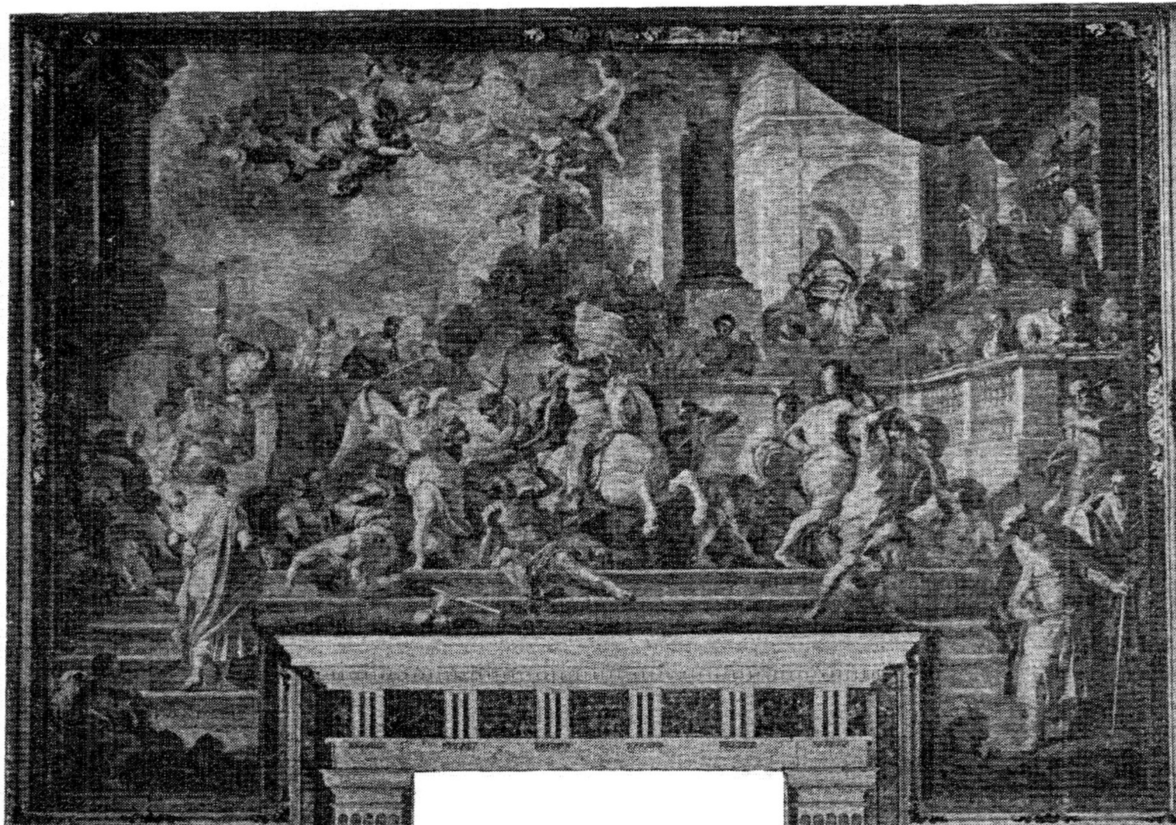

Photograph: Alinari

FRESCO BY SOLIMENA

IN CHURCH OF GESU NUOVA NAPLES

door and provided a spring-board for the fantastic leaping of the tiny man who had spoken. At the same moment a couple of old men were placing copies on the music-stands.

For a month past Solimena had been working on his fresco of the Expulsion of Heliodorus from the Temple. Some divinities had arrived on clouds, there was a mortal on horseback, and some Virtues half-way to earth. The temple was building, the roof nearly finished, and some cloud-children hovering as if at work on it. The marble pillars already exhibited their capitals nearly clear of the wrappers in which they had arrived from wind-swept quarries. Below this colonnade there strolled one or two turbaned Turks curiously looking between these pillars down out of the fresco. The church lay below them shimmering with light. It had the air of slowly sailing, like a ship, among those spaces that fire fell on to out of the clouds.

The artist was at work on a staircase, to lead from his fancy into the artificial world below. It lay with steep steps like the channel for a waterfall, and was built expressly for great surging crowds. Like a cascade it would collect all the colours of the spectrum, without the fabulous help of a rainbow. Intermittent music, that rose from falling rain to the thud of waves, now throbbed with a softer heart-beat in its intervals—a musician or two in broad-striped clothes played his guitar. The rush of the waterfall was even now cooling the hot marbles and sifting the stifled air in the church. This staircase, with its steep and breathless flights as yet unpeopled, seemed already to run with flashing water. The bare steps, empty and untrod, led past the temple up and above it to a fine balustrade. Over the heads of the people leaning on this a colonnade stretched back. Here, in imagination, you could see the source of these waters, and the splendid homes of the noisy crowd. The houses edged the brimming lake near enough to catch their echoes, and every open window was shouting into the little waves. A double town, and a prison-like harbour from which there was no escape, so close did the reflections fit, were in waiting for the sailors, who led a lazy life attended by the wind and sun.

It was a waterside such as Palladio would have built, such a Giudecca as he would have remodelled to ripple up the wave ladders in at the windows opposite. In deeper water there stood the colossal statues, the absence of which it is difficult to understand at Venice, where they made use of marble and water to every end but this. The tallest of them stood so high that clouds shaded them from the sun, better than trees, however drowsy. You could row past them, floating straight into the courtyard of a palace. When these walls rang as if hundreds of coins were thrown jangling on the floor, it was raining. There were striped posts to fix the boats to, fiercely coloured as if to accustom wild animals to this new haunt by pretending to belong to the sun-slashed woods in which they wandered. Sometimes a man and woman would be drawn here by unicorns ; sometimes a guest would alight from the air with one or two fire-like feathers still clinging to his clothes. There were fountains continually throwing like a feat of nature, and low music most of the night. Towards morning there were speeches, but no audience. Such long balconies led in front of the windows that by day children rolled their hoops along them. They were wide enough to dance on if a street musician passed beneath. So bright was the water and so glistening the windows that you knew you walked upon the rainbow, a far bolder bridge than any that joined island to island over the canals. To trundle a hoop along this was to play with the universe. There were other smaller balconies better built for talking, and high up. You could step straight out of a room on to one of these small anchored clouds. A balustrade is the inevitable accompaniment to a banquet, for each pilaster demands a cup or a dish to hold. Each corner pillar has a tub of fruit. From below, on the water, each fruit is a lamp for the balcony, or a star hiding behind a cloud.

You could see over low roofs, across the lagoons, to the mainland behind Venice. The summer palace of the Doges lay there. The canal on which it was approached glittered like a very far-off window caught by the sun. For the last furlong the canal led up a colonnade. Both wings of this were occupied by an equal population of statues. Their strange elongation only appeared transmuted to normal life when seen reflected. Withered, ascetic limbs in the water-version were smooth and young. The finest of them grew like flowers out of the water, but the wind never let them alone. Just when they burned with a clear flame against the sky, little ripples of water clouded them over again, and bent the reflection. After a dozen such experiences very deep-down marble steps appeared, rising broadly and slowly to the quayside. On these the forms were reflected climbing over, or lying upon shelves of snow. It was always a galley that passed along these waters. Had there been a boat drawn with a sail, this would have provided a cloud as a still background for these deities. With a wind strong enough to belly the sail, even the inside of a tent might be simulated. This should be pitched at the end of a heroic avenue, corded as a curtain against a shady tree. A plumed warrior crawls into it as if into a cave. Woods and orchards lie behind the house. There were barracks for the necessary shoals of boats, and stables for unusual animals sent as presents; but the frightful mountains far away to the north, with their ice as scorching as fire, brought one back to Vesuvius.

Why is it that this volcano, the indomitable point of every view, occurs to so small an extent in Neapolitan art? This nearer and more intimate Fujiyama is not iconified here as it is in Japan. No one of the gymnastic local artists has presented it seen perpetually like the inevitabilia of an icon. In Tokyo it looms horribly through every tree, between the meshes of every fishing-net, among the crests of waves, reflected in still pools of water, echoed on a dark cloud, or shadowed on the wall of a paper house. The artists of Naples and Tokyo, alike in many terrible facilities of their art, differ in this. Those of Naples are less willing to help themselves to the inevitable. They avoid, in this way, taking the lazzaroni and the grotesque and revolting freaks of slum life as background for their improvisations. Only in wax-work do the Neapolitans reveal the worst intensities of realism.

It is necessary to visit the Certosa of Bagheria to value this. All travellers who visit Palermo are snared into visiting Soluntum. The road traversed was perilous from brigandage as little as twenty years ago. Before half of the eight-mile journey is covered, the first indication of Bagheria appears on the right-hand side of the road. It is a small villa, high up, and approached by a disproportionate staircase. You climb from the road into a grotto, leave this grotto by the right or left, come into the open again, turn to the left or right, and meet once more on a platform over the grotto. From here the stairs lead straight in three great flights to the door of the villa—stopping twice for breath on two landings which seem to climb higher and higher from the sea as it is revealed to you more and more distantly. After a halt on the second landing you attempt the last flight and arrive in the house. There is nothing of interest inside. This, and the fact that on climbing down again and starting off in the motor the villa vanishes at once and for ever, may be symbolical.

Next come two villages, Ficarazzelli and Ficarazzi, of unending squalor bordering each side of this straight road. They might be villages in Central Africa. After two dreary miles of this, and a short breathing space in the country, comes the town of Bagheria. Here everywhere out of the low white houses rise arches and triumphant pavilions. Only last night the town must have been decorated for a festivity. There should be loud bands and flower-bombs, detonating as they touch the aim. Hundreds of lights glow in the air and from the roofs. From far off the town has climbed up one storey and hangs in the air. From the hillsides it appears anchored out at sea, and low down like a great barge escaped from a bridge of boats. From the deck of a ship it must look like a lot of swings and trembling platforms strung under trees. The swings move slowly, very gently, making the lights stutter a little. Then a soft wind turns the leaves, until the trees break into foam, just like the very slight waves to-night. But towards morning, as all the candles are guttering down in the lanterns, a damp breath of rain comes, and very soon last night's ornaments are spoilt. The hot midday sun then bakes them, half-dilapidated as they are, giving them permanence.

This is the impression Bagheria gives you. Half-way through the town, the road and the town itself turn sharply to the right. Here the decorations begin in earnest. On each side there are magnificent gate pillars rising out of nothing and leading nowhere. But the road climbs a little, and when it turns to the left again, many big villas can be seen farther on, a little way out of the town. A few more yards and you are out of Bagheria. An open space with the drives to three separate villas opens on the right. Suddenly bordering the road, facing this piazza, the wall falls back a little to the left and gives a breathing space. Beside the gate pillars, on separate pedestals, stand two statues—one of a Chinaman, and the other portraying a pierrot with more affinity to the vegetable than the human world. His head-dress is like the flower-sheaf of an arum lily, his ruff like a bundle of reed-flutes, and the rest of his body more of a flower-stalk than a human trunk and legs. He and his companion are markedly of a night-world, carved with the ragged and deep relief that looks best by starlight. This is the threshold of the wizard-world of Prince Palagonia.[1]

The circular court into which this gateway leads is like a native kraal. I suppose the gardeners and the keepers of the statues lived in these low houses looking on to the villa, with their roofs weighted down by these fantastic statues. The whole of the roof wall of this court is writhing with

[1] The traveller Swinburne, in 1779, says that Villa Palagonia was entered through a huge gate, on the plinth of which were fixed six colossal whitewashed statues of hussars or halberdiers to dispute the entrance of an avenue three hundred yards long—not of cypresses, elms or orange-trees, but of monsters. There are still signs of this to be seen at the back of the villa.

these monsters. They do not stand there to keep with their weight a roof above the peasants' heads during an earthquake or a fierce gale of wind, but their presence is an excuse for the hovel-building. It is the keepers who are in the cages. In many travel-books there are accounts of this villa, while one or two of them describe personally Prince Palagonia. They comment on his shuddering manner, as if ever in fear of hearing a dog bay, or something fall. It was the dislodgement of an ornament that he lived in fear of: like the Viceroy of Algarve in Beckford, he made his appearance "in grand pea-green and pink and silver gala, straddling and making wry faces as if some disagreeable accident had befallen him. He was, however, in a most gracious mood and received our eulogiums upon his relative, the new bishop, with much complacency." It is difficult to discover the secrets of his manias. Horns were another object of his collecting. He was anxious and willing to buy, for great sums of money, antlers of any rare animals. They hung in immense profusion in his villa. He must and would have every extant specimen of antler. Some of the walls seemed hung with dry snapping twigs, ready for firewood. The quantity of them drowned the fine aspect of these many-pointed spears given their ancestors, perhaps, long ago, as a protection against pterodactyls, and the huge winged and beaked air monsters. Perhaps Prince Palagonia feared some such steel-winged aggressor, for he is reported to have kept his wife in undue seclusion, and to have created the world of stucco and stone monsters to frighten her before childbirth. Many of them he caused to be copied from the fanciful Central Africans described by Diodorus Siculus. Almost a majority of the dwarfs, more to hypnotise and distract attention than to while away their own time, were playing on every variety of musical instrument. Besides these two, Prince Palagonia had a third formalised, and most objectively crystallised, preference — for mirrors. With music to disarm and mesmerise, and horns to press against beating wings to spoil their heroic clanging, he liked to case the walls with mirror, that no expression and no gesture could escape unobserved. The ball-room is roofed and walled with mirror. The head gardener, once butler in the last days of the family ownership, will tell you that fifty couples can dance there and see themselves again in the glass roof. The ceiling is coffered with great slabs of glass, making so many pools and lakes to use as mirrors in dark and tangled woods. But you cannot lie at the edge and look in at yourself, because the floor is like a whirlpool with dancing and movement. Out of the walls the Palagonia ancestors emerge from the waist, periwigged, in breastplates, wearing cravats, and brandishing swords or rolls of paper, adding fresh titles to the family name. These busts are of marble, but sadly marred by time, so that the features are hardly recognisable, although two centuries have not nearly passed since they were first put on the wall to gesticulate and watch their descendants. To members of the family these images, so voluble and chattering in their movement, were so many parrots taught to mock the voices of a hundred years ago, training thus the voices of a century later to the same intonation.

Besides the ball-room there are other apartments equally striking. Out of the ball-room leads the horseshoe-shaped dining-room, also adorned with mirrors, where once stood the curved dining-table adapted to the strange shape of the room. The walls were still ornamented with devices of china vases glued together, so as to give the appearance of very large and elaborately shaped Chinese porcelain. The furniture, chairs and settees, also inlaid with mirror, are, sad to relate, sold. On the farther side of the ball-room are a room with painted decoration in the Pompeian style, one or two bedrooms with Indian or Chinese papers, and a small square room hung with portraits of the Gravina Palagonia family, none of them, I think, previous to about 1660. Under each portrait is written in full the names and titles of the owner—Majordomo to His Most Christian Majesty Charles III. of Spain—thrice Grandee of Spain, etc., etc.; but all of them are irrevocably gone from damp, save only the portrait of the creator of this strange world who straddles and smirks cynically, just as you would imagine him.

The house is in many ways a fine piece of planning. It is remarkable how many big rooms are fitted into but a moderately sized house. The bedrooms are well assembled on one side of the big reception-rooms, I suppose for reasons of humanity and fear of ghosts. The outside staircase is elaborate, though fine in design. All the living rooms are on the first floor. The ground floor is occupied by stables and store-rooms, and by the inside court beneath the ball-room, while the whole ground floor is pierced by the passage leading to and from this court. Here again the ancestors of the family come out of the wall and talk to you.

But time, even in Bagheria, is limited, and we must drive on to Villa Valguarnera. This is one of the three villas opening from the piazza opposite the Palagonia—the centre one, to be exact. After a drive of some hundred yards you arrive in another of those circular courts like native kraals, so numerous in Bagheria. An old woman leads you past the house to the garden. The sea is down to the left, sweeping back to Palermo and Monte Pellegrino. Suddenly, on turning to the right, you see the garden in front of the house ending in a balustrade. Beyond it the sea appears again, having rounded the corner of the promontory in front of the town. It stretches away past Cefalu, thirty miles away into the distance. The very far mountains, rising like cliffs, have slight white clouds towards their base, almost as low as the fishing-boats. The wind that moves them so slowly must issue from caverns in the cliff side and blow them as if dancing to the music of her flutes. The classical proportion and colour of this view knock the breath from one's body. It is farther from these baroque contortions than another universe. Below the sweeping classical slopes, wind-swept, cropped close by herds, hoof-marked by centaurs, lies Cefalu, just such a fishing town as the Normans contrived to build everywhere between Whitby and Amalfi. One can see in imagination the Cathedral, with its head and body of Christ in mosaic in the apse of the church, filling the building from floor to ceiling with its superb and undreamable beauty. Such a goat-herd, turned to anchorite, might well inhabit the caves from which the wind blows forth.

Turning back again on this unrealisable paradise you see, to begin with, the belvedere of the Villa Valguarnera, like an artificial pinnacle on one of Nature's hills. Below are the Villas San Marco, Camastra and Butera. Their strangeness might tempt you to spend a whole day exploring their inanities. Here, first, was there mention of the Certosa of Bagheria, a piece of news which sounded too good to be true. Here must be the very monastery one had always known to exist—placing it in Italy, in Portugal, or in Mexico as the fancy moved one—photographed as near as humanly possible in the Churriguerresque sacristy of the Cartuja of Granada, or at Padula beyond and inland from Paestum. One renounced, therefore, the glories to be collected in Villas Valguarnera and Butera, and hurried off towards the Certosa. Arrived back in the piazza of the town, a large convent was pointed out. But this was not it. On entering the grounds, a number of nuns and their pupils fled to a garden at the back of the convent. At last one found oneself in a large walled enclosure, worked in by many men and boys, all of whom had heard of the Certosa, but knew not its whereabouts, except that it lay within these actual garden walls. It was very strange motoring up and down the only road of this garden, past its central well, expecting any moment to see the shell-like entrance to what should have been stranger than any water-world. At last a man appeared on the top of the outside staircase of a small house at one end of this walled garden, and by his fat movements betrayed signs of interest in our doings. After a lot of functioning like a semaphore, he could be interpreted as suggesting that the visitors should climb up into his house. There, sure enough, above the door at the top of the stairs was carved Certosa. The horrible waxwork world dawned from the very threshold. An evil-looking lay-brother stands in the hall, sweeping the corridor with a long brush. On each side of this passage there are small cells set out to illustrate the Carthusian life. In one of them the monks are at a table eating their supper of glass eggs and wax chickens. All the figures are portraits. The prior at the end of the table, with an empty and redundant profile, is Ferdinand of Bourbon; the monk nearest to him is the Prince of Butera, the chief noble of Sicily, a friend of the King and the creator of this monastery. Some of the diners are as if frozen in the act of conveying food to their mouths. Another villainous monkish servant stands rooted to the ground, as he waits to serve the eaters. It was a hot afternoon, and there were clear signs of perspiration on many foreheads and hands. Farther on there came the inevitable romance of this wooden life. Two figures in a small cell represented a monk and his former sweetheart who, on his entry to the convent, had disguised herself in male attire and sought refuge there also, in order to be near her lover, her identity remaining concealed till her death-bed. It was a relief to turn away from these nightmare creations and look at the prints after Giuseppe Velasquez, with which the walls were hung. Fastening the attention upon these one could creep out again, without interrupting the monks at their prayers or feasting. But at any moment the rostrum at the top of the stairs might become a pulpit for any of these automata, and his wheezing voice would follow, even to the garden gate.

This horrid scene haunted the mind for days after. Perhaps it is not necessary to come as far south as Bagheria for such sensations. The Cappella di San Severo, at Naples itself, can supply this. Many minds must have been disturbed by the sculpture there, as they should be by the mummies still shown in the sacristy of San Domenico near by. The sculpture in this Chapel of San Severo has a far Eastern deadliness of realism. Here is the famous piece of man fighting against vice, which shows a middle-aged and drab man flapping fish-like in a net in which he is hopelessly entangled. Near to it lies the statue of the Dead Christ covered with a transparent white marble shroud, and lying on a grey marble bed. Here, and at Bagheria, may the curious reap those sensations to be gathered by the on-lookers at executions. That it is art of the circumstances more than of the date can be seen by a visit to the Church of Monte Oliveto in Naples, where a pièta in terra-cotta, the work of the Modenese sculptor Mazzoni, may be seen. The principal figures are the likenesses of contemporary characters. Sannazaro is introduced as Joseph of Arimathea, King Alfonso II. as St John, and his son, Prince Ferdinand, as a young Roman soldier. The horrible Tussaud-like realism of Sannazaro's portrayal has the power of completely divesting his name of the warm and voluptuous colouring with which poetry has clothed his memory. All these are examples of the showman's art.

The travelling circus, like the showman, is Italian by invention. One town, Monte Cassino, still supplies the world with organ-grinders, but the Italian cities have relaxed their custom of contributing, turn by turn, a travelling artist to tour over Europe. Examples of this make a fine array of names from Torrigiani down to Tiepolo. But Naples came late into the ring, though it produced more than one celebrated pyrotechnician. For the predecessors of Luca Giordano there is little to be said in criticism. But as he is one of my heroes, and the spiritual parent of many more of them, I feel bound in honour to make mention of him.

There seems to have been a period in the seicento when the architecture of private houses was inquired into, dissected, and re-formulated. In England we notice it in the time of William and Mary. There was in particular an inquest on the bodies of staircases. It was decided that a staircase was, most certainly, of importance, but only momentarily so. You were impressed by a grand stair, but only while ascending it. Once on the landing all interest faded into the big reception-rooms at the top. For this reason the decorations of the stair must be important but evanescent. Walls and ceiling should be covered with a decoration that impressed, but repulsed the eye from too close an investigation. It is said that in many Italian palaces the reception-rooms were placed, of a purpose, as high as possible on a tiring stair, so as to weary the visitor, and for the time stop his speaking. With even closer insight, artists were selected to decorate the walls and ceiling of staircases whose work could never sufficiently attract attention to make the climber pause and investigate. It was of such an art that Verrio was the master. Antonio Verrio was a painter from Lecce, who studied his calling in Venice and in Naples, where he painted in the Gesu Vecchio. He tried his fortune in the south of France, and, according to Dominici, he turned Huguenot and was drowned there. Far from this being the case he had a career of enormous success in France and England for another fifty years. He worked at Windsor, Hampton Court, Chatsworth and Burleigh. For his frescoes at the last-named place alone Verrio received £18,000 beside his keep, and a carriage at his disposal. This vaporous Neapolitan art can be studied in England. The rattling of plates from Venetian banquets was audible as far as these islands. An arrival down the long pleached avenues was celebrated with Italian triumph. Virtues and celestial powers attended these functions like porters at great railway stations. The same task was allotted them; but they executed it more rapidly with the help of wings.

These pale reflections of triumph flickering in the long canals are but echoes of the stronger southern music. Moored to the landing-stage is the barge, yellow as if it had floated all day on the golden tide. Neptune at the prow has fallen asleep in the hot afternoon, and his beard and hair have been touched by high-flung flakes of foam. Cleopatra is led ashore by her general, who points the way with an air of possession, as if he ruled all the land as much as she smoothed and kept light the seas with her glittering barge. A page comes ashore carrying her crown on a cushion. When old enough he will grow into as fierce a warrior as Antony. Before his first breastplate is ready to buckle on, an eagle may carry him off into the clouds, sheathing his breast with her steel plumes. They will fly straight into the sun, and be lost to sight in the flaming mist. A black man holds back a greyhound, too ready to recognise his mistress. Up above shows the rigging. The ship is folding her wings away again, and the ends of ropes hang down, dangling among the spearheads of the soldiers. There is the standard-bearer of a legion—an Eastern attendant with a bag of gold and a glowing turban; and far away there are other turbaned heads, and a trumpet raised to the lips and shaped like an elephant's trunk.

It is still by daylight that the banquet is served. A negro hands Cleopatra the glass of wine in which she will dissolve the drop-like pearl she holds in her fingers. Antony is not looking at her. He is thinking how the whole day has been a climb up shallow and imperceptible stairs. Now the cool evening has come, and he finds himself safely on the terrace he has thought about all day. A fierce-moustached Oriental behind the queen contrasts with the garden term he stands against, and shows the multiple and varied Alexandrian life. To remind them of traditional Egypt a flashing white pyramid, as regular as a fountain, throws up underneath a portico on which are stationed musicians. There are some lutes with long necks that look like a halved melon. So sweet is their savour that they have been mounted on a spear or sword, that they may be handed to the thirsty who walk on terraces higher than the beds in which the melons lie. Then there are pipes and soothing violins. A splendid Cæsarean door frames and furnishes the banqueting scene. But on the far side of this door a narrow panel is painted with the buffet at the extreme end of the banqueting chamber. On this sideboard are great silver dishes piled up and ranged like plates of armour. A bearded cook, in almost sacerdotal white, hands a negro servant another flagon of wine, putting it on the silver salver, while the negro still looks back on the scene, and no doubt hears the measured classical music from the gallery.

It is difficult to give an impression in words of the miraculous skill with which Tiepolo handled these frescoes. There is a rippling prismatic effect, and the colour, never dazzling, by minute and detailed examination, is, in the mass, gorgeous beyond imagination. Nowhere is the drawing tricked or dispensed with. Effect is won by equal skill in drawing and painting. Especially is Tiepolo successful in his blues and whites. It is as if a whole world of snow had been brought by Cleopatra to temper the glaring Egyptian day for her warrior. Not that the snow is anywhere seen, but it is reflected everywhere. The marble walls and pillars are no longer broiling to the touch. The air is no longer too hot for the musicians to place their scaffolding and sudden cascades along its yielding surface. The sky, where visible, has lost its midday staring emptiness, and feels as if cooled here and there by fleecy clouds. Yet, at one word, if the heat grows too extreme just as the light is dying, she can make all the snows melt. It is the moment when she dips the pearl into the dissolving wine. At her word the springs lie low and silent, and the winds blow away the sailing clouds. Torches are brought, and then the torches from the gardens flicker across the sea bridge to her gleaming barge.

The water-world, as it is, lies just outside the doors and windows of this palace. A galley is tied fast to the quayside. After feasting in the gardens, the two lovers go back again to this trembling perch, at the mercy of high winds. A sudden gust will dip them into the curdling waves, just as a bird's nest on one bough is tossed by the wind into the green whirlpool on another branch. Other palaces, luckily, are too near for great waves to be born in the space between. Big trees cannot grow in narrow spaces. But other passing boats leave innumerable ripples and wakes like very light fluttering leaves on this stalk-shaped canal. Presently they will hoist sail and move out into the desolate sea on this white cloud. It will be very shallow there, and the reflections of the galley's lights will reach deeper than the waters in this wide lagoon. They will set a regular staircase out from the islands up to the cool deck. On these boards it is very smooth and quiet, like a terrace. There is only the sound of other feastings down on the low-lying islands, and very muffled whispers from the poop. Up there it is high and seems swift like a chariot; but to-night it is drawn by doves, not stallions, and the whispers are like fluttering wings.

Such is the Palazzo Labia of Venice and my mythical annexe to it. Its banqueting chamber shows the best that Venice could produce in its second Renaissance. Whilst Venice languished between these periods of productivity, painting flourished at Naples. It is impossible to discuss one centre without making mention of the other. After the great period was over in Venice, ending with the death of Tintoretto in 1594, painting drifted southwards, following the wandering footsteps of Caravaggio. From Rome it dropped to Naples, from Naples to Messina and Malta. In Venice, after the languorous Podovanino, there is nothing to interest us till the time of Fumiani, who frescoed the roof of St Pantaleone with such heavy and exuberant form. There were, of course, isolated painters of talent on the Venetian mainland, such as the Carmelite Fra Galgario, or Ghislandi, at Bergamo. But his work, and that of the Guercinesque students, Giuseppe Maria Crespi (il Spagnuolo of Bologna) and Piazzetta (of Venice), is too well known to students to write a detailed discussion, more especially as Piazzetta is now well represented in the National Gallery, and there is no lack of his drawings in the collections of amateurs. But while painting was (in Venice) in a few capable hands, in Naples, as I have said before, one of the greatest of all the Italian pyrotechnicians had flourished, and, on his decline, left a great host of brilliant and facile craftsmen in his wake. Luca Giordano is to be seen in every gallery of Europe from Hampton Court to the Hermitage. Is it not really true that he shares with Rubens, Rembrandt and Titian an almost universal diffusion of work? Is there a single European gallery where he is not represented? But putting in an appearance does not amount to being the greatest success at a party, and so I record his attendance, while remaining silent as to his competitive merits. He began young, did Luca Giordano! In the Church of S. Maria la Nuova in Naples, at the right of the high altar, under the organ loft, you may see two angels painted by him when eight years old. By the time he was twenty years of age Luca Giordano, from tremendous study, was the master of every style, and could counterfeit for you at a moment's notice Titian, Correggio, or any great painter of the cinquecento. In this connection one may mention his picture of *Christ before Pilate* in the Naples Museum as an example of his imitation of Albert Durer; *Justice disarmed by Love and Ignorance*, also in the museum, as an imitation of Spagnoletto; the two pictures in the Church of S. Teresa di Capodimonte in the style of Guido, and his picture of S. Michael in the Church of SS. Ascensione which he produced in the manner of Veronese. An anonymous biographer of Luca Giordano, under the heading of work done in 1681, records the dispatch of sixteen great canvases in the manners of Guido, Tintoretto, Veronese, and Spagnoletto to Charles II. of Spain at the Royal Convent of the Escurial. These imitative feats make it difficult to believe in the original talent of the artist, but every qualm can be quieted by visiting the huge saloon which he frescoed in the Riccardi Palace of Florence. As a piece of decoration this is little inferior to Tiepolo's masterpiece in Italy, the banqueting hall of the Clerici Palace in Milan. The fame of this protean artist burnt brighter and brighter every year, and he had the common reputation of not only excelling in merit all artists that had gone before, but of having surpassed their combined efforts in the number of pictures he had produced.

If any zenith to his reputation was possible, he found it a few years later, in 1691, when he was called by Charles II. to the Court of Spain, and set sail from Naples the following spring in a galley commanded by Don Antonio Gonzales. After improvising in the presence of Charles and his Court a picture in the style of Bassano, he was set to work in earnest on the great staircase of the Escurial. In about the space of seven months he had finished this huge piece of work, bringing it to a fine finish in a representation of various episodes in the battle of Saint Quentin, which he showed in a running frieze between the windows. His next order was to paint ten of the vaults in the roof of the Escurial church. This task, also, with the preparation of all the drawings and cartoons necessary to produce it, he accomplished in a very short time, and, indeed, these ten vaults of the church and the frescoes of the great staircase, together, occupied Luca Giordano for only two years. After this he was employed on a great number of works in oil and in fresco for the King's palaces in Madrid and for the convents and churches in that city. At the Palace of Buen Retiro he painted a casino with the foundation of the Order of the Golden Fleece, and at Toledo he frescoed the great sacristy of the Cathedral, his best work in Spain.[1] Then in the year 1700 Charles II. died, and Luca Giordano found his work interrupted, realised he was growing old himself and, with difficulty, obtained consent to return to his native city, where he was received as a hero by his fellow-citizens.

It is amusing to judge of his lightning effects where they may be contrasted with the exaggerated detail so beloved at this period. There is an occasion to do so at the Certosa di San Martino, overlooking Naples. The whole of this convent, now secularised and declared a National Museum, is unrivalled as a place to study the seicento art in Italy. Here is to be seen the work of every artist in the course of Southern painting, from the Cavaliere d'Arpino to Bonito, who died in 1789. But it is in the Treasury that the skill and effect of Luca Giordano can best be appreciated. The walls are cased with cupboards and presses of inlaid and painted wood—both executed with a terrible fidelity to fact, and with overpowering detail. It is the work of many years. Tradition says that two Carthusian monks spent twelve years of their

[1] Luca Giordano also executed nine excellent canvases for the Camarin of the far-distant monastery of Guadalupe in the wilds of Estremadura.

lives at this hard labour. There are landscapes cooled with rivers that run between rocky banks, overlooked by anchorites at the mouth of their caves. There are views of the piazzas of towns, which lie empty and quiet, waiting for the peasants to come to market. Below, on the lowest panels of the presses, are still-lives as formal and complicated as the Cubists'. They show piles of books and vases of flowers, while generally there is a guitar lying among them that Picasso might have left there. Above, on a small cupola, and on the wide roof of the room, is a great series of frescoes by Luca, which he began and completed in forty-eight hours in the year 1704, when he was seventy-two years of age. These frescoes are the last great work, and perhaps the masterpiece, of Luca Giordano—when he had returned from Spain loaded with wealth, but presumably too old to accomplish much more with his art. They are in good condition, with unimpaired colour, and as fresh as when newly painted. Though but the work of a few hours, in invention and subtlety they surpass and crown this meticulous labour beneath. The sacristy presses, like the inlaid choir-stalls of Italy, are ever very trying to the patience. In the Certosa di Pavia there are portentous and gaudily inlaid stalls after the designs of Borgognone, who sketched a saint in full colours to be inlaid above the head of each monk as he knelt at Mass. At Bergamo, in the Cappella Colleoni, there are outstanding examples of this laborious inlay in the shape of two landscape and figure panels by Fra Damiano, and work of the same kind is to be seen in the Ducal Palace at Urbino, where the Duke's study has marqueteries of weapons of war, musical instruments, and whole suits of armour, jangling and dangling together—the whole room a-clatter with strings and iron. It is reassuring, at Naples, to see this insect labour accompanied and surpassed by Luca Giordano's non-stop decoration. He has, on purpose, picked out the greens, which look so false and stained in the dyed wood, and painted his ceiling in this key of colour. The whole composition is cool and pleasantly undetailed. His use of green as setting for the figures is as if a delicate grass had sprouted up there in the two days Luca was at work. The action of the frescoes is in the open air, and as vague as at a garden-party.

No establishment, indeed, could be more suited to such an entertainment. The cloister garden and the cool long corridors seem expressly made for talking, singly or in groups. The traveller, Sir John Swinburne, who visited Naples in 1779, tells us that in his time the annual income of the convent, though reduced, reached the total of £130,000 sterling. After providing, amply, for their own comfort, this sum was devoted by the monks to the benefit of the hundreds of beggars who infest and crawl about the rich suburb of Vomero. Even this could not exhaust their supplies of money, and the balance was applied to the benefit of the female relations of the monks. Sir John Swinburne says it was rumoured the Royal family intended shortly to inquire into and appropriate the surplus income of the convent. Swinburne's remarks are significant. A few years later, in 1799, the social ideas of the monks got the better of their political common sense. When the French had entered Naples, and proclaimed the Parthenopean republic, the monks, out of the church wardrobe, prepared the red, yellow and blue flag which the French soldiers hoisted on the Castel Sant' Elmo near by. But this was not all. When General Championnet arrived, they celebrated his coming by inviting a party of both sexes to the monastery. That evening the Carthusians gave a supper to about forty persons, male and female, and afterwards a dance was held in the prior's apartments. A printed memorial of the occasion remarks that the monks, full of joy and admiration, seeing such pretty smiling women dancing among them, could not help rejoicing, more than the rest, at the coming of Liberty. A water-colour drawing which accompanies these remarks shows the prior's apartments, richly hung with pictures, and filled with patriots of both sexes, who dance, under the delighted eyes of the monks, to the strains of a small and energetic orchestra.

This tarantella was overheard by the Royal authorities. On their return to Naples, in 1800, they dispersed the brothers among other charterhouses, leaving only five to perform the religious duties. In 1804 they were permitted to return. But the Bourbons had helped their supporters largely to the monastic funds, and the income was now only 57,000 ducats instead of the 95,000 of former years. Their subsequent adventures, how they were turned out by Napoleon in 1805, restored again by the Bourbons, and finally suppressed on the last day of the year 1866, were on a par with the fate they had precipitated upon themselves by their gay living.

It is, nevertheless, the effect of their passion for amusement that makes the Certosa di San Martino so interesting a study. There it stands, up above Naples, on the hill of Vomero, looking like, and functioning as, a Neapolitan white-city. All travellers to Naples were led up here, as to the chief sight of the town. Later years have added a whispering gallery to its attractions. A little balcony, beyond a room fitted with statues of the heroes of the Risorgimento, juts out over the face of the cliff-like bastions on which the monastery is raised. Some fifty feet below lie the monastic vineyards, and then a second and deeper precipice falls straight down into the town of Naples. On the balcony every sound from the town can be heard—you can distinguish the cries of salesmen, the clatter of donkeys, the asthmatic coughs of old men, and now and again a snarling tenor voice singing one of the facile Neapolitan songs. I believe this gallery to be a late addition to San Martino, but the sights which drew travellers here in past centuries were of the same order. The huge roses carved in marble which are to be seen, some ten feet above the ground, on the pilasters separating each pair of lateral chapels, are still, as they must ever have been, a source of pride to the population. It is related that not one of these numerous blossoms is the same as any other. This is a strangely debased criterion for art. In Spain, where decadent Italian taste was carried to its extremes, the barrel-vaulting of the sacristy in the Cathedral of Siguenza is adorned with rosettes and with three hundred heads, no one of which is a repetition of another. Things can go no further than that.[1] San Martino is very far behind in this race; but it gains on other counts, and the custodians still remember the cost, in thousands of lire, of each of these marble flowers. The sculptor Fansaga was, they say, responsible for their design. But this was in or about the year 1625, and their production took time. Giuseppe Gallo finished one in 1652, after Fansaga's death, and the last two were completed by Alessandro Rondone in 1702. So they seem to have been the work of three generations of sculptors. The state-custodians of San Martino add a quality to these marble rosettes which it is difficult to believe was unintentional and ignored by the carvers. If you stand on a chair and tap the marble petals with some metal object — for example with a key, the symbol of monastic seclusion—each petal gives out a different and very pleasant bell-like note, like the softest of xylophones, or the watery notes of the musical glasses that you can still hear played in cheap music-halls or at country fairs. The marble rail separating the body of the church from the Tribune is another work admired for its cost and difficulty of execution.

This is, also, I believe, to the designs of Cosimo Fansaga, who drew the pattern for the elaborate inlaid floor, and was responsible for the great cloister garden with its groups of statues. There is a great deal of the work in Naples of this period, for which Fansaga was responsible. The two guglias outside great churches which are described in the opening pages of this book are the works of his hand. He must have had a peculiar facility for expressing the wants and sentiments

[1] Another example of this nature is to be seen at the Palace of Peterhof, near Petrograd. One room in this palace contains a series of eight hundred and sixty-three portraits of Russian women. These were painted to the order of Catherine II. by the Venetian, Count Rotari, who, for this purpose, undertook a journey through fifty provinces of Russia. Rotari was a pupil of Solimena, and died at Petrograd in 1762.

of his period. Many features of his art have a more Spanish than Italian air about them, with their barbaric and southern exuberance. But his mingling of bright colours with his sculptor's sense of design seems a necessity in an air which is so sparkling with the bright colours in the sea and sky. The series of great rooms, sacristies, chapter-houses and the like through which the church is approached are an interesting study of the mass of Neapolitan painters, now forgotten and despised. Here are to be seen their best works in the original places destined for them.

First of all there is Ribera, best known and best spoken of out of this tumultuous school. In the choir one finds his *Communion of the Apostles.* He painted also the Twelve Apostles in the angles of the ceiling of the nave of the church. The church and the series of chambers leading to it contain the best work of Lanfranco, who had such a great name in the time of Walpole. There is to be seen a reckless prodigality of figures, using every excuse to be found in Biblical history for their existence, by Corenzio, Caracciolo and Massimo Stanzione. The two former of these composed, with Ribera, the Neapolitan triumvirate who had determined to exclude and expel from Naples all capable competitors. To this end they were prepared to exploit every means.

Annibale Caracci was the first to fall into their toils. He came to Naples on an invitation to paint two of the churches, and was driven away by the threats of Corenzio with such a violent haste that he died soon after reaching Rome from the effects of his hurried journey under a burning sun. The Cavaliere D'Arpino was the next. He was compelled by the threats of Corenzio to fly from Naples, leaving the ceiling of the choir at S. Martino, upon which he was engaged, in an unfinished condition. Guido—a mild and perhaps rather tempting object for persecution—was the third. He had come to Naples to decorate the chapel of S. Gennaro in the Cathedral; but he had scarcely begun the work when an attempt was made to poison him, and he received a warning to prepare for death or leave Naples. He obeyed this order by returning instantly to Rome, leaving his pupil, Gessi, with two assistants, to complete the work. The latter were enticed on board a galley on their arrival and never heard of afterwards, and Gessi, of course, threw up his commission and also returned to Rome. Domenichino—a more gentle Guido in character—was now invited to Naples to execute the commission which had proved so unlucky to others. To reconcile him to the dangers of the task he was promised payment on an immense scale, and the especial protection of the Spanish Viceroy. He had completed four paintings and three frescoes when he was compelled by the threats of Spagnoletto to take his departure secretly for Rome. He was soon recalled with a renewed promise of the Viceroy's protection, but he died shortly after under strong suspicion of poison. Lanfranco, a life-long enemy of Domenichino, was the next to continue work in the Cathedral, but, luckily for Lanfranco, Carracciolo and Corenzio soon died, the latter by a fall from a scaffolding in the Church of San Severo, and Spagnoletto shortly afterwards had to flee from justice to his native Spain. One of Spagnoletto's last works of vengeance, before the trio was broken up by these two deaths and his own flight, was his destruction with some corrosive fluid of all the works of Massimo Stanzione, of whom he was jealous because of the popular success of his paintings in the Certosa di San Martino.

The later school of Naples is copiously represented at San Martino. But for an adequate idea of this school the monasteries and churches of the kingdom must be visited, and also the private houses of Naples, and the Palace of Caserta.

After a detailed survey of these we may state the sum-value of our impressions as to the worth of Neapolitan art. It is unfortunate, for our purpose, that German monks from Beuron, in Hohenzollern, should have so recently converted Monte Cassino into the semblance of a North German Lloyd, with their ship-mosaics and porthole windows. But the upper church is still untouched, with its marbles as rich as any in Europe. It is a queer sensation to walk in here, after the long and wearying drive up the bare mountain. You would as soon expect to find an expensive box of chocolates on a rock just uncovered by the tide. The mere manual labour of dragging such marbles to this height is striking evidence of tyranny or devotion; and it was a cunning merman who tied up these chocolates with coloured ribbon to such purpose that they are not wetted. In the opinion of experts the marbles here in variety and richness surpass S. Peter's, and rival the Certosa di Pavia. The nave has its roof painted by—who else?—Luca Giordano, and by the same hand is a "masterly" fresco over the doors, illustrating the consecration of the church by Pope Alexander II. Four great pictures by Solimena hang in the choir.

The monastery of Monte Cassino shares with two other famous convents, La Cava and Monte Vergine, the privilege of being the only three religious houses not dissolved by the present kingdom of Italy. They owe this immunity to their great libraries of MSS. and early charters, of which the monks are now suffered to remain the guardians. At La Cava there is shown in the small picture collection a fine sketch in oils by Solimena for some big fresco.[1] Such a work is not in existence in the convent of La Cava itself, and I believe this to be a study for some destroyed painting in the great convent of Padula, which was wrecked by an earthquake, and finally sacked by the French in the time of Napoleon. The inlaid stalls and the Abbot's Throne in the Chapter Hall of La Cava, which are of very curious design, have also found their way here from the Certosa of Padula. This great convent now lies like a ruined city waiting for the spade of an excavator, but there are few travellers intrepid enough to find their way to this modern ruin, which is a day's journey south of the antiquities of Paestum. Even by fast motor-car it is a journey of five hours to reach the long valley in which Padula lies at the foot of the hill on which the town of the

[1] It is, perhaps, more probably, the sketch by di Mura for his large picture of the rebuilding of the church which is over the organ in the Church of S. Chiara at Naples.

same name stands. All the guide-books and authorities that mention the Certosa of Padula exaggerate its ruinous condition, so that few travellers are tempted so far away from civilisation to see a convent which, from its description, should be roofless and uninhabitable. It is all the more surprising to find this huge building still standing, and with all its decorations and marbles in place, when you have reached the Val di Diano in which it lies, after crossing the stark and bleak earthquake country which fills a great part of the sixty miles between Salerno and Padula. The shepherds in their goatskin breeches, and the occasional hawks and eagles which you see hovering and staring as pointedly as the shepherds at the unfamiliar form of a motor—both these elements of surprise at your coming seem to enhance the iron inhospitality of this bleak mountain district. But as you come down the hills towards Sala Consilina, the capital of this district, the country takes on a happier appearance, and then, in the midst of this fertility, the domes and long roofs of the Certosa become visible, and in a few minutes more you are in front of the façade of the building. This has a peculiar and extravagant brilliance, which calls to mind Vanbrugh's buildings, and reveals, as in a flash, what lost talent there lay dormant in that architect whose genius was more especially designed for the building of the great convents which he never had the opportunity to start upon; for Vanbrugh was, by nature, the most glorious of the paladins of Jesuitism.

The interior of the convent contains three immense arcaded courts, out of which lead a church, in the most inlaid of Carthusian styles, and a refectory of surprising size. Round and about the first two courts lie the prior's apartments and the Foresteria or guest-house for travellers, all of these in the same redundant provincial manner, a little heavy in detail, as are all buildings by provincial architects, but with the same large scale-planning and full-dress appearance that the façade would lead one to expect. The third and last court is the greatest in size, and stretches out its huge quadrangle till the ends of each corridor meet each other like railway lines receding into the distance. These open corridors provided the monks with exercise in the summer, and in the winter they could walk in the closed-in arcades above. Upstairs and down, the passages are lined with the cells of the Carthusians, with a large piece of garden to each apartment, with a terrace, several living-rooms and a bedroom, with its canopy for a four-poster bed. Half-way along the south side a corkscrew stone stair leads up into the library, and the smooth stone-work of this circular staircase looks like the labours of a bookworm in some massive folio. Then at the far end of the passage, facing the road travellers come along from Naples, is an open-work belvedere containing a double staircase of the school of Sanfelice, so that if you are tall you can stand on the half-way landing, stoop down and look along the passage on the ground floor, and then, standing on tiptoe, look through the open doors at the top down the parallel corridor above. If you had walked down the upper landing you would come, after a few minutes' straight walk, to the little ante-room leading off to the right, into which the literary members of the community would leap as if out of the floor as they ran up the spiral stair on their way to the library, where you could hear their sandalled feet treading cruelly on the majolica cupids of the floor-tiles. Even now, when the whole convent is deserted, when it has been riven by earthquakes and is still desolate after being sacked over a century ago by the troops of King Murat, it is a peculiar sensation to look up and see the dazzling, reinforced blue of the sky imprisoned in this square shape between these flashing white stucco walls, when outside there are nothing but black hills and the terrible contorted mass of Monte Alburno, which Vergil often mentions in admiration of its stern and unyielding endurance.

At La Cava one is filled with a dislike for the ascetic spirit which could build the convent down a gorge just out of sight of the incredible view to be seen from the road as it reaches the crest of the hills and leads down again to the ledge where the convent stands. Farther south still, and so far away that it seems out of Europe altogether, is the famous monastery of S. Stefano del Bosco, destroyed by the earthquake of 1783. It was here that S. Bruno first established his order, and within these walls he died and was buried.[1] It was the centre, therefore, of a multiplication of the Carthusian particularities. The convent had the air of a fortified castle; it was defended by artillery, and had an income estimated at over one hundred thousand ducats. The paintings and marbles were worthy of the sacredness of the site. The buildings must have glittered out to sea as far as the convent bells could be heard. Now they are destroyed and in ruins, and only a fountain built by the monks at the convent gate is still in working order.

The neighbourhood of La Cava is the country of Solimena, for he was born within five miles of here, at Nocera de Pagani. It is a very strange district hereabouts, with the large monasteries lying outside and above each town on steep hill-sides. The huge masses of masonry resemble the monuments of this nature in Thibet, where, also, large monasteries overhang villages of revolting and awful poverty. The hills around La Cava contain three other varieties of buildings besides monasteries. The steep conical hills support the ruins of mediæval castles, dating from the Angevin kings of Naples. The flatter, lower hills are covered with round towers, whose mysterious purpose is to snare pigeons. Each tower is occupied by a slinger, who, as the birds approach, slings white stones towards that part of the hill-side where the nets are spread. The pigeons are always caught by this stratagem, and pursue the stones, being themselves snared by the nets during their search. The fourth variety of buildings are the hermitages, which lie on the highest and most inaccessible pinnacles. Every night there is to be seen from the town of La Cava a bright light glowing, apparently, in the sky, over beyond and above where the railway runs. It

[1] S. Bruno founded it as the second Chartreuse in 1094, and officiated as Abbot till his death in 1101.

burns in the early hours of the morning, and probably all through the night. From its intensity and steadiness it must be due to electricity. The presence of electric light among the anchorites is a subject worth investigating, but the ascent to this stylite would waste a whole day for the traveller. After a long day's climb the anchorite might remain compulsorily silent to all questions. Perhaps he would decline, till the next day, to show the only descent possible from his retreat; and in any case there are no nets spread to catch the person who tries to float down like a bird from these natural battlements. So an uncomfortable and chilling night would be the price paid for such fantastic information. Among the hills between Brescia and Salo on Lake Garda I have passed beneath another such lighthouse on the rocks. It proves that the early hermits had the foresight to prepare for the air-monsters that would one day be flying over the hills through the darkest night.

Most of the churches and convents in the neighbourhood of Nocera must contain work by Solimena and his pupils. Beside two or more disproportionately large churches, each small town contains invariably one or two fine houses. Angri, the next town to Nocera, has in the centre of the town a Royal villa, formerly belonging to one of the younger sons of the King of Naples. This building is ventilated with exceptionally fine ceremonial balconies for musicians to play from, or for the owner to sit and be seen during a *festa*. Proclamations to the sound of trumpets were delivered from here.

Monte Vergine, the third of the convents mentioned as being still unsuppressed, lies farther inland than Avellino. Here the interest of our period is centred, not in the actual convent of Monte Vergine, but in the Loreto or "ospizio" lower down, a large octagonal building designed by Vanvitelli.[1] This is the home of the abbot and a greater part of the

[1] It is ascribed by some writers to Domenicantonio Vaccaro. The Loreto contains a set of apartments, hung with fine tapestry, in which King Bomba and his family sometimes stayed.

monks, and here the valuable archives of the convent are preserved. Up above, at Monte Vergine, the court of the monastery is covered with snow for six months of the year, and it is the extreme cold which made the construction of the Loreto necessary as a home for the older and more infirm members. Even the younger monks are allowed to live up in the snows, four thousand feet above the sea, for only eight days at a time. The sight of this elegantly elaborate octagon makes a fitting introduction to Vanvitelli's masterpiece—the Palace of Caserta.

Luca Giordano—for I have not finished with him yet, though his character is concealed in the furious steam from his own speed—is, nevertheless, a figure represented in most of the galleries of Europe, and the details of his life lie easy to the explorer's hand. But what is there to be said in explanation when we read that the gallery in the palace of Prince Brunaccini at Messina contains fine works by Monosilio, Comandé, Rodriguez, Onofrio Gabriello, Fulco, Maroli, Suppa, Scilla, the two Catalanis, Giannotto, Menniti, Filocami, Tuccari, the two Cardillos, Tancredi, Quagliata, Bova, Paladino, Polidoro [1] and Barbalungo? [2] Those times of splendour seem very far-off halcyon days in contrast with the miserable modern town of wooden huts that would shame a backwood in Canada. Those were the days when Messina was still an emporium for trade with Asia Minor and the Indies; when Egypt was still productive; and when Malta was the richest republic in Europe. It was the early part of the seventeenth century, and the occasional sojourns of Caravaggio as he passed through Messina on his way to or from Malta kindled an enthusiasm for painting. There are still preserved at Messina, and farther to the west, at Syracuse,

[1] The splendid gilt coach which was used by the Mayor and Corporation of Messina, and is still in existence, was built in 1742, and is painted inside and out by Polidoro, the younger.

[2] There is a learned book on the painters of Messina published by a local enthusiast in 1821 at Messina. This work contains full details of every artist of the town, with portraits of several of the more eminent of them.

some of the paintings that Caravaggio executed in the last years of his very brief life.[1] Such was the wealth and the spirit of that time that the romantic life and adventures of Caravaggio awoke longings among the young men of Messina, and those of them who became artists suffered from no lack of commissions for pictures. This was the period of the huge Jesuit churches and monasteries which are to be seen in every Catholic country of Europe bearing the stamp of the same style, as if all of them had been ordered and delivered by the same firm of contractors. Messina is no exception to this rule.

Sixty miles to the west, along the coast, lies Catania, and this town we can select as a typical example of the effect produced by the practical realisation of my theories as they bore result in one of the great southern towns of the Mediterranean. In subsequent pages I shall investigate the town of Lecce in order to see our subject from as many different points of view as possible.

Catania is still, at this time, an exceedingly rich and prosperous city, carrying on a very extensive trade in sulphur, and with a port that is continually full of a varied shipping from every European and African port on the Mediterranean. But the rare phœnix of this stretch of coast is the Benedictine monastery, that lies high up on the outer slopes of the town. And it is not without reason that the people of Catania call it the phœnix, for this immense building has risen again from its ruins after the earthquake of 1693 in an even larger and more luxuriant form than before. In actual dimensions it is larger than any monastery in Europe, except the palace-convent of Mafra in Portugal, in front of which we shall stop for a moment on our voyage to the Latin Americas. But it is the nature of the building that is interesting and not its extent. There is an extraordinary quality about this work

[1] The Church of S. Andrea D'Avellino contains *Christ before Pilate*, considered to be Caravaggio's best work at Messina.

The monastery church of S. Lucia at Syracuse contains, over the high altar, Caravaggio's picture of the burial of S. Lucia.

that is to be found nowhere else in Italy except in the very far southern towns. There are distinct traces of the championless Churriguerresque that writhed over from Spain to Mexico late in the seventeenth century.[1] As an expression of the guitar music of these hot towns it deserves more credit than it has been, so far, allowed. For the extravagant processions of their *festas* it is as admirably adapted as any class of building ever has been for its purpose. The energy and love of art, which is responsible for the building of so important a structure as this convent in a town of the size of Catania, deserves the same credit that is voted to the builders of the great Gothic churches of the small towns of Northern Europe. The architects responsible for the design were natives of Messina, and their plans seem to have been corrected and passed by a competent artist from Rome. The classical lines of the building are flowered over with a strange profusion of designs, just like the frost flowers on a window-pane. The straight lines of door and window-panes are filled with carvings, and the iron-work of the balconies is an excuse for the most elaborate festooning. Inside the convent there is a staircase the walls of which are worked with elaborate stucco bas-reliefs in a style that the Cambodians would recognise and admire. Under the landing of this double stair a passage leads into the enormous cloisters of the convent. In the middle of the first one there is a fountain canopied and worked over with a mosaic of flashing tiles. The arcading of the upper cloister is, unhappily, filled in, and so the effect of the double cloister surrounding this fountain is lost. Upstairs there are vast dormitories six hundred feet in length—so long that they finish in a point of light. They are like long

[1] This style of building may be further studied at Catania in the palace of Prince Biscari, which he opened as a museum for his fellow-citizens in 1758. Being smaller in scale, it is even richer in detail than the Benedictine convent. The palace contains a theatre, a fine staircase, and several finely painted saloons, chiefly by an artist called Pastore. The rooms are filled with the archæological discoveries of Prince Biscari, and there is a small picture gallery, one room of which contains sixty paintings on boards by Polidoro.

telescopes laid out towards the view of some brilliant star. The immense size and the expense of this building are very strong evidence of the popularity of monastic life among the ordinary townspeople, as well as among those of their relations who were lucky enough to be able to lead this life, in which there was little work and all necessities were provided. It was forty years after the earthquake before this convent grew up again on its ruins, but a great part of the cost was provided for out of the subscriptions of the townspeople. The church was on such an ambitious scale that it is still unfinished, but inside there is the famous organ, and there are two tiers of carved stalls, with accommodation for two hundred singers. It is such details that give the key to the solution of how and why a building of this size should exist in a town like Catania. The convent provided for the townspeople processions in which everyone took a part and which were highly enjoyable—theatrical entertainment with all the pleasures of opera—and there were large receptions held in the convent, to which all persons of importance were invited. Whilst providing these forms of entertainment the monks, at the same time, if prevailed upon to do so, could furnish the pardon which was necessary for too free an indulgence in any of these pleasures. They could, at the same time, encourage you in your weaknesses, and then forgive you for your excess in pandering to them. No wonder that they were seldom without money to enlarge their scope of work.

Having dealt with the monasteries of the kingdom, let us examine the churches of Naples. They are, for the most part, crowded into a small part of the town lying between the Toledo, the main street of Naples, and the Central Railway Station. Inside this small circumference there is a bewildering plenty. So great is the profusion of work of our period that I am forced to conduct a bird's-eye promenade over the roofs of this quarter of the city, making it understood that by some X-ray process the insides of all the churches may be seen without moving far away from our post in the air. I can point out, therefore, everything of interest without having to conduct the party down side-streets and through the haunting slums. It is an inspection which repays the trouble, for there are very few foreigners who have turned their interest away from the classical and the mediæval to the later Neapolitan work.

In the Church of S. Maria la Nuova, in the Largo of the same name, at the right of the high altar, under the organ, are to be seen the two graceful children painted by Luca Giordano when seven years of age—and yet he lived to be an old man and to complete, when ten times this age, his non-stop forty-eight-hour run over one of the cupolas in the convent of San Martino. Santa Chiara, not very far away from S. Maria la Nuova, is like the most inviting of ball-rooms. All the early work of Giotto was destroyed long ago by a Spanish magistrate, who said the colours made the church look dark and melancholy. Behind the high altar a small window gives on to a great decorated hall, where the nuns can be seen sitting at their needlework and praying. This, indeed, is the only sight that you can get of them, for they are strictly cloistered. High up in the air, as you turn back to look down the church, there stand the opera boxes, through the gilt lattices of which the nuns watch and join in the service. Behind these bars they can turn and hide from spectators, as if armed with the most subtle fan. Higher up still, the roof and choir are painted in fresco by Conca and Francesco di Mura, the foremost of Solimena's pupils. The large central fresco of the ceiling shows David dancing and playing the harp before the sacred Ark. This is Sebastiano Conca's work.[1] Huge draperies, filled out by the wind till they are the size of clouds, are blowing round the correct classical colonnades into which David is leading the procession. The inevitable stone steps, always used by these artists so as to place the chief characters high up in the middle of the composition, are crowded with a host of unnecessary

[1] At Holkham Hall, in Norfolk, there is a picture ordered from Sebastiano Conca by the 1st Lord Leicester, at Rome, representing Orpheus and the nine Muses, with Lord Leicester himself as Orpheus.

spectators, each one of them offering an excuse for some exploit of Conca's technique. Di Mura and Bonito have supported their chief's action with supplementary frescoes to each side of it. The best painters of the eighteenth century in Naples are, therefore, to be seen in their most typical moods on this one ceiling in Santa Chiara.

Five minutes away, travelling towards the fourth and last church that we shall notice, is the Church of S. Maria dell' Annunziata. A disastrous fire in 1757 utterly destroyed this church, which contained a vast quantity of the most successful work of Luca Giordano, Corenzio and Solimena. Vanvitelli rebuilt it, and a hall at the back, frescoed by Solimena, and the still existing treasury and sacristy, with their paintings by Corenzio, illuminate what we have lost. By this time we have reached our destination, the Church of S. Severino e Sosio, in front of the huge Benedictine convent of that name. There is a slight slope falling away from this church down to the harbour, and a tufa balustrade of queer design protects this small precipice, seeming to assume that the congregation will leave Mass precipitately and with a dangerous force, which must be arrested before it can do them harm. These tactics are continued inside the church. Great altars on each side are so arranged that a halt and a prayer at each are unavoidable when the church is crowded with a moving audience. From the door to the high altar is like a difficult railway journey, with six changes before you reach your destination, and an equal number before you can get home again. At this time one or more sermons would be in progress and a great crowd would be listening to each preacher. Neapolitan preachers were famous. The author of a *Voyage to Italy in 1714* describes the scenes he was a witness of in exactly these churches we are visiting: "The preachers here, indeed, have some natural endowments that have a tendency to form parts of oratory, but seem perfectly ignorant of sublime eloquence. Their motions are extravagant. The variation of their voice throws 'em from the loudest treble to the lowest bass twenty times in a quarter of an hour. 'Tis true every

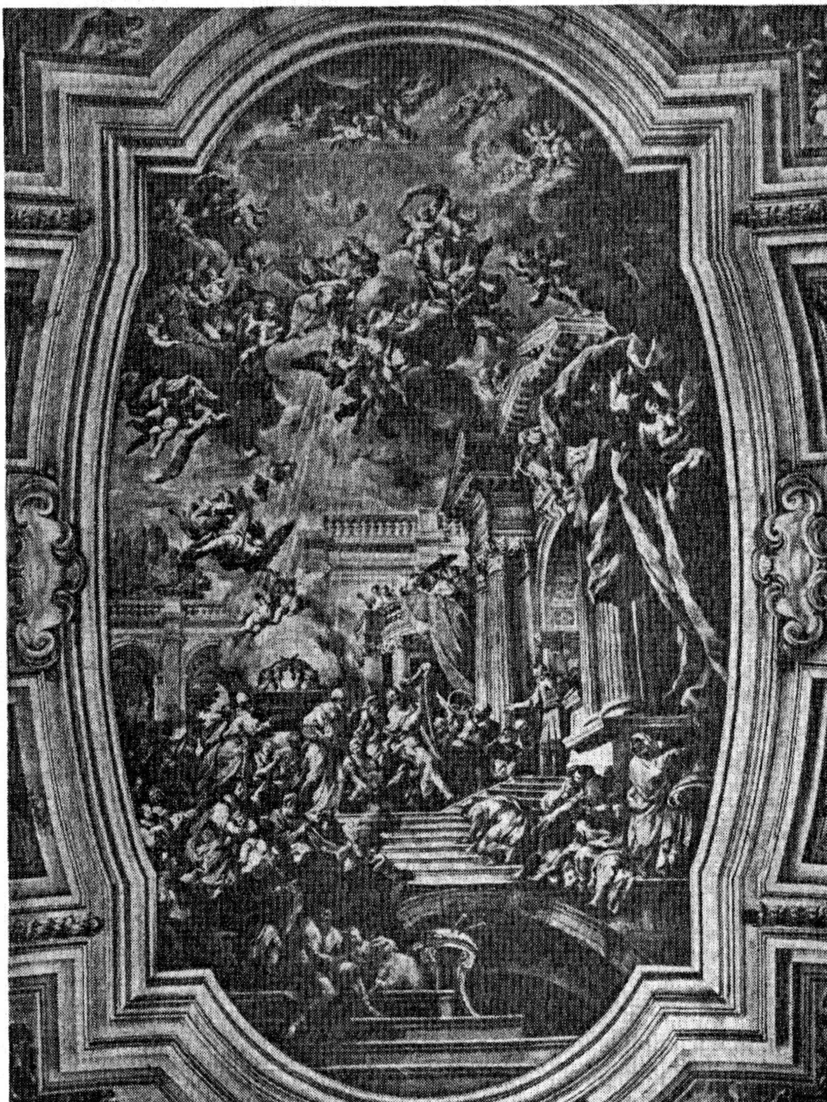

Photograph: Alinari *S. Chiara, Naples*

DAVID DANCING BEFORE THE ARK

BY SEBASTIANO CONCA

Order of monks has a particular way of preaching; the Jesuits are esteemed very good declaimers, and their gesture is not so extravagant as that of other monks, but their style is the most swelling. The Capuchins are everlasting thunderers, and preach nothing but Death and Destruction, if it be not a day for Buffoonery. They pull their beards, clap their hands, and roar out hideously. I found t'other day a very pleasant remark by an author, who says: 'When a Capuchin preaches, the dogs run out of the church.' They bawl, they torment themselves, their pulpits are for the most part so many balconies, in which they run from one end to another with great noise and heat." It was from the ceiling above these balconies, with their ranting preachers, that the painter, Corenzio, fell and was killed. This artist, who loved his own craft enough to make him attempt Guido's life with poison, left his best work on the ceiling of this church.[1] His is curiously dateless and so illustrative in his treatment that you might expect to find his work engraved to illustrate Scott's novels or some historical romance in an early Victorian annual.

The hundreds of other churches to be found in Naples are all of the same pattern, and contain work by the same sculptors and artists that we notice in the four big churches visited. The work of these painters is more interesting when it is secular in subject, and to be sought for in a palace rather than a church.

There are in Naples a great number of palaces which repay to the full those who are willing to investigate their bad architectural reputation. The Palazzo Monteleone, for example, the property of the descendant of the Conquistador Cortez, has an entrance doorway with the heads of satyrs composing capitals of the columns, their eyes representing the volutes, their hair the flowers and their beards the leaves. This doorway remains like the overture to what must have

[1] But these are now obliterated by the work of di Mura, whose best frescoes in Naples are on this ceiling, obscuring the previous set by Corenzio.

been a very amusing double comedy, for the palace contained frescoes by Paolo de Matteis, illustrating Virgil's Æneid and the *Gerusalemme* of Tasso, that were long since destroyed by fire. One may imagine the inside of this palace furnished, by the wealth of the Indies, with feather tapestries and all the exotic paraphernalia of Mexico; but I keep this interior closed, and shall only unlock it when we meet again—those of us who can survive the journey—in Mexico, in the last chapter of this book.

The chief palaces of Naples are in the Piazza of San Domenico, and here is the gloomy and terrible Palazzo Sansevero, the property of the family who built the chapel, with the realistic sculptures that I have described. This palace was the scene, in 1590, of a drama that should be of interest to students of music. In that year Carlo Gesualdo, 3rd Prince of Venosa and the nephew of San Carlo Borromeo, who was then living in this palace, discovering his second wife in the act of adultery, killed her and her lover on the spot. He then fled to his castle of Gesualdo and there murdered his only son, in whose features he fancied that he recognised a resemblance to the seducer of his wife. In expiation of this deed he founded two monasteries at Gesualdo, one for Dominicans and one for Capuchins. In the church of the latter there still exists a large painting representing this double tragedy. The Prince died at Naples, and is buried in the Gesu Nuovo in a chapel built at his expense from the designs of Fansaga. Ever since this sinister story the palace has been associated with bad fortune to its occupants. It is a magnificent and substantial building, and has many rooms decorated with frescoes by Belisario Corenzio; but in spite of the solidity of its appearance quite half of the building collapsed in the eighteenth century, burying many victims in its fall, and the lurid sequence was brought down to modern times by the last Duchess of Sansevero, who, while watching a procession through the square in 1878, fell from a balcony and was dashed to pieces on the paving-stones beneath. The Palazzo Maddaloni in the Toledo, now used as a bank, is the finest of this period in Naples, and has splendid frescoes by Micco Spadaro, Giacomo del Po and Francesco di Mura, for every building in these streets is a palace of some once powerful family, and their crumbling cornices and shuttered and apparently deserted interiors are in the strangest contrast to the appalling slums which are crowded into this small area of Naples. The chief streets leading round and towards the square, the Strada dei Tribunali and the Strada Trinità, have also the same huge family palaces, where, in some instances, the framework of the classical entrance doors rises higher than the second floor of the mean houses on the opposite side of the street. One palace there is in particular, that of the Roccella family, where the doorway, with faun caryatides upholding its cornice, has, on either side, a fabulous monster in stone, waiting with open mouth for the letters that it should carry to the family upstairs, for they are too mythical to venture farther afield than their own threshold. As if to verify this guess at their habits, from inside the court you can see another pair of monsters at the foot of the stairs, and then the staircase itself growing more fantastic at every turn, until it disappears on to the lowest landing, at which level they find it possible to live safe from the crowds outside.

Not many years after the building of this palace, to justify the Roccella family in the refuge they had sought, the transcendental staircases of the architect, Ferdinando Sanfelice, began to grow in all the newest palaces of Naples. This indigenous invention in building became the study of every foreign architect who came to Naples for the next century, but they are now long since forgotten, and strike one with their real peculiarity again, unspoilt by too much praise. The finest of them all, as to the materials with which it was built, is the Serra Cassano Palace, in that high part of Naples near the villa of Lucullus. Out of an octagonal court at the back of this palace there flows a double geometrical staircase, like two streams gently urged uphill by an unknown means, so that they meet again in the happier air above. It is edged by a running balustrade rising with each spring of the stairs and swift enough to dash out the torches of the servants who stand on each step when there is a reception in the huge rooms above.

In the part of Naples lying behind the museum and towards Capodimonte there are many more of these geometrical staircases to be seen,[1] but the finest of the whole number is in the palace built by Sanfelice for himself, which has two of these stairways, each one for the use of a portion of the house, big enough to contain several palaces within its walls. From the court the stairways have a strange appearance, for they consist of three cones of masonry, each hollowed out, for the staircases are open to the air; the openings of the two outer cones corresponding with each other, but being different from those in the central mass. At every turn of the stair, as it follows its twin on the opposite side, and they thread their way together through this intricate maze, there are masks laughing or frowning at you out of the walls, but the children of the tenements, into which the palace has long been converted, have thrown stones at them until their surface is almost flat with the wall and they are but faded portraits of a race that is unknown now. At the top of one of these staircases—it is impossible to discover which—is a room covered with frescoes by Solimena, who was the master of Sanfelice; but now that the palace has become a slum settlement, numerous attempts to push one's way into the burrows in which whole families live, and innumerable attempts to inquire a path from room to room, were alike unsuccessful, and the frescoes remained an unshattered illusion.

Such were the houses of the rich and such the convents in which the younger sons of the family, having paid their entrance fee, lived luxuriously for the rest of their lives in the southern parts of Italy, before Naples had once more, after

[1] The double geometrical staircase of the Palazzo Spagnuolo in the Strada de Vergine, and the Palazzo Majo near the Church of Santa Maria della Vittoria, are two good examples of Sanfelice's skill and originality.

two and a half centuries, become the residence of a king. This sudden transformation in the fortunes of Naples, bringing her under wise rule to one of the foremost cities of Europe, came as a climax to so much activity in building.

To give a deeper shade of probability to the account of such strange lives I shall draw a parallel between these Spanish kings and the nearest approach I can find to them in other lands. It is in Hungary, which the Austrians reclaimed from Turkey and treated as if they had recovered it from the sea, that we can discover the nearest approach to these would-be Olympian lives. A few of the noble families of Hungary were allotted gigantic estates and allowed a semi-independent condition. The most famous of these families were the Esterhazys. An enthusiastic and perhaps impressionable Frenchman describes a visit that he paid to the head of this family at their country seat of the same name. It was possible for any foreigner, on obtaining an introduction from the Embassy of his nation or from some respectable person in Vienna, to proceed down to Esterhazy for a visit to the palace and gardens. Some twenty miles from the house he passed the frontier into the Esterhazy domains and his papers were examined by the Prince's pickets. At length the façade of the palace came into sight down an immense avenue, which at length divided, to leave a fountain in the centre, and joined again, where it came to a stop under a double staircase which led up to the saloon on the lowest of the three storeys of the house. But a little before this point would have been reached the visitors were met by the servants and taken towards one of the wings of the palace, where the hotel for visitors was ready. Lieutenant-Colonel Rosetzki, the gentleman-in-waiting, and the Sieur de Nagy, the superintendent of lands and properties, two impressive Hungarian gentlemen, with hair shaved, but wearing fierce moustachios, were waiting to receive the visitors. It is probable that every guest regretted his arrival for the moment before this military reception. Rooms were distributed among the travellers and after this they were free to do what they liked. The chief rooms of the palace were open every day, and the house and grounds were crowded all through the summer by visitors from Vienna.[1]

The palace and gardens were the work of Prince Nicholas Esterhazy-Galantha, the then owner of the property, and they were still unfinished at the time, 1784, that this Frenchman visited them. The first foundations had been laid some twenty-five years before his visit. The view stretched down towards a distant lake and vines could be seen outlined against the blue waters, for, again in the Frenchman's words, Ceres had withheld her beauty from the hill-slope that led down to the lake. The view down the chief avenues extended for a three-hours' journey and came to an end towards the town of Oldenburg. At various points, including the door of the guests' hotel, day and night, were posted sentries of the Esterhazy Grenadiers. This regiment consisted of one hundred and forty-six men, forty of them over six feet in height, and none of them less than five feet eight inches. Their uniform was blue, with red facings and white brandenburghers. Every morning at eleven A.M. sharp they performed their ceremonial drill at the command of Lieutenant-Colonel Rosetzky under the Prince's windows. The drill was performed to the music of a military band, for which Haydn was responsible. It was the chief spectacle of each day and became a parade of the visitors as well as of the soldiers. After the drill was over everyone walked in the gardens. There were four splendid temples to the Sun, to Fortune, to Diana, and to Love. There were elaborate parterres, bordered and intermingled with colonnades, trellises, and labyrinths. The rose-garden was an enclosure, like a labyrinth, in one of the lateral alleys. Farther down the slope, in an oval space, was the Chinese Pavilion, La Bagatelle. Eight colossal statues were just being put up there, and also four grottos in the Chinese taste. This was at the bottom of the garden, and the town of Oldenburg was just visible among the distant trees. A few miles

[1] In the Frenchman's words—"Le palais fourmille d'étrangers pendant tout l'été."

from there, at Forchenstein, was the Prince's treasure tower, on a high mountain. The next avenue led away towards Eisenstadt, the other great family house, where the Dowager Princess Esterhazy, the former Countess of Weissendolf, was in residence. Half the Esterhazy Grenadiers were always stationed there as a mark of respect towards her.

Walking up the slope again, with your back on the deer park, through which all the avenues ran, you came to the winter-garden, which was on the right wing of the palace. This was full of parrots, shell-work grottos, swings, little streams, and Chinese bridges. Next to this was the orangery, with a marionette theatre inside, in which Italian and German operas were performed every night. This theatre for *fantoccini* had no box or gallery, but a parterre of shell-work, like a grotto.

After this tour everyone rested through the hot hours of the afternoon. When it grew cool again they resumed the inspection. An avenue to the left of the palace led away a distance of three leagues to Monbijou, a hunting pavilion. Here was a garden with elaborate parterres, fine statues and two grottos, one of which was used as a chapel. The stables, from which this particular avenue led away, were filled with splendid and glittering coaches. There was the coach of the Empress Maria Theresa, in which she was dragged through the grounds by eight men dressed like satyrs. Then there was a carriage for eight horses, with a circular glass cabin to hold ten persons. Out to the left, on the edge of the garden, were the Champs Élysées, full of swings and flying chairs under the trees. The workmen were in the process of setting up two gigantic cascades through the midst of this. Next to the Champs Élysées was a schoolhouse for forty children and, in a grove beyond, a hermitage built according to all the rules of this class of building. In this wing of the palace were the library, the chapel, and the studios of the artists and sculptors, mostly Italian and Bavarian.

Of course the palace itself was full of works of art (galleries full of pictures and rooms of precious Indian woods), but the fact that the Prince was in residence and liable to walk into any of the rooms in an informal way seems to have deterred the Frenchman from a detailed description of their treasures. He says, though, that so tactful was Prince Esterhazy that when the visitors did not wish to see him he was nowhere to be found, but when wanted he was always at hand. He was ready to take his part whenever occasion needed. The more gorgeous the ceremony the more splendid his dress. The climax was a complete uniform of pearls for himself and his horse. This was reserved for the reception of the Emperor.

Every evening there was opera, German comedy and Italian tragic, or buffo opera, on alternate nights, in a house which held five hundred. This night it was the first performance of the opera *Armide*, by Haydn. The effect on entering the theatre was most splendid. It was brilliantly lit by candlelight and big enough to hold five hundred persons. Haydn himself conducted, and struck up the Overture as the Prince came in, attended by his page, Auguste, a negro from the British West Indies.

The *dramatis personæ* were as follows :—

ARMIDA . . .	*Mathilde Bologna*
RENARD . . .	*Prospero Braghetti*
UBALDI . . .	*Antonio Speciali*
UDRINE . . .	*Paolo Mandini*
ZELMIRA . . .	*Costanza Valdesturla*

La Specioli, Poceli, Negri, and Morati did not sing that evening. It was their night off. The scenery and the heroic costumes left nothing to be desired. Next door was a café, where refreshments were served during the intervals, and there were two billiard-rooms for enthusiasts. The performance finished with a grand mythological ballet.

. . . .

Those who object to the conscription of labour in Russia can take pride in Caserta, built in the last days of despotism. It is the work of slaves, some of them negro, but in great proportion European. This last great work of slave labour is heartless, as you would expect. The staircase, with its ceremonial landing, the chapel and the theatre are famed for their marbles. The stair is formed of single blocks of the Sicilian marble of Trapani, called Lumachella ; on each landing are marble lions, distinctly to be known as such. On the side walls are to be seen the best breccias of Dragoni and the marbles of Vitulano *in principato ulteriore.* There are twenty-four Ionic pillars adorning the centre of the vestibule made of the red breccia of Mons Garganus, in Apulia, and sixteen of the porticoes are of the yellow breccia of the same mountain. The marbles of the theatre were, in large part, stolen from the Temple of Serapis, at Pozzuoli. The porticoes leading through the house recall drawings by Bibbiena. Beyond them lie the gardens, rising for two miles up a hill, and of such length as to necessitate a carriage. The innumerable groups of statuary on successive landings along the cascade become monotonous. The water drips down slowly past you, passing from basin to basin, between the two straight roads that border it. Arriving at last at the height of the hill, where a mere fall of water into the topmost basin precipitates this small avalanche, there awaits you the biggest and most imposing of the statue groups. But it is the view when you turn round on your ascent which is the culmination of this immense work. Very far down the avenue, just filling the space between its two arms, lies the palace, absolutely still and uninhabited. On the left there is Vesuvius, like an ink-pot with a cut-down quill pen in it. Then the eyes naturally travel again down the groove laid for them. The trees of the avenue, as they fade and go smaller in the distance, have an air of gently spinning like tops in a slight mist. But the dropping water and the hot afternoon turn them to hundreds of bells, smaller than almost any leaf. These millions of little tongues are lolling, or beginning to chatter, and the whole volume of their song, swinging as it goes along all the little bells it touches, eventually jumps right off the trees over the palace. And there, in the heart of the mist, over the middle of the palace roof, far enough at sea for this music to be heard, lies Capri, looming out of the mysterious sea like a huge whale's back. Trundling back down the side of the cascade induces sleep, and it is only the wide steps of the great staircase and the necessary effort that awakes one. Here, again, it is the summit that is interesting. There is a huge landing, walls lined with marble, and the floor space divided by groups of pilasters. On to this landing there open numerous very large doors. The way down the dining-room to the chapel, and from the state apartments to the Royal bedrooms alike, led across this landing. It was the centre, for this reason, of that formal etiquette which Louis XIV. had invented, and which his descendants had brought from Versailles to Spain and thence to Naples. A door would open and the King would pass with his Court between lines of halberdiers from perhaps the chapel to the Infanta's nursery. Half-an-hour later he would be returning from the Royal nurseries to the dining-room. The marble floor seems to be laid out with a view to assisting in these progresses. There is a regular track marked out from one door over to another, like an insect's path or like the dotted track which you must follow on a pianola roll to regulate your playing. You discover yourself waiting in this deserted vestibule for a conjurer to produce the King. At any moment, to the trumpet's sound, one of the doors will open and then your presence in the middle of the path they must traverse will embarrass you. You will be seen on the staircase; your shabby clothes betray you anywhere against the gorgeous marbles. The only escape lies through one of these great doors, which may magically open for you. If you follow their invitation and go through them it will be more difficult to return than you anticipate. You think of the priest who fled through a secret door into the marble walls when the Turks first entered S. Sofia, and was immured there, never to be seen again. And there is only one afternoon train back to Naples.

When Charles III. of Bourbon came to the throne in 1734 Naples became the chief city in Italy for wealth and population. No king had been in residence there since the days of the Emperor Charles V., and it was a very calculating diplomacy on the part of Elizabeth Farnese to design this kingdom for her children. Charles left Parma with a delighted speed, taking with him the art treasures of the Farnese House. He drove out the Austrians with but little difficulty, since the twenty-seven years of the Austrian interregnum had not been appreciated by the Neapolitans. In addition they were flattered at being once more the capital of an extensive kingdom. There were a great many improvements to be made before the town might be considered fit for the residence of a king, more especially a Bourbon. The palace must be extended and a theatre must be built. Both of these schemes were a very short time in execution. The theatre of San Carlo was actually completed in one year. Then Charles drew up plans for the summer residences of the Court. He built the Palace of Capodimonte and employed Antonio Canevari as architect at Portici. In 1752 he, in person, laid the first stone of Caserta. By 1759, when he was called back as King to Spain, the first storey was already completed. It was left for his son Ferdinand, and for Joachim Murat, to finish this vast palace.

In one of the rooms in the museum of San Martino there hangs a bronze head, or rather the bronze features, for the back of the head is not shown. At first sight it is quite impossible not to mistake this mask for a ram's head from the prow of a galley or the architrave of a building. Then you see underneath it the name of Charles III., and at your eye-level, below this mask, is the death mask of Ferdinand, his son, with an only slightly diminished resemblance to this animal. Remember when you look on his features that this is the most intelligent, save Louis XIV., of the Bourbon family. His mother, Elizabeth Farnese, was, in her person, no contradiction to the Farnese tradition of obesity. But her son, Don Carlos, had from her his brain and his direction of power, without the family fatness. There is a remarkably fine portrait of this interesting prince by Goya. It shows you the contradiction of his silly, heraldic features with the immense competency and sense of duty which were his good qualities. He stands in a landscape where his gun has just sounded in pursuit of game. He has stopped for a minute, so it seems, on the slope of a little hill, rather out of breath and anxious for a look around in search of more victims for his gun. He looks untidy, slouching, pious and almost idiotic, but has intelligent eyes. Beckford, visiting Madrid in 1787, a year before the King's death, writes an account of his rooms in the palace. The King was away on one of his eternal shooting expeditions, but Beckford so well describes the palace atmosphere that the absence is not noticed. In every room he passed through stood cages of gilded wire, and in every cage a curious exotic bird in full song. Mingled with these warblings was heard at certain intervals the low chimes of musical clocks, stealing upon the ear like the tones of harmonic glasses. No other sound broke in upon the stillness except, indeed, the almost inaudible footsteps of several aged domestics, in court dresses of the cut and fashion prevalent in the days of the King's mother, Elizabeth Farnese, gliding along cautiously and quietly to open the cages and offer their inmates dainties such as highly educated birds should relish. Returning to Spain eight years later Beckford describes a visit to the Palace of Aranjuez. While seeing over the rooms of this palace he inquired after a remarkable room called the " Salon de los Funciones " or " El Coliseo." The ceiling had been painted by Raphael Mengs and was one of his chief works; here Ferdinand and Barbara, the most musical of sovereigns, used to melt in ecstasies at the soft warblings of Farinelli and Egiziello. Alas, for Beckford's pleasure! Not later than the previous summer this grand theatrical apartment had been divided into a suite of shabby, bandboxical rooms, for the accommodation of the Infant of Parma. No mercy had been shown to the beautiful roof. In some places legs and folds of drapery were still visible, but workmen and stuccadors were working at a great rate, and in a few days whitewash would cover all this former glory.

These few sentences of Beckford produce before you with wonderful reality the illusion of the strange lives passed

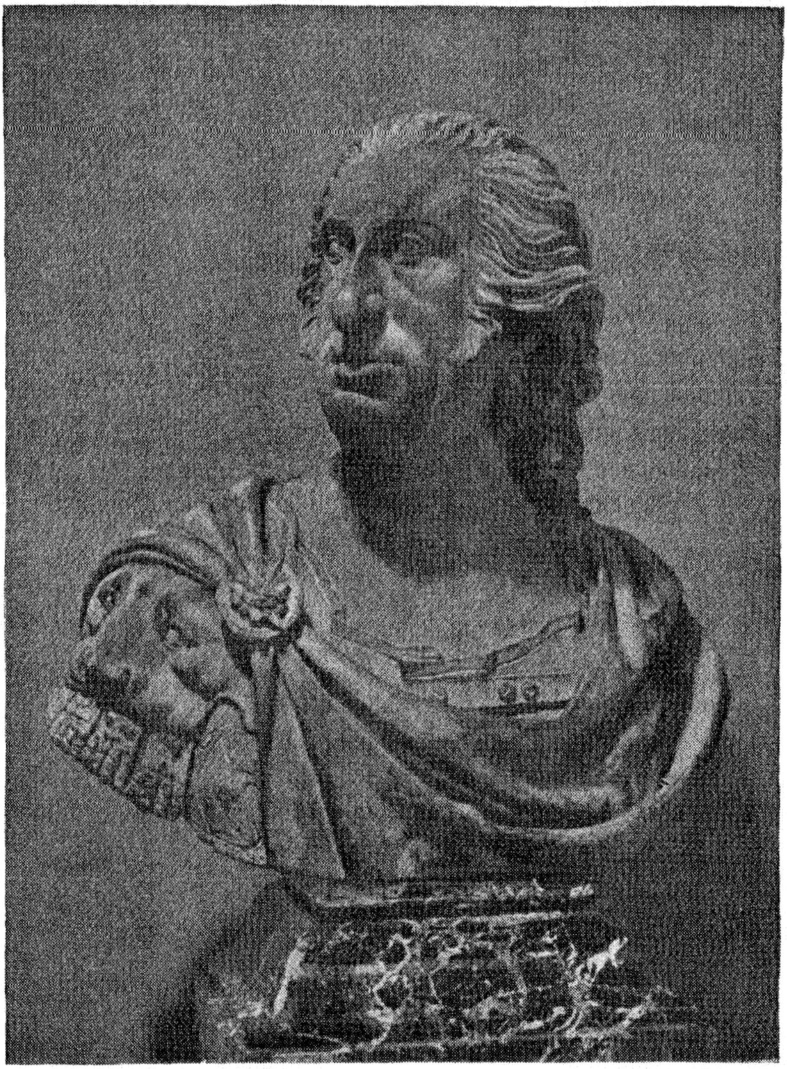

Photograph: Alinari

FERDINAND I. AND IV. OF NAPLES

BY CANOVA

within such walls. During an age which, in Southern Europe, has the name for poverty and decadence in industry and agriculture, the most remarkable feature in Charles is the extravagant size of his buildings. To house himself and provide a barrack for his Court, no expense was considered too great. He planned to build, not the palace alone at Caserta, but a whole town to supply and house his Court. In Vanvitelli's book on Caserta there are plates showing the proposed parterres in front of the palace, down past where the railway from Rome to Naples now runs. With their intricate embroidery they are like carpets spread to walk upon, and it is a surprise when the tall and dandified courtiers in the prints skirt and avoid this carpet—going, in fact, to any lengths to avoid walking upon it. All of this parterre—if, indeed, it was ever carried out—is destroyed, and the town of Caserta shows no traces of the Royal scheme. On the other side of the palace, the actual garden front, there remain a few great scrolls and flourishes in high topiary work. They stand there, tall enough for a man to hide behind them, and every few minutes they shake and move a little, like a person walking in a crinoline.

There is a print, often to be seen in Naples, of Ferdinand I. (the son of Charles), with his family, walking in the garden just outside the palace front. The King, very burly and clown-like, walks in front with his queen, and the children are disposed in perspective, according to their age and height. Other prints may be seen of the Royal family enjoying a gala performance at the San Carlo theatre. Behind the chairs of the King and Queen are the children and the persons-in-waiting, sitting upon low stools and quite obviously debarred from any view of the stage. It is tedious to describe the process of dressing and undressing which Louis XIV. underwent each day, but this same procedure was in force at Naples. A fact which made it particularly freakish and funny to the English visitor was that the pious Charles did actually occupy a bed in the same room as his queen. This was out of tradition with our notions of the degenerate foreigner.

The love of formal roads for processions of triumph was a part of the emulation felt by this age for Rome and its emperors. A long straight avenue decorated with arches and tunnels was, to them, like playing with trains to a modern child.[1] There had been, for a moment, talk of a road to lead direct from Caserta to Naples, between rows of trees. In this way a straight line some twenty miles in length would be scratched on the surface of the earth. The long, bar-like garden on the other side of the palace would make this longer by another two miles. When the day came to remove from Naples for the summer, a caravan was

[1] Avenues are a subject that may be studied in England—in a typical instance at Badminton. I quote from Reginald Blomfield's *The Formal Garden in England*: "The approach to the house was formed by a triple avenue, the centre avenue 200 feet wide, the two side avenues 80 feet wide. The entrance gates to this avenue were placed in the centre of a great semicircular wall. The distance from this gateway to the house was 2½ miles. After passing through two more gateways the avenue opened on to a great oblong open space forming part of the deer park, with avenues on either side, and the entrance gate to the forecourt of the house opposite the end of the main avenue. A broad gravelled path, with grass plots and fountains on either side, led from the entrance gate of the forecourt to a flight of four steps leading to the pavement in front of the house. A print shows a coach and six approaching the entrance gate, apparently not on the road, but on the grass of the park. To the right hand was the base court with stables and outhouses; at the back of the house, the kitchen and fruit gardens and the pigeon-house. To the left of the house and forecourt were the bowling-green and pleasure-gardens, with the grove beyond. The latter was divided into four plots with fourway paths and a circular space and fountain in the centre. Each of the plots was planted with close-growing trees laid out as mazes, and trimmed close and square for a height of some fifteen or twenty feet from the ground. Opposite the centre alley was a semicircular bay divided into quadrants, each quadrant with a basin and fountain and great square hedges trimmed to the same height as the rest of the grove. The whole of these immense gardens were walled in, with the exception of a fence round the grove. Wide gates were set at the end of all the main paths, and from these, as points of departure, avenues were laid out in straight lines, radiating and intersecting each other in all directions. Some of these avenues extended beyond the park to the villages in the adjacent country, and were six or seven miles long" (pp. 63-64, 1892).

formed.[1] The Neapolitans, with their love of fireworks and the cheaper emotions, fired salvos from the fleet at anchor in the bay at the moment when this caravan appeared beneath the arch of the palace at Naples. Long before the tail of the procession left the palace, the report of the guns would roll up the long avenues to the model town of Caserta. Great numbers of lazzaroni ran beside the King's coach, picking up the coins he threw to them and joking with him in their dialect, which he spoke like a native. Before the two hours of the journey were up, the Mayor and Corporation of Caserta were waiting some half-mile from the entrance to the palace. The Mayor would leave his tall glass coach and wait on foot, talking to the most influential of the councillors. The procession looked as if halted half-way down the avenue, so slow was their progress. But, of a sudden, they were within a hundred

[1] Some idea of the manner of Royal processions in Naples can be gathered from the accounts to be read of the famous Festa of Piedigrotta, which took place on the 8th September each year. It was started by Charles III. to celebrate the victory he gained at the head of the Neapolitan and Spanish armies over the Austrians at the battle of Velletri. In honour of the day, all the available troops of the kingdom on this side of the Faro, amounting generally to thirty thousand men, are marched into the city, and after having defiled before the King and Royal family in the piazza of the palace, they proceed to line the streets from the palace to the Church of Piedigrotta, including the long line of the Chiaja. About four o'clock, His Majesty and the Royal family, in their state carriages, attended by the Ministers and great officers of the Court, and escorted by flying footmen, set out in procession through this double line of soldiery, whose brilliant uniforms give unusual gaiety to the scene. Each prince drives in a separate carriage. The coachmen, and footmen too, are without hats, but wear full-bottomed powdered wigs, a relic of Spanish etiquette. After performing their devotions in the Church of Piedigrotta, the Royal family return to the palace in the same order, and the rest of the day is a scene of unrestrained rejoicing to the thousands of gaily dressed peasants who come from all parts of the kingdom to attend the *festa*. In fact, the country people look forward to it with so much delight that at one time no marriage was ever solemnised without a condition being made by the bride that her intended husband should annually take her to the capital to be present at the festival (*cf.* Octavian Blewitt's *Guide to Naples*, 1853, p. 113 *et seq.*).

yards, and the rattle of wheels came louder and louder. Just before it was loud enough to drown all other sounds some white puffs of smoke jumped into the air, far away back in the bay, and the report of guns arrived very slowly and menacingly. By this time the escort of cavalry, crowing their trumpets like a farmyard, were already past, and a great many outriders and postilions pulled the King's carriage to a halt. It was just like an arrival by canal. The Mayor made an obsequious speech, thanking the Royal family for benefits conferred on the borough by their choice of a residence. The King grunted a few words in reply in the Neapolitan dialect. Then the procession moved on again. The coaches containing the Royal children and court ladies flashed along the dusty road like raindrops rolling down a window. With an immense rumble they all arrived safely in the main courtyard of the palace. The Mayor and his attendants arrived last in their coach ; they climbed out and, going through a small side door, were supplied with wine and refreshments by the King's order.

During the summer Caserta experienced great increase in population. Besides the regiment of foot and a squadron of cavalry the town was lively with the uniform, dating from Philip IV.'s days, of the Royal Halberdiers and the Suisse. In addition there were in residence for the summer a great many Neapolitan nobles, all of whom, without exception, spent their fortunes, great or small, on dress and entertainment. A few years before Charles took possession the one kingdom of Naples alone contained fifty princes, sixty-five dukes, one hundred and six marquises and sixty earls. Ten years before, in 1707, the numbers were, one hundred and twenty-four princes, two hundred dukes, two hundred marquises and forty-five earls. By the middle of the century, in spite of many sumptuary laws and regulations concerning the use of titles, Naples had still a large population of these needy but extravagant paragons. The almanac for each year contains long lists of the dazzling titles by which the King was surrounded. Every excuse and temptation for spending their money were given, and in this way the Royal family received entertainment, while they need never fear conspiracy. All travellers noticed the luxury and licence that obtained in Naples. Long after Venice was bankrupt the Neapolitan nobles found enough money to support the most lavishly produced opera in Europe. The immense palaces of the nobles, still inhabited, but still inaccessible, are, even now, a proof of the magnificent lives led by these ill-educated and hot-tempered fellows. Spending the summer at Caserta in attendance on the King they obtained free lodging in the palace and could indulge in yet richer clothing.

A grand serenade was given in the evening to celebrate the arrival of these visitors. To begin with, at five o'clock the privileged were allowed in to watch the King at his dinner. Innumerable anecdotes of his family make us certain that the King acquitted himself well in this part of the entertainment. While this went on, a military string band played in a conversational undertone. Whilst the band did the talking, the brothers and sons of the King handed him the dishes. He embarked on these adventures with a Gargantuan zest. His audience were appreciative; for a Bourbon without a nose and without an appetite would have disappointed them. No doubt they felt that in return for the huge salary they paid him as figure-head he must do what was expected of him. He looked like a fat, empty horse filling himself from their sleek pastures. He made an almost vulgar advertisement of their wares. There he sat, by himself, eating away as if he were being fatted for the slaughter. They could not grudge him his wine or food, however costly and excessive. For generations no pains had been spared to ensure a suitable marriage for his sires; prematurely condemned to a princess who was certain in herself to produce the race they admired. If they did not resent his breeding, they could not object to his diet.

By the time it was dark and the Royal family were formally to enter the garden, this immense affair was so crowded and so moving with colour as to give the air of being bedded out, for the occasion, with numberless and varied flowers. Enough lights glittered for a galaxy of stars. Theatre art had been called in, and some very satisfactory platforms and gangways were in temporary existence. Till the moon rose it was very dark, but the cries of fruit and drink sellers acted like so many signboards giving the name of each bed of flowers and showing the gardener his duties. Occasionally a murmur that their automaton had left his booth blew among the crowd, passing from lip to lip like a wind among dry leaves.

The monotony of waiting was whiled away with music. It was to the dispersion of such moments of tedium that the genius of the Southern composers was most readily adapted. It is remarked of Mozart by his biographer, Edward Holmes, that, in the spring of the year 1782, he embarked with the greatest pleasure on a speculation with a certain Martin, who had received the Emperor's permission to give twelve concerts in the Augarten of Vienna, and four grand serenades in the principal squares—the orchestra, excepting bassoons, trumpets and drums, to be composed of mere dilettanti. These garden fêtes at Vienna took place on Sunday evenings in the spring and early summer. A stand for an orchestra was built up on some green space among the trees, and the first beat of the conductor's baton was the signal to stop talking and gather round the musicians. Mozart's genius, in its lighter moments, was peculiarly fitted for the composition of this style of music, meant to attract and divert the promenaders. He was able to transmit a new elegance even to those who were dazed and dusty after a church service — for Holmes remarks that the pleasures of this promenade and the enjoyment of the air and sunshine regularly succeed the observances of religion.

For this style of music, for his serenades and *divertimenti*, Mozart was much indebted to his experience of Italy, gathered during his young life on the frequent tours on which he displayed his infant virtuosity. Such *festa* music was remarked by every traveller through Italy at this period. The Neapolitan composers were, so to speak, educated to produce light music of this description, and *opéra bouffe.* For a *festa* such as this annual event celebrated at Caserta, every composer of note who was not engaged in Russia or Vienna would write a piece. Perhaps this summer Cimarosa would be resting in his native town, luxuriating in its heat, while he prepared the opera which he was to produce at Tsarsköe Selo in an amphitheatre of ice before the eyes of the Empress Catherine and her Court. In the park and within sight from the theatre door was the Chinese village of twenty-four houses perched on rococo scrolls, with their roofs ringing in the wind with the hundreds of small bells fastened to them. To sleep inside one of these houses would be as difficult as sleeping beneath a waterfall. The palace itself had rooms of tortoise-shell and amber, with floors inlaid with ivory, ebony and other woods in a carpet of great spreading flowers and leaves. The bedroom in which the Empress held her receptions had pillars of violet glass, and was so lavishly mirrored as to appear liquid and clear as a drop of rain. Outside her glass bubble the statues and every cornice and window-frame—everything, in fact, which presented a suitable surface — was coated with gold-leaf. When, in a very few years, the gold-leaf tarnished and a renewal was necessary, the ostentatious vulgarity of Catherine made a joke at its cost incumbent on her.

The retailment of such preciosities is very necessary in order to gain the true proportion and scope of the work undertaken all over Europe by the travelling artist from Italy. Here, in Naples, the Court lived in a Spanish tradition of splendour and aloofness, which they exhibited up till the very fall of the dynasty sixty years ago. A great many of the nobles, besides being Roman princes, were grandees of Spain, and held extensive properties in that country. Some of them pushed their international ramages still farther afield. The title of Marquess of the Valley of Oaxaca, which was granted to the Conquistador Cortez in 1529 by the

Emperor Charles V., conveyed with it a vast tract of land in the valleys of Mexico and Oaxaca, containing twenty large towns and villages and twenty-three thousand vassals. The male line of his descendants failed in the fourth generation. The title and estates descended to a female, and were united by her marriage with those of the house of Terranuova, descended from the "great Captain," Gonsalvo da Cordova. A later marriage carried these united estates into the family of the Pignatelli, the greatest nobles in the kingdom of Naples. The present possessor is the Duke of Monteleone, who lives in Sicily at Castelvetrano, near the ruins of Selinunte, and still enjoys what is left of these estates after Royal repressions and republican revolutions. Such evidence should persuade us that the fandango was not unknown among the dancers of the Neapolitan tarantella, and that the harnessing of sledges was familiar to a few, at least, of the donkey-drivers in this torrid and dusty town.

A flight of rockets which shot up into the air and then dangled below a trellis of cloud, like clusters of grapes, was an abrupt signal to all the onlookers that the ceremony had begun. The King's state descent of the staircase was arranged and coaxed with a loving care. Both sides of the stair were lined with halberdiers, and the retinue in front and behind made it all but impossible for him to leave the track. But the precautions taken imparted an air of danger to the proceeding, and at the same time magnified the condescension of his act. If you can imagine what steps should be taken to drive a large iceberg down the St Lawrence and over the Niagara Falls without splintering its bulk, so that it might survive the fall and reach the sea in safety, you may realise the care and resource displayed over this use of the staircase. He negotiated it with a complete success. In a few seconds he was out of sight, floating down among the rocky colonnades towards the gardens. Impetus and current carried him quickly away, while, for a very short time, his train jostled about, splashing and foaming from the descent. Then they arranged themselves in proportion and precedence, and

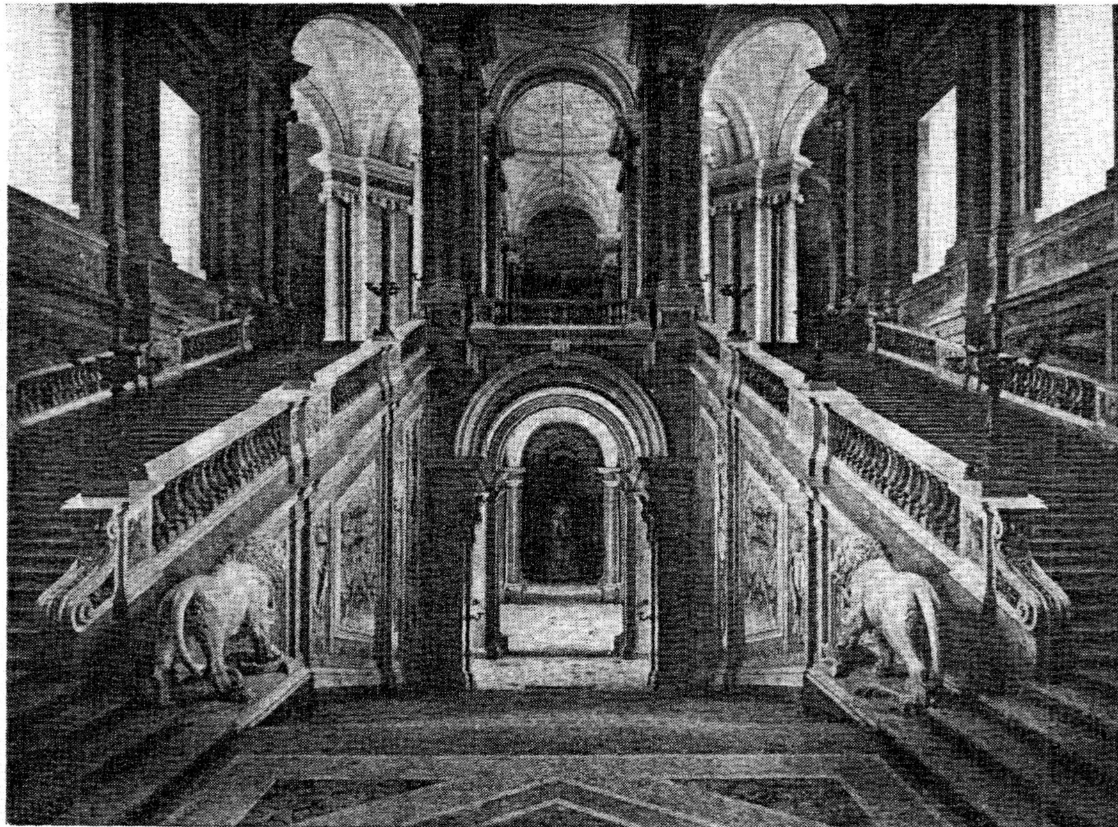

Photograph; Alinari

CASERTA

THE GREAT STAIRCASE

themselves were drifted and floated away. The broad gravelled walk in front of the palace was just such a beach as you would expect, and the strength of the river ran the whole lot of them right on to the edge of the sea, over these shelves of sand.

A short halt to see what lay in front of them, and then the procession set out among the waves and breakers. A route was prepared for them, touching at various fountains, at certain whirlpools, with a halt beneath wooded islands. The parterres were so many quicksands to be avoided, and this was easy, because they lay bare there with no waves of people breaking over them. Every fountain was throwing inordinately high. The jets of water curved down again at the height of their flight and broke into leaves of foam. These flakes glittered more and more brilliantly as they fell, until, just as they reached the basins, they opened out like a wheel of fans and spread their plumage like a bird's tail.

The trees, laid out only thirty years before, were now high enough to give shade. So close and even was their planting that they seemed like the piers of a low causeway, along which, most evidently, it was the Wind's custom to run. This much you could tell by the sudden shivers and whirrings that travelled along their avenues, keeping pace with the flying feet that ran along them. The purpose of his journeys was hard to tell, unless these bridges were a quicker road to bring water along. I presume that he ran very swiftly over them, carrying his goatskins full of rain.

More often than not the caravan that I am describing passed by little wooded islands, trimmed and clipped to shape. Some of them are worn ragged, and the tear is patched with a lattice window. Moving past quickly, you had just time to see through this window, a crinoline like a ship in sail, or a powdered wig like a young tree dusted with snow. There was a whole archipelago of these clipped trees, and they lay in front of the palace, before the open cascade-sea had begun, like so many islands in the delta of a great river.

Passing these fountains, whirlpools, and islands, the night

was constantly lit up by the chariots of fire that rushed up to the heavens with their flaming horses. When high enough in the void they let loose the birds they carried with them. With glittering wing and proud crest these birds coasted down towards the earth, as if eager with messages of the sights they had seen up there, but the rush of their fall was too impetuous. The flaming wings were shrivelled and put out, and when only the height of a steep cliff above the gardens, each plume vanished into a wisp of black smoke. In this way all the fireworks burnt out before they came back to earth, and could sit chattering in the trees or burning in the fountains like a boat hung with lamps. Nevertheless there was a continual shower of these rockets, hopeless as it seemed that one of the birds they released should reach safety again and describe what he saw at the end of each radiating avenue that led away from the house.

After the tour of the gardens was finished there were a few moments of complete silence while everybody concerned sat down and made themselves comfortable. It was quite dark, but the whole façade of the palace was illuminated, and each separate window was as light as the most alluring balcony. The strains of the grand serenade now started, as even and flowing as a flight of aeroplanes from their sheds. Each instrument as it entered the contest left the ground sharply and cleanly, and took up its post in the assigned formation. A few heavier and more blatant instruments made their entrances like bloated masks. There were sheds or archways full of zanies waiting for their cues. At the bars of wine-shops were gathered the doctors of Bologna, alert as at the dissecting-table. There were fiery harlequins leaping like smoke above springboard flames. After the vast fireworks and flights of glittering birds it seemed natural that most of the comedians were beaked. They had stolen down plumed and cloaked like the phœnixes that had flickered out before they reached earth again. To perfect this disguise their voices were rasping, for the more brilliant the feathers, the uglier and more dissonant must the song be. Once these creatures landed, they had for a time to ingratiate themselves, imitating their nearest neighbours, as at an unfamiliar church service. More of these bird-men had arrived by water, swimming here down the canals, with their clipped wings too heavy to take the air. There were yet others who had run here, jumping from tree to tree, or, like an aerial acrobat, from cloud to cloud. There were assembled in great force that particular race of humorous Neapolitans, the punchinellos. These were dressed in the plain white clothes that must be worn under the most torrid sun. The voluminous coat and trousers, as big as a sail for the wind to play with, were fit for a Turkish sultan. But instead of the turban, as tall again as himself and gaudy with jewels, they wore the beak of a particularly voracious bird. This would crack even the hardest of fruits, and, while like a bird, wore equally the set sternness of a humourless Roman soldier.

In a letter addressed by the famous Count Algarotti to a friend in Vienna, describing in ecstatic language the latest additions to his collection, the Count concludes on a note of triumph with the remark that he had lately acquired some drawings of punchinellos by Tiepolo, who was, he adds, an expert in this line. All lovers of Tiepolo will agree with this dictum, bearing in mind his superb Carnival pictures, of which two were lately in the possession of the Princess Mathilde in Paris, while yet another pair belong to the Papadopoli family in Venice. But the ethnologists who study this race of bird-men will find the best specimens for their examinations in the Museo Civico Correr of Venice, where are preserved some frescoes by Tiepolo's son, Domenico. These used to ornament the family villa at Zianigo, on the Brenta, where Domenico lived in retirement for thirty summers after his father's death in Spain. There is one fresco especially, an octangular panel for the ceiling of a small boudoir, and this composition seems to say the last word on the subject. It represents four of these comedians seen vertically from below, as the population of a ceiling ever should be. So steep is their height that only the sky and the topmost, thinnest tree branches lie between you and them. They are the four finest specimens of their race, which the Tiepolo family, always on its travels, discovered at Naples, and gave permanence to, here in the north. And that is why I find it necessary to tell of them, whilst we are spectators of this scene at Naples.

In this set of small frescoes, painted when he was an old man, Domenico has incarnated the fruit of all his impressions of this tribe. For so many years Domenico had followed his father round Europe, travelling like a family of wealthy gipsies. There were, in addition, the second son, Lorenzo, and the daughters, who were trained to pose for their father in any rôle out of an immense repertory. They were, thus, a family accustomed to take up a position among the clouds at a moment's notice. But I suppose that, in time, even a Venetian grew weary of riding clouds and floating among waves. Sufficiently dressed in the silks and brocades that the family wardrobe took with them wherever it went, the daughters would recline upon banks of cloud as easily as lie upon grass. Sparkling in the air, or rising out of the windy snow of the sea, their lovely legs and arms gave an air of safety to the most perilous positions. The duty it was of the two sons to assist their father in copying these ravishments on to the surface of a ceiling. This subordinate work did not allow fair scope for the independent vision of Domenico, and in these frescoes of Zianigo he has shown what he can accomplish, working on his own taste. I shall transfer this scene directly to Naples. It gives the widest interpretation to our midnight music.

A number of bird-men had climbed into the trees. You could see their beaks silhouetted directly against the sky. They hung, swaying, on to the branches with their hands and feet. They were a very hard and fantastic fruit for such slight boughs, but they dangled only for a moment. This lattice of boughs was a set of trapezes for them. They were springing from one to another, calling out with their sharp, bitter voices. One of the spectators, who had spent the whole evening at Caserta and watched the King at his dinner, had a fantastic explanation of these sights. The bird-men were, in his opinion, the Royal cooks. These had issued in a body from the kitchens to gather fruit for their master. The crush was too great to allow of ladders being carried, and they had climbed straight into the trees. To protect their eyes from the branches, and in order to frighten away the voracious birds, the cooks and scullions had provided themselves with these masks. But this was an insufficient excuse. At the very moment his explanation ended, one of them swung himself straight off his branch on to a cloud, and was carried, croaking in triumph, right across the canal to the trees opposite. A second afterwards, another of them leant as far as possible out of a low branch and quenched his thirst by catching one of the fountain jets in his mouth. Two of them appeared rowing an intoxicated companion in a boat on one of the small lakes to the left of the palace. They hoped, no doubt, that the cool air off the water would restore him. They disembarked at a small island and propped their friend against the foot of a pavilion. Some more of them in a second boat upset the deep baskets of fruit they had filled. But one of them dived into the water and glided as smooth as a swan over the surface, whilst he craned his long neck to look for the lost fruit. They were too at home on the water to be human. At the same time they were too free with the clouds to be of angelic origin.

By this time music was well in the air. It was a serenade quite different in intention to those we are accustomed to—a public affair, and not a private undertaking. There was no need for a Leporello to keep alert and watch the colonnades. That was a night when each turning of a window latch echoed like a footfall. At such sound he waved and whispered to his master, and the music stopped suddenly. The last notes carrying his song still hung in the air a moment before they collapsed and fell back again. It was like a rope-ladder which he hurled into the air. It spread out, mounted, and reached the railing of the balcony, but, failing to grapple on to this iron fence, folded itself and slipped back into his arms. It was a long moment for them both before the sound was dead and they were safe again.

Nor was this serenade sung under a blaze of sun by someone standing in the strong rivers of light. On that occasion it was from a marble seashore—from a quay rising straight out of the waters, and giving directly on to the sailing ships. The naked wintry masts, like tall trees without their leaves, made a hedge of wooden spears against the Turkish sea. The sailors, with their baggy trousers and burnt bodies, were slowly hoisting sail, and the evening wind was strong enough to occupy them and keep from them the real meaning of this Italian music. As sometimes happens in tropical lands, the wooden fence, under the effect of the warm sunlight, began to sprout forth. The sails opened out like giant flowers, and the fence of dead masts became changed into a flowering thicket. Each huge flower was held up in the air by a dizzy web of ropes. The wind hummed among them like a swarm of bees. The serenade died away of itself, outdone by the songs of the sailors, by the creaking ropes, and the flapping petals of the ships.

This was a music, moreover, that answered itself with a clearer voice than any echo. Both invitation and reply ran with light feet along the wires of the mandolines. There was, at the same time, no occasion and no interval for an answer. The façade of the palace was too regular and too long to allow a personality to any particular window. The shuffling feet of Doctor Bartolo could not be heard. His authority must assert itself in a little space. A door would open, while he stumbled out into the piazza on his tall staff. But by now the wires were still again and the square empty. From upstairs, but not of a certainty from his own house, sounded the stately cadences of semi-music. Someone was playing the recitative of an opera on the harpsichord. The porticoes and terraces down which this conversation was conducted sounded innocent enough, and Doctor Bartolo went off with confidence to his coffee-house. In another moment the serenade had begun again, and two figures came round the corner, out of the shadow of the colonnade. Instantly the music inside the house stopped and the two musicians felt the eyes of the player in the house upon them. The song went on, carried by its accompaniment on the guitar, until it died away in a provocative silence. There were a few seconds of doubt, in which the footfall of anyone creeping to a window would be heard. Even without such warning the window was thrown wide open and Rosina answered them. It came like the sudden fulfilment of one of Nature's labours. It was as cool as the cloak of snow which lies on every hill if you climb up high enough through the heat. Every fruit-tree seemed to protect its burden with a sheath of snow. The trembling leaves were not strong enough lattices against such hot and hungry hands. To taste their ripeness you must break through these lattice cages, which run in bars like strong sunlight in a wood, and then brave the other alternative of cold. The song which answered from the window was the more refreshing to the taste, as if the cool fruit they longed for was sheathed in snow, protecting it from heat, and making it colder still to the taste. But when just in their hands, there came a crash, followed by a frightened scream, and the singing stopped all at once. Somebody had broken in and disturbed her.

This clandestine spirit was not in the air at Caserta. There was music from as many directions as there could be birds upon the trees, and they sang on without fear of a gun, in spite of the English visitors who were present in the grounds. A great band of music was continually flying far overhead. This, at any rate, was the effect produced on far-off members of the audience. Of course the nearer you stood the better you could hear each instrument take to the air. There were one or two punchinellos still clinging to the trees, as if exhausted with their energy. From time to time they joined in the music for a few bars, rattling their guitars and singing in tired, cracked voices. Nearly all the fruit on the stalls beneath was sold. It was surprising to see the fountains still at work and the cascades as full of water as ever.

Midnight was past. The final piece of music began. The avenues were already full of people returning to the villages near by, in untidy regiments. It was so late that only those who lived within easy reach could stay and listen. Consequently the cascade and the terraces became almost empty of an audience. The winds lay panting, like the punchinellos on the trees. By the time the music was half done the crowd had dwindled down to the palace-dwellers and the most obsequious or inconsequent of the townsmen. It was so quiet that the water-birds, ruffling their feathers, floated out again into deep water from the reeds. Now that the sounds of springing and running water could be heard, everything round began to revive. The trees seemed to wind up again like springs; they were spinning once more like tops along each side of the avenues.

The straight roads which led down them like black tunnels looked more mysterious than any archway. The soft strains of this final serenade seemed to float great parties of people away as on a canal. A few of them, dressed in paler colours than the rest, were flowing steadily away with the even motion that a swan makes moving over the surface of the lake. By degrees they were washed nearer and nearer to the bank, until they disappeared in an eddy down a distant creek, and soon reached their different villages.

In the meanwhile the music had finished and everyone in the palace was about to go to sleep. Even the King had nearly finished the tedious ceremonial of undressing, and was on the point of sleeping naturally and without assistance. There remained a great quantity of scaffolding to be taken down in the morning. Over and above the bandstands and the platform for the Royal family to place their chairs upon there must have been, to those who listened attentively to the ceremony, all those artificial contrivances which lend their aid to such entertainment. The language spoken was that of a land as full of balconies, colonnades, and grots, as a

Palladian park. All these had disappeared before morning, save the bandstand and the King's platform. But all through the night there were small staccato noises. Musicians who had climbed into trees and slept there, lulled by the last music of the evening, woke up in the chilly morning hours and called to each other. Then with creaking limbs they climbed down to the ground and stumbled home. They slipped off their masks and looked more haggard still.

By this time the King was asleep and dreaming in a masterful way. Like—and he almost said, in his dream—an ancestor, he would ride right out over the bay towards Capri, on a bridge of boats. As always, he would advance between a double line of halberdiers. At the end of this pier he would cause a floating island to be built on which to perform his daily ceremony of eating, still in public, but in a novel situation. The island would be hung with lights and the sea would shimmer as if he had caused his guards to throw gold into it. Music there would be; but besides a military band in procession with him there should be other, lighter strains. Instead of the musicians among boughs at the mercy of the wind, he would be serenaded by a shoal of boats. These should play their music to him as fitfully as the waves allowed. They would be lifted higher on the crest of a wave than they could ever swing to on their trees. It would be a still sincerer address to a more perilous balcony.

Part ii

" Les Indes Galantes "

Part ii

"Les Indes Galantes"

The Spanish night is so deep and so pompous as quite to browbeat the noisier light of day. The buildings, which always look clear-cut and newly built, become, against the dark stress of evening, brilliantly crisp and more brittle than glass. A long line of white buildings will tower up to threaten you with its proud, wave-like bulwarks. At every corner, behind the dark trees that are deep, still areas of water, there will rise up another of these strutting waves out of the depth. In its turn it will draw up, holding itself to full height before it launches a leonine assault on your puny presence. Then it will hold itself back from you before the superior strength of the next glittering wave that you meet, as you walk through the brittle moonlight. In this way the slowest progress through a town will be running the gauntlet of a whole pack of hungry shadows.

Sometimes the light will be cut off for a moment as a stray cloud stands in front of the moon. This sudden darkness will enhance every effect of shadow and make the light seem more dazzling, still, when it comes back. One might imagine the rays of moonlight like a sharp-pointed sword as they pierce into every dark place and investigate its mysteries. Then, of a sudden, the moonlight dies and the Spanish captain trails his cloak along as if before a tired and dying bull. His arrival gives a new and unexpected turn to the atmosphere of the evening, and the shadows and the white squares of light, that are continually changing into each other's places, become so many pawns capturing each other on a huge chess-board. This is, indeed, a true parallel to the lives of those who are sleeping inside these palaces. It was a continual warfare between the wearers of glittering turbans and the cavaliers who wore helmets with glancing plumes that were a tribute, like steam to a train, of the speed and ferocity of their attack. This warfare lasted through many centuries, until the knights who wore turbans were driven out of their houses, which the richest among them had built in the manner of an artificial honeycomb, and the plumed horsemen were left to offer up their prayers of thanksgiving for victory. This they continued to do before altars on which they expended all the energy they had displayed in battle. There are many of such altars, still now in use, that rise sixty feet from the floor of the church almost to its roof, and are gilded and inlaid up all this height, like a parade breastplate by the most painstaking of armourers.

The awful soul-searchings of this people to discover if they were still fitted for a war against pagan destroyers resulted in the secret courts of the Inquisition. Their energy in the field was diverted into the service of the religion that they all practised. In this way there was at the command of art a never-failing eagerness to embark upon the most fantastic difficulties of construction, and this was coupled with an endurance that lasted until every difficulty was overcome and every task completed. But these qualities of faith and endurance have also the mark of slavery in their inhuman obedience to command. And just as slave-work is always the fulfilment of an alien mind forcing its will upon a machine-like crowd, so all art in Spain is a pattern sketched out by some imported foreigners, which the Spaniards fill in with all the workings of their imagination.

For a long period the great and directing influence on Spanish art came from Flanders. The visit of Van Eyck to the Peninsula in 1428-1429 is the inception of this Flemish invasion. The Spanish Gothic was like a forced blossoming of the plant that was already vigorous enough in the more northern country. There are tapestries and pictures to be found all over Spain and Portugal that give an added illustration of the strength of this influence. It may nearly be true that the Spaniards had, at this time, no national expression in art.

"Les Indes Galantes"

The dark trees and the sudden flashing houses provided a most suitable background for a rehearsal of the sudden revolt that was necessary to foist these violent characteristics, that are supposed to be Spanish, upon a world that can never have suspected them. Gradually an influence from Italy crept in. We may tell how, to begin with, the Italian artists arrived in Spain as humble itinerants. It was a long time before they came in magnificent circumstances. To parallel their mode of invasion we will say that, first of all, Savoyards and organ-grinders appeared with, occasionally, that most significant Italian product, the man who plays many instruments at once, using hands, feet, and head to produce his effects. Then, after a long preparation of the soil, Spain was ready to receive the more ambitious pioneers, and those glorious circus artists came over, whom we have discussed in the previous essay. Luca Cambiaso and Luca Giordano played to a crowded house for years, and they came back to Italy loaded with riches and honours. Between the times of these two artists the resistance had been broken, and from now onwards Italy, instead of Flanders, was to influence Spain. This victory had been brought about behind their backs, and the Spaniards did not realise where was the battle-field on which the fight had been waged.

As this was a victory of equal importance to those which ended in the expulsion of the Moors, it is very necessary to enlarge upon it. Like all victories, many of its fruits were unexpected, and the course of events afterwards was not at all upon the lines that might be imagined. It was a success fraught with greater possibilities of a change in the aspects of life than is the case with most of these secular triumphs. But this was not a battle of swords or a contest of words. It was a battle conceived of, organised and carried to a successful termination, by painting. As I have said, it was a battle behind people's backs, and the fruits of this victory, though important, were far different from what you might expect. The beginning of this essay was in a garden; and until it is late enough for the nightingales to be heard—for their song and its success is my main theme—I shall pitch this previous battle in and among these dark woods, where it is quiet enough to call everything to imagination. Then, as soon as the nightingales begin, the trumpets will be heard proclaiming that the second battle has begun, and I shall run off to watch its results.

Now the first battle to be treated of was fought on behalf of the Spaniards against the Gothic armies that had collected from Flanders and Germany. The Spanish predominance in the sixteenth century was won, not so much by the quality of her inhabitants, as by the fortunate marriages of her princes. It was through these alliances that Germany and Flanders, the Two Sicilies and Holland, became parts of the same Empire. Under the rule of Charles V., who was himself a Fleming to the exclusion of any Spanish note in his personality, there was, at first, great resentment among the Spaniards at the favouritism shown to Flemings. This race were advanced to all the posts of administration in Spain, until serious trouble arose, and Charles had, in future, to cultivate his Spanish blood at the expense of his natural feeling, which was an inclination towards Flanders.

In numerous unexpected towns, throughout Western Europe, statues of Charles V. are to be seen in the rôle, which circumstances forced upon him, of a Roman Emperor. At Palermo [1] there is a fine example of this dramatisation, and Charles presents a very strange appearance, with his gaunt, Gothic jaw showing under the Roman helmet, and with his legs showing beneath the heroic Roman kilt. The expedition which Charles undertook against Tunis was like the top stone of this pyramid of glorification. It was one of those spectacular and dramatic feats which are calculated to win fame, with no regard to the expense, or the failure to retain success. It was the same motive at work in Charles V. that sent Napoleon to Egypt. Charles was accompanied on his expedition by a great concourse of international notables, and by

[1] This statue is by the sculptor Livolsi, and stands in the Piazza Bologni.

several artists. There is a series of twelve tapestries representing Charles's campaign and a set of engravings by Hemskirk, who is said to have gone with Charles on this adventure. Giulio Clovio completed twelve large miniatures of these battles, which were stolen from the Escurial during the Napoleonic wars and are now in the British Museum.

The fact of such elaborate records being preserved shows the romantic importance which was won by this escapade. Giulio Clovio's work on this subject is the most elaborate that he ever executed, and there is little doubt that Greco must have seen either this volume or the series of engravings and the set of tapestries representing the same campaign. The expedition to Tunis was the most impressive to the imagination of any of the events of this period. The Field of the Cloth-of-Gold was as nothing with regard to the cost of its splendour, and that other crusading venture comparable in importance to the taking of Tunis, the Spanish Armada, was not yet fitted out in harbour at the time when this battle I am describing was painted.

The picture of *St Maurice and the Soldiers of the Theban Legion*, which Greco painted for Philip II. and which Philip rejected, is, in its most direct meaning, not a battle picture—that is to say, that although there are quantities of armed soldiers represented, they are not shown fighting, for there is not even an enemy within sight. The scene is divided as to its grouping into two compartments. On the left-hand side St Maurice is shown watching the execution of his men. His hands are stretched out, half in blessing and half to show the warriors where to kneel before the executioner's sword. In the other part of the picture, on the right-hand side, St Maurice seems to be remonstrating with his captains, pointing out the bravery with which the soldiers face their death, and trying to win them over by argument. To the extreme right, and just to the left of the standard-bearer who stands at the edge of the picture, there are three or four men standing looking straight out of the canvas at the spectator and not taking any part whatever in the discussion in progress. It is impossible to describe this work in more detail, and from the bare account of its composition it would be hopeless to gather an impression of the immense importance of this picture and of the manifold problems of which it represents the first successful solution.

The picture was never intended as an illustration. Greco painted it to portray the subject that had been ordered from his brush, but in doing so he tried to invest each figure in the composition with every importance that he could devise. It thus shows many more histories than that alone of St Maurice and the Theban Legion, and Greco took advantage of the fact that this story dates from classical times to make the legend an excuse for the most fervent representation of all the mock-Roman posturing of his age. It is a picture, therefore, that one may understand more perfectly by a knowledge of all the imaginary and intricate beliefs of the period. The easiest explanation of its apparent lack of meaning is to draw a parallel of the age that it presents.

To start with, then, it is evident that the painter of this picture should be tracked down as to the source of his knowledge and with regard to the scenes from which he drew his inspiration. It is important not to over-estimate the value of his work by reaction against the ignorance and contempt with which it was regarded until recent times. If he had shown a supreme genius for painting all through his early life, it is unlikely that he would have been suffered to leave Italy, where was the most understanding market for artists, in order to proceed to Spain. He was a person of sporadic inspiration, producing, as a young man, many not particularly interesting religious pictures. Although a rapid worker, he was not a prolific producer. It is important to understand that he was over-sentimental, over-sensitive, and easily to be influenced in his art. Even in his apparently most extreme feats of personality there is latent some trace of its inspiration. In his great landscape of Toledo, for instance, which strikes many people who see it as the most independent and aloof picture of its kind, it is evident that Greco had let his

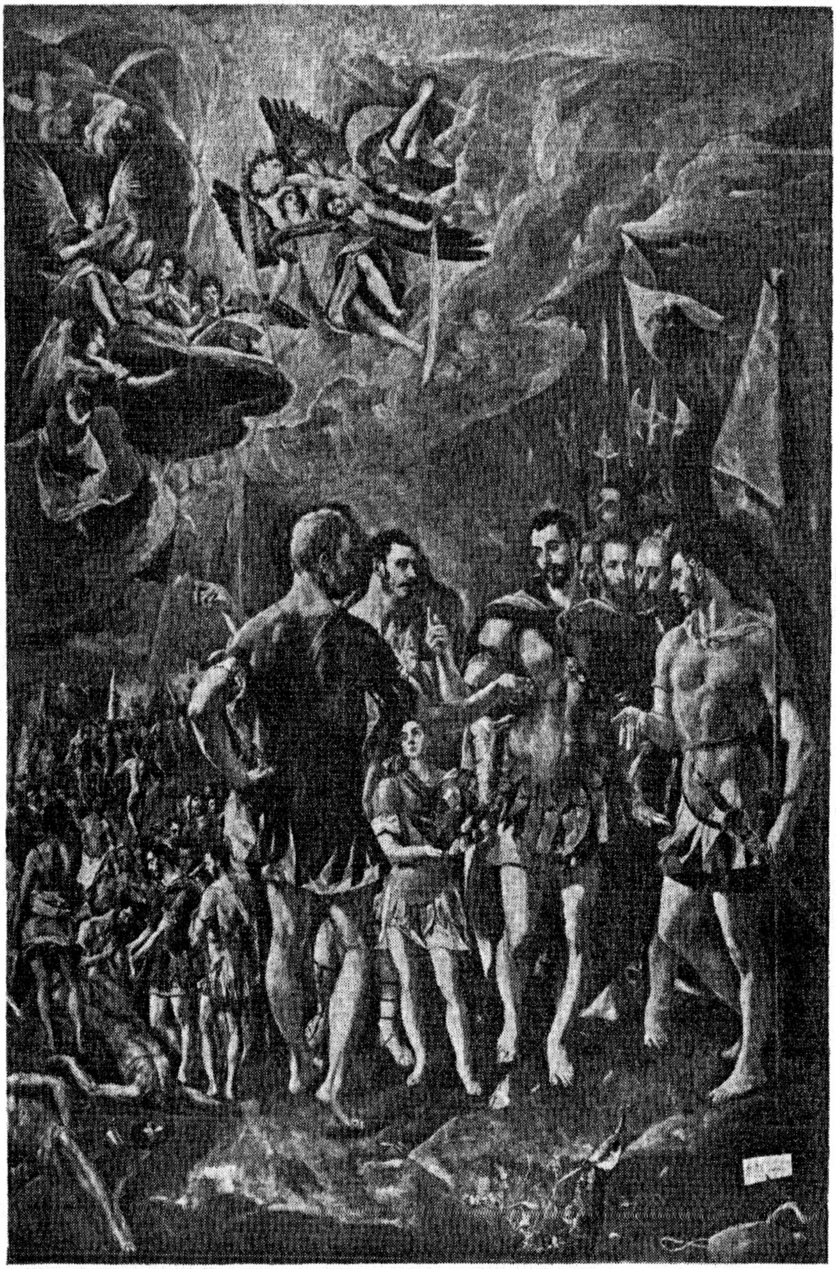

Photograph: Anderson *Escurial*

S. MAURICE AND THE THEBAN LEGION

BY EL GRECO

individuality run on a theme that is often to be met with in Italy. The views that Vasari painted of various Tuscan cities, in the Palazzo Vecchio of Florence, must have been known to the painter of this picture. I am taking the *St Maurice*, therefore, more for its manner than because of any anecdotal interest in its handling.

There is at Bukarest, in the collection of the King of Rumania, a small picture by Greco, bought probably from the Spanish Gallery of Louis Philippe. This is no less than a later rendering of the *St Maurice* at the Escurial. But in an unskilfully written catalogue of the collection, M. Léo Bachelin [1] gives the subject of Greco's picture as the Forty Martyrs, and proceeds to give a fantastical explanation of the subject. But he rightly calls attention to the cold, hard colour that is gleaming from every inch of the picture. And it is precisely this quality which is noticeable in the earlier and larger one.

I was just comparing these two canvases in my mind and thinking how Greco, in his later version, had put all the warriors into Elizabethan hose, when the whole wood became, quite suddenly, tormented with sound. Hundreds of blaring trumpets were thrashing the trees with their long blasts, more unmercifully than the cruellest wind. Very soon it would be as empty of trees as the barest field.

Now this battle that I have staged in the Pardo Woods was to determine the whole future character of Spain. She was, as a result of this contest, to drop the Flemish influence, which had been so powerful, in favour of a particular brand of southern æsthetics which, now for the first time in history, became a visible agent. To everyone who is interested in the history of æsthetics one unaccountable feature of this latter sixteenth and early seventeenth century is the total inability of the contemporary painters of sacred subjects to represent anything more than the subject, alone and simply, that they were paid to portray. Anything like the emotion or the

[1] *Peintures anciens de la galerie du Charles I., Roi de Roumanie,* p. 220. Par Léo Bachelin. Braun, Clément & Cie. Paris, 1898.

superstition of the large town populations of, say, Bologna or Naples, is quite unrepresented. The fervour and the hysteria, with all its pagan accompaniments of an un-Christian import, which were part of every religious festival, seem far away from the immaculate and perfectly executed works that the Caracci and their school produced.

It is at Naples principally that any element of this feeling creeps into Italian art. I have tried to illustrate this in the first essay. The object of this second essay is to describe how much of a similar spirit can be found in Spain and how narrowly a transcendental and supreme elaboration of this nature was missed. I have described how Caravaggio, with his melodramatic realism, was the subject of feverish emulation as he proceeded farther and farther south from his birthplace in Lombardy. Under the hands of many skilful disciples his style obtained a victory that lasted for the lives of more than one generation of artists. The voyage that Greco made to Spain should have resulted in a victory more sensational, and more deserved, than those which accompanied Caravaggio on his travels. I think it is possible to describe the small fruits of what victory there was, and at the same time point out what things might have ensued if the victory had been properly followed up to its finish. But Caravaggio had many captains under him, whereas Greco had but one disciple, and not an enterprising artist at that.

Let us examine, now, what positive effects followed Greco's adventures. Whereas the towns of Northern Europe, and the great monasteries over the countrysides, had developed a style that perfectly interpreted their feelings, it can be said that the great towns of Southern Europe remained without any means of expression peculiar to themselves. Gothic art was not fruitful in its southern forms. The art that succeeded it was too much the creation of the scholar fired with his classical discoveries, and it was not until the power of the Jesuits and the counter-Reformation movement that the population of the great southern towns of Europe began to be taken into consideration when a church was to be built, or an altar-piece painted.

Greco, who had, not improbably, visited Constantinople and Alexandria, and who was familiar with all the great contemporary achievements of Italian art, was the most likely person to give possibility to such a development. It is the fault of the Spaniards that they did not cultivate what was purposely designed for their benefit. The huge size of Spain and the difficulty of travelling there, when compared with Italy, for example, is one reason why this influence did not spread as it should have done. Greco was a person most easily susceptible to influences and must have been quick in his seizure of the peculiar qualities lying dormant in Spain. One of the very few stories recorded concerning him deals with his fondness for the local music and distorts his partiality for it into an idiosyncrasy. So there is evidence enough of his power of diagnosis.

It is a subject of thrilling interest to imagine what possibilities there were for a total alteration of most of the visible apparatus of life under the hands of so adaptable an artist as Greco. He had the powers to produce an absolute culmination of all the history of Italian painting had he been successful in his dealings with Philip II. It is well known that the *St Maurice* was painted, at the King's command, for one of the altars of the Escurial church, and that on completion it did not please Philip II., who refused it a place on the altar it had been destined for. If this picture had met with Philip's approval it is probable that the whole of the work at the Escurial would have been placed under Greco's superintendence. Such an outcome is worthy of, at any rate, fulfilment in imagination.

Let us suppose, for a moment, that Greco's picture has met with the approval of Philip II., and that the heroic figures out of the *St Maurice* are still in the midst of their argument. The sound of trumpets that I have just described was the signal for them to drop their discussion and return home. It should be possible for us to take each one of them by the shoulders and walk him home like a marionette to his box. Now the subject attributed to the smaller version of this picture at Bukarest, that of the Forty Martyrs left out on the ice, is singularly at one with the hard, brittle colour of the larger one. So, at this point, I shall fuse together the two legends of this same picture, combining the two with the manifestly false meaning attributed to the latter, and out of this double opportunity I shall try to extract the fullest interpretation of the possibilities lying dormant in such art.

If the brain which produced this picture had triumphed over the Caravaggesche realism that gave a Grand Guignol intensity to every sacred drama or farce, the whole character of succeeding taste would have changed. If Philip had encouraged this painter in his mannerisms, the next century would never have been concealed by the periwig, which was introduced as a kind of unobvious mask to the true expression of people; for a periwig was most efficacious for the machinery of cynicism, and to this day it remains difficult to arrive at the character of those portraits which are preserved, nicely masked by the flourishes and scrolls of horse-hair. Philip, the greatest figure of his time, had it in his power to dispose of the future by adapting the plans of an artist so essentially parallel to the real Spanish feeling as was Greco. But it was as hopeless to expect the King to encourage and appreciate Greco as it would be for the present Royal family of England to commission a series of caricatures of themselves from Max. There can be truths too flattering for appreciation.

The blare of the trumpets grew in violence and intensity until their warning had penetrated to the farthest of the figures concerned. The hot, glaring day was just over, and another of those nights was beginning which are so cold as to turn even running water to ice. The warm, moonlit nights of Andalusia seemed as far away as another continent. There were huge, crackling fires lighting up the slopes of the burnt-red hills. They were flickering in front of the openings of tall tents, of which a long Spanish infantry spear formed the pole. Inside these tents you could see great forms sprawling, or they were in the doorways, warming themselves before the fire. Some of the rough-looking tawny sheep that are always to be seen on the hill-sides in Spain wandered past the fires on the search for good grass.

The merest glance at the country in which these heroic figures were found—and which differs little over a great area in the centre of Spain—suggests many sites for a Thebaid. It was precisely in the most unlikely and difficult situation to be found that Philip would wish to build his retreat. The most luxurious countries in the world he was resolved to govern from as far away as possible, and from the place most contrasted to their plenty. The rich plains of the Low Countries, Germany and Italy, and the unmapped discoveries in the Western Seas, all of these were to be given direction from a kind of military hermitage. He would build a whole barrack for anchorites as near to the granite pinnacles of the Sierra as the size of his building would allow. The whole concourse of anchorites singing together would be drowned by the icy wind sweeping its harp-strings among the jagged granite rocks. He would allow no flowers in the garden, but to effect a change from the stark summer heat there would be the cold cloak of snow stretching away from the peaks above, towards Madrid; and every granite boulder that had rolled down ages ago on to the plain would seem like the footprint of a hungry monster looking for food.

We must imagine the Escurial, then, garrisoned by a host of these military ascetics, who, when there was no war to contest in, competed against each other in feats of privation. They would run long races over the plain of ice, letting their bare feet be cut by the sharp, sword-like edges. In the summer they would exercise all day long, bareheaded, going through their military routine in the hottest hours of the day. They would spend whole days climbing like goats among the highest rocks, and when the chill night fell they would sleep out there without a fire or coverlet.

The race of these Crusaders was engendered from the mind

of someone who was continually justifying and tallying his fancy with the dire necessity of such an order. Crete itself did not fall to the Turks till nearly seventy years after El Greco's death, but Turkish slavery was a menace that was always present, and which must have formed the nightmare of every person with foresight. Greco's insistence upon his Greek origin is seen in his signature and in his professed inability, at the hearing of a law case, to speak Spanish after a residence of several years in Toledo. When twenty or twenty-five years of age, the artist left his island and sailed to Venice; but to a person who took pride in his Greek blood the real capital of his race must have been Constantinople. It was in the character of the defenders of Christianity against the infidels that Greco understood the Spanish austerity, and in the picture of *St Maurice* he presented an idealisation of this particularity of the Spaniards. This casting of a rôle gives the fervency and the assured enthusiasm that we can see in the picture.

At the time when Greco was a young man in his native island the great figure in the Oriental world was the Sultan Solyman the Magnificent. It was under this Sultan that the Turks attained to their greatest power. They conquered and annexed Hungary, and they entered into a dangerous rivalry with Venice.

The situation was so grave, with the prospect of the Turks gaining a foothold for invasion in Western Europe, that the necessity for a crusade against them was discussed generally. In such a case the Holy Roman Emperor would assert his mythical authority over Europe, and the Spaniards, who had so lately extended Christendom by driving out the Moors, would be the most enthusiastic embarkers on this new expedition against paganism. But in spite of the danger, no steps were taken by the various European states, and the Turkish menace grew to greater and greater dimensions all through the sixteenth century.

Solyman the Magnificent, and his cruel and splendid ancestors, were not without effect upon the imagination of the period. Of all the states of Italy which came into touch with the East it was Venice that in her turn drew most influence from contact with the Mohammedan world. The painters of Venice were able to fix their Biblical scenery in a more convincing reality from their knowledge of the dress and manners of the East.

Gentile Bellini went to Constantinople with two assistants in September 1479, at the invitation of the Sultan Mehemet, the conqueror of that city, and at the expense of the Doge and Senate. He did various drawings of important persons at the Sultan's Court and completed a picture of the reception given by the Grand Vizier to the Venetian ambassadors, as well as the portrait of the Sultan now in the National Gallery. Bellini returned to Venice after an absence of a little over a year.

It has been suggested that Carpaccio also visited the East as the pupil of Gentile Bellini; so that by the middle of the century at least two of the most important artists of Northern Italy had seen the East and were able to draw their impressions from life. By the time Greco was to visit Venice as a student the Oriental influence was at its height. The world had learned again to imitate Roman luxury, and Italian princes and nobles emulated the Eastern satraps as much as the Roman emperors.

The Sultan and his extravagances excited the same thrall of interest over Venice that all other nations were to feel one day for Louis XIV. His armies, of which the cavalry alone ran to more than one hundred thousand, were sweeping the rich plains of Central Europe up to the very walls of Vienna. The whole earth seemed ringing with the glitter and success of his arms. The Venetians, who were so often worked by the jealousy of other states into a semi-alliance with Turkey, were especially liable to be infected with this ostentation. The joining of East and West was to produce a second Byzantium for dignity and display. An explosion of colour was on its way, so violent and blinding that it seemed as if the mind of all those Eastern parts of the earth, whom their religion had prevented from seeking an expression in painting, were at last breaking down their enforced convention and allowing the accumulation to break out. It was as though the Venetians were at work, not only for themselves but for all those races of the East that had been prohibited for centuries from this exercise.

Travellers from the East always told stories of the splendours of the Sultan's outer life, and the mysterious reticence of his private living; descriptions of the invisible beauties from Circassia, who lived in the Seraglio, were in circulation through every port of the Eastern Mediterranean. It is possible, from numerous descriptions and from the still existing remains, to piece together some idea of what the Old Seraglio, or Palace of the Sultans, may have looked like in the day of its greatest magnificence. This huge collection of kiosks and courts was surrounded, on all sides but one, by the sea, and was guarded from the waves by a wall thirty feet high, outside which there ran a quay where artillery was mounted, so that it was protected against man as well as against water. On the land side, the entrance to the Seraglio led through the Bab-I-Humayun, or Sublime Porte, and the exterior of this gate was decorated by huge heaps of skulls and guarded by fifty *kapujis*, or porters. Through this gate lay the first of the four courts of the Seraglio: on the right lay the Treasury, the infirmary and the bakery; and on the left were the timber-yard, the stables, the armoury, and the Mint. Fifty porters guarded the second gate, beyond which lay a court with a cloister on marble columns, and with its centre laid out with grass plots, cypresses and fountains. The kitchen and offices were on the right; the Record Office, the Hall of the Divan, the Treasury containing the robes of honour, and the office of the Grand Eunuch on the left. These two first courts were more or less public; it was in this second court that the janissaries were received, and here it was that, when a foreign ambassador was received, the janissaries used to dart forward like wolves to seize the food which was placed for them upon the huge kettledrums, this furious agility impressing foreigners with their potential ferocity in battle.

A gate led from here into a third court, in which were placed the Seraglio mosque and library, four huge halls for the four chambers of pages, rooms for the two corps of eunuchs, a huge series of baths and the Imperial Treasury. At this point the formal distribution of buildings gave way altogether, and towards the far end the court became like a garden, with buildings hidden away among the trees. Down in one corner of this huge enclosure, in a place called " The Boxwood Shrubbery," were the *kafes* or cages for the sons of the Sultan. Each cage was a pavilion containing several rooms and a small garden, and the whole was enclosed in a high wall and guarded by sentinels. In these pavilions the young princes passed all their early lives in seclusion, unvisited, except by the old men who came to teach them, and served by some young pages and twelve odalisques.

This court was the last stage before Paradise, and a gateway, called the Gate of Felicity, and guarded night and day by black eunuchs, led into the fourth and last enclosure. No man except the Sultan was ever allowed through it. The gardens sloped right down to the sea, and in numberless places, hidden away in groves of trees, there were pavilions for the Sultan's use, made out of the rarest marbles, and with the rooms they contained made of coloured Persian tiles, of inlaid woods, or even of mother-of-pearl and tortoise-shell.

These four enclosures, taken together, must have given lodging to thousands of retainers. In the way of music alone there were numerous bands attached to the Sultan's bodyguard, the principal of which consisted of sixteen hautboys, sixteen drums, eleven trumpets, eight kettledrums, seven pairs of cymbals and four great timbrels. Lutes, mandolines, and rebecs were the instruments most in use with the ladies of the harem, and to these male and female musicians there were added other purveyors of music, as is indicated by two posts of importance in the Sultan's household—the keeper of nightingales and the keeper of parrots. The military bands

I have described were, naturally, used principally for processions and ceremonial occasions. When the Grand Vizier was summoned to confer with the Sultan he arrived at the Seraglio with an imposing train of attendants and preceded by a tremendous band of martial music. Just in front of him walked the two chief heralds, in long fur-trimmed robes and white cylindrical hats, striking the ground at regular intervals with their tall silver staffs. The corps of chief porters, five hundred strong, and confined to the sons of viziers and pashas, rode with him on these triumphs in their robes of cloth-of-gold trimmed with sable, and wearing curious gilt head-dresses, with enormous white plumes splayed out like an umbrella over their heads. Walking at his side were some of the one hundred and fifty *peyks*, or couriers, who wore helmets of gilt bronze with black crests and carried gilt halberds. Their dress is said to have been copied from that of the bodyguards of the old Byzantine emperors. Within the walls of the Seraglio there lived the chief cook, an important official with one hundred subordinates, and five hundred comfit-makers and confectioners, all of whom wore the uniform of their profession—a green cloth robe and a pointed white felt cap shaped like a giant champagne bottle. There were two thousand five hundred gardeners, who acted also as sentinels and as watermen for the Sultan's barges, and their distinctive dress was made more prominent still by high cylindrical caps of red felt, with a long flap behind, which reached down to the waist.

When the Sultan made a progress out of the Seraglio he was followed by the sword-bearer, who walked behind, in scarlet and gold brocade, holding the heavily jewelled scimitar by its point, so that the hilt hung far over his shoulder; the huge head-dress that he wore was further ornamented by two locks of artificial hair that hung down to the middle of each cheek. The corps of one hundred and fifty tressed halberdiers came behind him, with long locks of artificial hair dangling like the sword-bearer's. The Master of the Turbans walked carrying one of the Sultan's most gorgeous turbans, which he inclined slowly to left and right as a salutation to the crowd. By this time we may imagine the procession could be seen from our standpoint far ahead, curving round a corner, and in front of the whole train march the fifteen corps of *chawushes*, or heralds.

In case he was fatigued on returning to the Seraglio the Sultan would be examined by the chief physician, who worked with eighteen doctors under him, and derived the best part of his large income through the presents he received in exchange for the china vases containing a preparation called *ma'jum*, made of essence of opium, aloeswood, ambergris and other spices, which he prepared, with the help of his assistants, and sent out at the Festival of the Vernal Equinox to the Sultan's family, to the ladies of the harem, and to the chief Ministers of the state. All of these officials were allowed only in the first two courts of the Seraglio, and there was a guard of janissaries and porters set over the various buildings; but beyond the third gate no janissary was allowed, and the eunuchs had charge of the further pair of courts. The corps of two hundred black eunuchs had special charge over the harem, and their chief, the Grand Eunuch, had the rank of a three-tail pasha, and administered the mosques and many of the holy cities of the Empire. His dignity was suitably emphasised by a white robe, trimmed with sable, and a huge white muslin cylinder, twenty-five inches high, as a turban. There were also in this part of the Seraglio a corps of eighty white eunuchs, with many dwarfs and mutes.

On his campaigns the Sultan's train was increased by a corps of six thousand Bulgarian slaves, who acted as servants and tent-pitchers to the janissaries. The tents of the pashas were all of green, and from the spearhead of their tent poles they flew the three-horse-tail ensign that was the mark of their rank, and a number of glittering gold balls—according to their importance—were strung upon the tent pole below the horse-tail device. These tents were more in the nature of a palace than their name suggests, and they contained many rooms, all ornamented with extreme splendour, as it is interpreted by Turkish taste. In the absence of anything approaching building on a large scale, as understood in Europe, it may be true that the Sultan's encampment when he was on his wars was not much less elaborate than the collection of pavilions which formed his palace at Constantinople.

The booksellers of Germany and the Netherlands had sets of woodcuts of the Sultan on his progresses always in stock. It was a special line of business, like that of the hawkers who sell printed programmes and accounts of the fashionable London weddings, or of the Lord Mayor's show. The traveller's account sold with the prints was a parallel in splendour. In front would come four hundred archers and one hundred and fifty running footmen; after them, seventy guards with gilded helmets and gold-headed spears. Interspersed among these was a band of one hundred drummers and trumpeters. In the midst of them all, with officers of the guard walking at each stirrup and three youths running before him carrying his cloak, his water-bottle and his bow, rode the Sultan, so glittering with gold and gems that, in the words of his Court poet, "he was like the sun shining through light clouds."

The extravagant head-dresses of the Sultan's followers gave additional weight to any theory that might attempt to explain their disputed origin. Those of his train who wore the huge white cylindrical turbans seemed like a race of aquiline birds half-hatched out of the enormous white eggs in which they had arrived. The more important of this train, whose hats were decorated with magnificent plumes, were full-fledged members of this tribe of birds. The Turkish camp was a terrifying sight for their enemies to look down upon from the overhanging hills, because the peculiar form and colour of the tents and the huge head-dresses of the greater part of the Turkish army looked like the arrival of a ferocious troop of eagles or vultures who had built their nests and laid their eggs in the plain below. Meanwhile the Sun, in his natural rôle of a parent, would be doing his best to hatch these peculiar monsters out of their matrix.

"Les Indes Galantes"

The famous kettledrums of the janissaries sounded in the early morning, when it was still too dark to determine the origin or direction of these hysterical rattlings and thuddings. It was like the persistent nocturnal noises that some birds and insects keep up, tapping with their beaks on the trunks of trees, or rattling their wing-cases and the armoured joints of their legs. The kettledrums were calculated to kindle the ferocity of the janissaries, as a maddening intoxicant would affect one, if dosed strongly with it before properly awake. No Polish or Hungarian knight could stand against them for the first two hundred years of their stormy career, and, vulture-like, these hordes would pick clean the bones of a conquered country, destroying everything of value and taking back with them any portable plunder and all the suitable women and children—the girls for the harem and the young boys to train as future members of their corps.

A book of engravings of the early sultans by Ja. Jac. Boissardo devotes special attention to the rendering of their ceremonial head-dresses, and gives very well the extraordinary appearance of these aspiring, eagle-like, and lean Cæsars—lean, because this was before the sultans became lazy and fat, in proportion to their self-indulgence. We can imagine quite easily the progression of a scene that has just been suggested as taking place in the Sultan's war camp. One by one, thanks to the kindness of the sun, we may think of these roc's eggs tapped upon and broken from within. Out would creep the young eagles, half-feathered, and ruffled as if washed to and fro in a strong sea. As the sun rose higher above the horizon their plumes grew more sleek, until, as soon as light had penetrated into every crevice and valley of the earth, their whole bodies were perfected and clothed with the feathers, and glittering as if dipped in the gilded morning air. By the time the full glare of light had come they were crying out and practising their wings. The huge noise of the metal kettledrums was marching down the valleys like a moving fence of steel rain that one can imagine some god carrying about in front of himself as a screen behind which he could rehearse his miracles. Very soon their music reached the hills, and they became drenched with this terrible shower.

Meanwhile the Sultan, who had been sleeping in his tent, was awake, and stepped out, fully dressed for war, just as the Sun at the far end of the plain was at the height of his forehead and had begun to gather force for his splendid climb over the hill-tops into the unencumbered air. The Sultan glittered like another sun, taking into action with him all the stars that did duty in his system ; he was moving out to war with every satellite that shone in his honour in an attempt to impose his authority upon some new tract of space. Every imaginable jewel glittered from the folds of his turban, from the rings on his fingers, from the hilt of his sword and dagger, and from the trappings of his horse. He scintillated and gave out light at every movement. The Turkish army, on his appearance, at once began their preconceived advance, throwing out huge encircling horns of cavalry on either flank, and offering a hollow centre to the enemy ; so that their whole line of attack was like a crescent moon moving in the direction of its two corners, and showing a concave cutting-surface like a blow from the back blade of a curved Oriental sword. The Sultan and his guards showed up by the brilliance of their clothing near the main body, acting the traditional star to the Turkish ensign of a crescent moon. The beating of the kettledrums rose to such a pitch of loudness that it struck the enemy outposts upon the hills as coming upon them from somewhere on the same plane as themselves ; it did not sound tired and breathless after its steep climb from below.

The Turkish admiral was as fierce and as redoubtable as the general. Their ships of war were usually built to the designs of Greek or Genoese experts, but the Turks, in their years of conquering, developed a particular adeptness in naval affairs, and chose for their sailors an even more international mixture of all the evil and criminal outcasts of other nations than that which formed a large proportion of their land army. The admirals were really so many freebooters, with a Royal licence to embark upon any marauding and slave-raiding expedition whatsoever, and in return for this lavish freedom of opportunity they were on oath to acknowledge the rule of the Sultan and to hand over to him a certain proportion of their plunder. It was a buccaneering organisation, not without the additional excuse of a wish to proselytise. The Sultan in person, of course, never proceeded on any but the most important naval engagements, and then he sailed with a huge armada of ships-of-war and with a train of barges laden with the beauties of his harem. All through the night this great fleet rowed, flickering with lights, over the sea. The sailors, in their baggy trousers, had occasionally to climb up to the sails by which the heavy boats were helped on their way when there happened to be wind. They clambered up higher and higher till the lamp they took with them looked like a little burning spark. It was remarkable to see the way in which they would glide through the meshes of a rope-ladder out on to the arm of a mast, in spite of the awkwardness of their dress. They were as adroit at this as any of the baggy-trousered clowns who go tumbling through their hoops and are admired for their neatness.

After these campaigns against Rhodes or Cyprus the Sultan returned victorious to the capital, and would retire for a space into the secrecy of his private life, rewarding himself for the hardship and privation of his campaign in a paradise of Circassian pleasures. The chronicles relate, in a jealous and gloating manner, the way in which he would walk down a double rank of the beauties of his palace until he met with the echo of his wishes, and would signify his choice by placing a gold handkerchief upon her shoulder. That night the Caliph would not sleep in a great bed, lit by four candlesticks of a man's stature, beside which four eunuchs would be standing to watch his movements and put out the two lights on the side on which he was lying. There would be no doctor waiting, mutely, in case he was wanted. The Sultan himself used to choose the pavilion in which he would prefer to sleep that night, and it would be got ready for his arrival, with a supply of food and with a small train of slaves accompanying the gold-veiled figure that he had chosen for companion. Here he would remain undisturbed for two or three days together, not attending to any but the most urgent of political considerations. The garden of his retreat was walled round, and protected even higher than the wall, by gilded lattices, while the black eunuchs on guard at the gate and at intervals round the whole enclosure made this paradise completely inviolate. From a balcony above one of the courtyards the Sultan would play a game of chess upon the black and white marble squares of the pavement, using twelve odalisques against the set of twelve slave girls who were controlled by his Sultana at the opposite window. The knights, the pawns, and the castles assumed a more human importance, and were more valuable than ever to win or lose. As a change in the monotony of these games and the contests of archery, in which a rich prize fell to the most skilled shooter at the gilded apples and the bright shining fruit of all sorts that hung upon the trees, the Sultan would spend the afternoon upon the water. They would come out from the side of a small marble quay down a creek into the wide waters of the Bosphorus. Their craft was a profusely carved and gilded barge, with an open-work pavilion in the middle; and the crew consisted of black eunuchs, and down below at the oars some eunuch members of the corps of gardeners, who pulled the boat along in place of galley slaves. There was voluptuous and lingering music played from the Sultan's airy cabin, and its strains seemed to keep time with the gentle flow of the waters more than with the rhythmic monotony of the oars. Coming to a small island thickly wooded with cypresses, the Sultan and his party disembarked, and while the boat's crew rested and refreshed themselves, the same lingering music floated out from the trees like a latticed protection to the bathers, who could be heard splashing, and must be guarded against surprise.

I have given these details of the Sultan's magnificence because they are of the highest value in studying the minds of the foremost Venetian artists. There must have been innumerable stories in circulation regarding the splendour and the wealth of Turkey. There was justification in always expecting such legends from that part of the world. The Italian states had grown up accustomed to this condition, as the small states of Greece were used to the luxury of Persia. It seemed as if there had always been magnificence in the East, ever since the times of the kings of Babylon. The capture of Constantinople by the Venetians and their bamboozled allies, the Crusaders, gave the guarantee to every story of wealth that went from mouth to mouth.

For three hundred and fifty years, from the conquest of Constantinople till mid-sixteenth century, Venice had been combining in herself the Latin and the Oriental interpretations of what was desirable in the world. There was consequently more than a suggestion of the Mohammedan paradise in their art. The most splendid exaggerations of Roman buildings were prepared to receive these Eastern guests. By the time that Greco reached Venice, the palaces were not only built but actually in occupation. Greco had it in his power to transfer these scenes to Spain, which was then in possession of greater riches than Venice had ever heard of from the East. There were all these potentialities behind him in his battle, but the force of his blow was too overwhelming. The enemy went down, while the victor himself was crippled by the strain.

Now, in examining the forces that were at Philip's command, we must consider every branch of his organisation. We have seen that, apart from these provinces of Italy which the Hapsburgs ruled over, they had, in the person of Greco, access to all the secrets of Venice, which was their enemy, and to all the expression of wealth, of which the Turks had learnt the manner from the mediæval Greeks. There was enough of the Oriental in Spain to replace all that was lost when the Moors were driven out. In addition, the whole force of Flemish art was at Philip's service. There remains one other factor, and this was derived from the Spanish occupation of Portugal.

In 1581 Philip went, in person, to Portugal to receive the allegiance of the Portuguese on his accession to their throne. The town of Thomar was chosen as the scene for this ceremony. There is in this place one of the most venerated churches in Portugal—that of the Knights of the Order of Christ, who were the successors of the Templars in this country. It was here that the Spaniards first came into contact with the strange architectural style only to be met with in Portugal, and called Manoeline, after their splendour-loving King Emmanuel. There is built on to the ancient church of the Templars the most perfect example of this style to be found in the country, in the shape of the choir and chapter-house of the Knights of the Order. Here it is that the Manoeline manner may be studied in its most typical elaboration. The famous Prince Henry the Navigator, who was responsible for all the Portuguese voyages of discovery, was Grand Master of the Order, and this choir and chapter-house were built, partly under his direction, and partly as a tribute to his memory when he was dead. At every available place the cross and the armillary sphere which formed the device of the Prince were worked into the design of the building. As if to typify his great enthusiasm for the sea-voyages of exploration, great stone cables like a ship's ropes are carved. The doorway is enclosed in an arch, of which the under curve has an elaborate pendent ornament. Over the door, and within its recess, figures in niches stand under canopies, and upon pillars, in which all these and many other devices have been employed. Coiled cables, bossed spirals, floreated pinnacles, armillary spheres, and crosses stand out in high relief. The lower window, which lights the interior of the choir, is a tangle of outstanding ropes, each point being crowned by the cross and the armillary sphere. Around one of the corner towers, a great chain, each link carved entire in stone, is braced, and around the other an equally tremendous buckled belt, representing the Order of the Garter, which the Prince, who was descended on the female side from the Plantagenets, was presented with. The upper window, which lights the chapter-house, presents an extreme instance of this manner. It is a window of great depth worked into the surface of the wall, and represents upon the sloping inner face of the circle a series of bulging staysails, each held down by a rope.

The Manoeline was a style most admirably adapted to display the sentiments of the small race of Portuguese who had risen into a sudden importance by their daring in embarking upon long-distance voyages. They owed everything to their skill in shipbuilding and as sailors, and, as if in proof of this, the whole method of building at this date seems to be a tribute, taking the form of imitation, to their vessels. The coiled cable recurs over and over again wherever buildings of this date are to be seen in Portugal. When inside a cathedral, this race of sailors liked to imagine they were on board ship. The well-known "Cappellas Imperfeitas" of the Abbey of Batalha are an instance. A large central chapel with ten smaller chapels round it rise to only half their intended height and remain roofless, for when King Manoel died—in 1521—the work stopped and was never continued. Toward the top the clustered columns of pillars start up again higher, in form like a bundle of reeds, and with an altogether Indian elaboration of detail. The upper parts of the chapels are so many tremendous masts decorated with galleries round them, and sacrificing every convention in order to conquer the necessary height. From such an elevation, on the stillest day down below, there would be a strong wind blowing, and the great stone cables, the flying buttresses, and the carved staysails gave the most convincing imitation of a ship in full sail.

For the first half of the century the King of Portugal had been the richest prince in Europe, and on succeeding to the Portuguese throne Philip found a great addition to his already existing wealth. The trade with the Indies, and the wealthy colony of Brazil, were added to the huge possessions that already belonged to the Spanish Crown. Spain was without a suitable harbour, except Cadiz, to cope with the great trade with America, and the Indies. Had the national prejudice of Spain not prevented him, Lisbon would have made an ideal port for this commerce. There is no finer natural situation for foreign trade in the whole of Europe. It is perhaps fortunate for Portugal, which was to assert its national independence again, that Spain did not take this step to absorb her, which would have been altogether to the Spanish advantage. At any rate the employment of the Portuguese wealth on their buildings cannot fail to have impressed every traveller who visited that land with the strange development that this country had given birth to in architecture.

I think that we have now summarised every influence that could have been brought to bear upon the most powerful prince that Europe had produced since the time of Imperial Rome. In spite of the partition of the Empire at the death of Charles V., Philip was a more important figure than his father, because of the increasing wealth of Mexico and Peru, which, under Charles, had only been discovered and not properly exploited. Having diagnosed these conditions, it now becomes possible to discuss the state into which affairs might have developed had Philip made use of the person who was most capable of giving direction to the Spanish peculiarities, whilst blending them with his complete working knowledge of all that the Renaissance had created in Italy, and of all that the Mohammedans had destroyed in Eastern Europe.

The retreat which Philip designed for himself was both less luxurious and more practical than his father's retirement at Yuste—that is to say, the Escurial was the scene of real austerity, while at the same time it lay near to the capital, and was ostensibly designed as the control-centre of the Empire. It must, therefore, be splendid in scale, however ascetic in detail. There must be every appearance of wealth to impress people, as if to magnify the sacrifice for future life which was shown by such insistence upon discomfort on the part of so important a person. It was calculated to induce resignation from those who were cast for a difficult and poverty-stricken part in this life.

Greco had been painting his *St Maurice* at the Escurial itself. It had occupied all his time for many months, and, having once begun, he had put his best work into it. He had been painting probably in one of the large and then unfinished halls of the building. He worked without any preliminary drawing: had one been submitted, it is not improbable that his commission might have been taken away! The workmen were not a little impressed with the miniature-like finish of the principal heads—painted so minutely with the smallest brushes that the glistening of the eyes was visible as far away as in an actual person. The heads seemed to contrast curiously with the apparent speed with which the figures were improvised. Actually there was more brush-work than in the most finished Flemish picture, but the fact of there being less ruling of lines and less copying of a highly finished drawing gave a bravura air to his work which was misleading. There is a depth in the picture which is not to be found in the Netherlandish masters, who conceived a picture in the terms of a drawing. It is a picture conceived in terms of painting, and not as the tinted enlargement of a photographic negative. The picture, during the months in which he was at work on it, never suffered from any of the ills of indecision on the part of the painter, for he seemed to arrive down each day in exact knowledge of what effect he would produce. This came from the complete mental visualisation which he had achieved from the practice of never preparing in more detail than a slight oil-sketch, however important the picture in hand. He had to depend, therefore, upon an entirely finished programme in his head.

Once the picture was in place upon its altar a furious battle broke out, in which the more devout a Spaniard might be, the more bloodthirsty was the warrior he became. It is true that the warfare, at first, hung fire, but it is my duty to pour all the oils of Mexico upon the flame, because the brighter the fire, the more we can see by its light. There were whole battalions of matadors marching to the fight from every monastery in Spain. The most convinced inmates of the many Thelemas that were hidden away throughout the land were stirred out of their pleasures by the universal clanging and bruit. The church doors were everywhere opening wide to let out the Crusaders, whose arms had just been blessed. In the biggest churches of all they were blessed to the strains of the loudest music that the building could hold. They were revived by the censers that dangled high in the air and were swung from below with ropes. Meanwhile, the second and more noisy sort of bells were pealing out very loudly; they looked as if pretending to jump down and crush the crowd with their weight each time they swung free outside the brick arches that held them. The procession leaving the church was just the drop of water that a wave had left on the bows of a boat falling back into the sea again, so vast was the crowd. Then the music suddenly rolled out through all the open doors. It gathered force as it spread out after these narrow openings. Then it caught upon the wind, climbed up, and rode it as a horse; it was soon galloping fast, far ahead of the procession, the flying clothes of the rider spreading out over the heads of the crowd, till the music caught them like a great sail flapping lazily in the wind. The music was a force that held every vessel straining at its ropes, and very quickly the pulse of every person in the crowd was rattling like a mandoline. The martial music had the power to brace up and kindle the heart of every person there. The square was as if latticed and festooned with taut wires, for every effect of marching to music is like walking a tight-rope, from which you dare not look down. The bells rolled out louder and louder, till their very metal was molten as if to beat into sword-blades, and when the whole volume of sound died suddenly, its last breath blew away, dwindling in force till the hills at the end of the valley were reached.

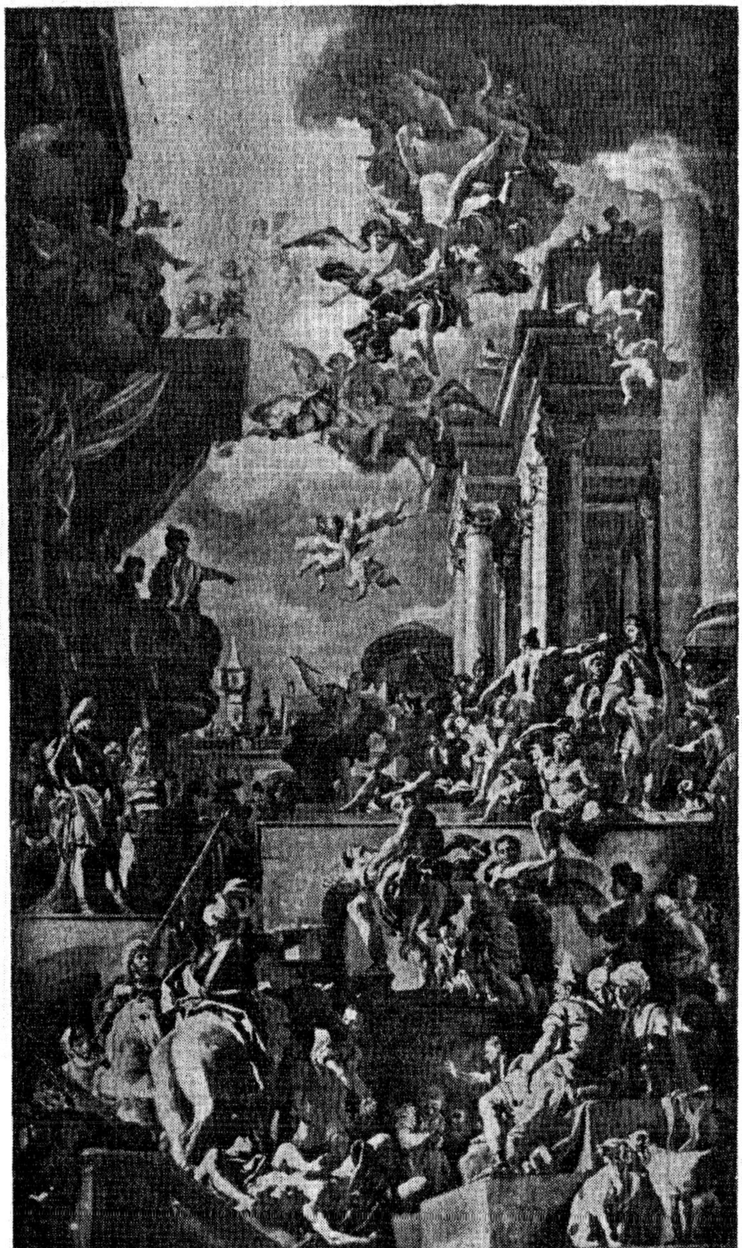

Photograph: Alinari *Museo Nazionale, Naples*

THE MASSACRE OF THE GIUSTINIANI

Over the other side of the mountains were marshalled the Gothic armies that were offering battle. An army completely clothed in steel is a sight more familiar to the insect than to the human world. When they moved at the word of command the noise of armoured joints was as loud as a fleet of ships manœuvring. Their spears were the barbed stings that an insect threatens its enemies with. They looked ready to emit poisonous stenches, or hide themselves in a cloud of black liquid at a single discharge from their fanged bodies. Their arms must be furnished with saws instead of fingers, that they may the easier dismember their foes. The horses, too, were trapped and harnessed in armour. With the rider encased in steel plates, they were too heavy to run over the plains as quickly as the centaurs they resembled. If a horseman was knocked from his saddle he lay too heavily lumbered to rise again, and the horse walked solemnly, as if at the funeral of part of its own body.

The gloomy and tangled edge of the woods became more provocative than ever by reason of the confused sounds that came from within. Far away through the black night that the trees made there were castles standing up in richly flowered oases. Their orchards stretched away down long avenues and through patterns and archipelagos, like the star clusters on the map of the universe. The signs of the zodiac were laid out in a belt of flowering trees, so that you could see their green forms splashed against by the blossoms. From up above, at one of the windows, you could see down the long straight alleys, where the leaves glittered with dew, as if the shining fruit was already hanging among them. Between these alleys there lay the different devices of the zodiac, like so many islands lying between the avenues that flowed like strong currents through the sea. Each island in its turn lay there with its leaves like fields of green and with its shore snowed under and broken upon by perpetual waves of blossom. Sometimes the castle walls rose straight up out of the waters of a lake, and in their fantastic newness they looked as if carved out of chalk cliffs by a serious sea, far deeper and more salt than this mockery dug and dammed among marshy ponds. On particular gala nights, before the winter came on, there was a splendid searchlight display by the moon. Sometimes it would play its beams upon the banks of cloud that began to loom up heavily as soon as it was dark. It was like levelling a great gun at a ship in full white sail. Then it would come down lower and run out across the water on its electric bridge, reaching the trees on the far side in a second or two. Here it would show a party of men snaring game with their spider-web nets. Rising higher again it lit up the tops of all the forest trees, showing them like a sea of tumbled billows above the quieter waters of the lake. Before disappearing altogether behind the cloud bank it would lift up its beams and show the whole of empty space lying there like an easy ascent to those floating terraces that were lying above, at the mercy of any wind that passed by. Later on in the night there would be one or two more displays of moonlight as soon as the clouds had drifted far enough away. But by this time everyone would be asleep, and it would play all by itself to a seemingly empty house.

Such galas caused the romantic feeling to spread about, infecting people with its extravagant fever. Clothes assumed fantastic and hyperbolic fashions. Rich young men wore their cloaks and sleeves cut like the sharp edging of a leaf or a fish's transparent fin, and their shoes were so long and pointed as to necessitate the toe being connected with the knee by a golden or silver chain, so as to keep it curled up above the ground. No prophecy of the aeroplane was too unlikely for the design of women's headwear: in extreme forms they compromised between the aeroplane and the fullest rigged sailing vessel.

A window looking on to the orchards would open very high up in the fortified wall. There would be, of course, someone waiting below among the fruit trees or on the sands of the lake. The window was too small for the woman to stand there with even a simple head-dress. She would lean out and loosen a long torrent of hair down the grey walls.

It was the golden mane of some animal trembling with its speed and the effort of climbing so high. This molten river ran down shimmering in the strong and fresh sunlight, while the wind blew little rivulets aside against the dour stone.

This was a direct challenge. Before long a tournament was arranged to settle the dispute. The knights arrived in their heaviest armour, while the ladies were disposed upon the turrets of the wooden castle built for the occasion. It was an arsenal stocked with flowers in place of engines of war. A flourish of trumpets, and the entrance of each pair of gladiators was the signal for a shower of flowers: there was a second downpour as each hero limped away. At the end there was a regular battle of blossoms. Some trees near the wooden stand had been arranged and strung for the occasion, and the jesters were high up, hidden by the leaves. They were sitting on the branches among these huge quivers, that were filled with flowers tied beforehand to the alien leaves. Small bows and miniature catapults were the weapons with which they propelled these arrows over the battlements and between the turrets. Wounds were given that left marks as red as blood, and the air was coloured with flying petals as if dropped down from the lap of the sky.

At this particular time, though, there were different sounds drifting out through the trees to the edge of the wood where we were listening. There was a feeling of departure and change quickly to come. Very soon the castles in the woods would be deserted. The knights went out to fight, and the ladies were removed to safer and more humble refuges. Even the hermits, living in their huts made of leaves, were occasionally interrupted in their meditations by a knight passing by, with his servants carrying the heavy armour that he was taking to the wars. All the hunting parties, late and far afield, arrived back at last to find they must set out at once on a longer and more dangerous expedition. The tapestries were rolled up into long tubes, with only their border showing, so that they looked like big bundles of dried flowers. The explorers who were for ever travelling in search of the fountain of life, the champions who were out to challenge the Green Knight when they could find him, and the musicians who walked through the woods listening for the voice of Orpheus and the sight of the wild animals waiting entranced —all of these adventurers came home for the last time, and started out again to the war.

In the middle of spaces, that had grown into deserts since the barbarians had passed that way, were huge monasteries, like the outlying colonies of the early mediæval kingdoms. The ablest as well as the laziest men of each district were gathered into these centres. In the course of three or four centuries they had developed into semi-independent states. All the land they had reclaimed was theirs, and they could depend for their existence upon constant streams of fresh blood, as they were celibates and far removed from all family cares. They were a drain, therefore, upon the whole male population of their state. They were as fierce soldiers, and more numerous, than were at the disposal of many kings and princes. It was in such communities that art had often attained its fullest development, under ideal conditions brought about by wealth and prodigal labour. These paradises lay far away, and could only be reached over the mountains by foot or on muleback. They had outlying farms with yards stacked with ricks and bundles of dried grain. The trumpets blowing in the dawn were as strident as any that ever awoke the farmer and his wife and children. But here they sounded more in the manner of a military bugle, for the farmers woke up at the sound and went out to their work, but there were no farmers' wives and no children.

Every town there had a church in proportion to its size, but very much too big for the population. Sometimes they stood out above the town on a little hill in the middle, sometimes they lay close to the river, and occasionally they stood high up on the cliffs like an iron screen to keep the fierce sea-wind off the town. The style and manner of their building had set out slowly from a centre in the north. In early days they aimed at height, and stormy weather was their most redoubtable enemy. The extraordinary means by which they sought to hold up these vast weights of stone were an encouragement for every antic of extreme weather. Over the carved doors was a rose-window, which on windy nights it was possible to spin like a huge wheel or a propeller. Just before nightfall it was distinctly to be seen beginning to turn round and round. The huge glass sides of the building, glass nearly from floor to roof, were riding like the bows of a ship through wave after wave of wind. There were buttresses flying up from below with their desperate attempts to hold up the stone-coping and the heavy roof above the brittle glass walls. The wind had only to throw one of its ropes round a buttress to direct the building as you steer a horse by catching at its rein.

As this style of building spread out in every direction from its place of origin in France, it altered a little, accommodating itself to each climate. Travelling farther south there was no longer necessity to keep in mind the great winds of the north. The winter had not to be considered, nor was there a crushing load of snow to be carried upon the roof all through the darkest months of the year. It must have been a memory of some such place lying with all its roofs knee-deep in snow that prompted the people of one torrid town, famous for glaring summer heat, to build their cathedral in imitation of one of the snowbound mountains which looked so cool all through the hottest days.

In extreme instances, as I have described, by way of a tribute to the sea, from which they derived all their prosperity, they attempted to build their churches, making use of every device and symbol that suggested the adventures of ship-going. Knotted ropes and coils of cables occurred as frequently in their ornamentation as they do on board a real ship. Cordage seemed to hold the towers and pinnacles together as much as the masts on a vessel. Everything was tied and lashed into place. The whole structure was only lying at anchor, and tied to the buildings round about that acted for her as buoys. She might set sail at any moment with loud music swelling out of every porthole and with her glass sides glittering with lights from within.

It was the men from such places as these that were some of the many foes gathered together in Spain for this last Crusade. There were ranged, against the art that was to conquer, all the romantic and literary influences that had held back mediæval art from the complete expression of all that had gone before it. Every person of discernment will recognise what a loss to civilisation was involved in the fact of France being unified and centralised into a nationality by Henry IV. and Louis XIV., instead of a similar condition overtaking Italy before she had exhausted her strength and sunk into decadence. The cultural war that was raging at this time in Spain, just on the extinction of Venetian power, held as many possibilities that were lacking in fulfilment. Had these chances only been followed up, the whole tradition of art that the Italians had gone over and learnt from Constantinople would not have been wasted. Instead of a collapse into realism, painting would have continued to transcendentalise Nature. I must contradict historical reality to a still more marked extent.

The conversion of *St Maurice*, then, met with a warm approval from Philip II. No sooner had the King seen it than he recognised its merit. Greco was appointed Court painter and Superintendent of Royal Buildings. He was awarded a generous salary, and it was paid promptly. Complete licence of expression was allowed to him, and he had only to suggest a scheme to be allowed to undertake it. The King treated him as a friend, and took pleasure in conversing with him upon every conceivable topic.

Often it is painters of the second order who find it most easy to found a school. A supreme artist who is not so much tied down to his date and to his local conditions is a more dangerous person to impersonate. The swifter a thief can run the more difficult he is to catch. I do not mean that Greco was a slow thief or an ordinary artist, but each of his posturings was carried to such a point that imitation should have been easy.

Many London theatres have still the bad manners to entertain their customers with imitations of other actors and actresses who can only be known to the most persistent of theatre-goers. Somebody is always found to laugh at this exhibition—a professional connoisseur. But it is evident to the simplest eye that it is not the best actor who supplies them with the most faithful imitation; it is usually of someone unknown to the unprofessional public. In the same way we may imagine an entertainment offered to connoisseurs of the date of these histories—a feature in which would be imitations of well-known painters of the day. We may be sure that the presentment of Greco would meet with frenetic applause, because he is the more obvious and the most distinguishable of artists.

He met with no difficulty, then, in a search for disciples. The strength of his art lay in a refusal to muddle and intermingle one art with another, having a very clear understanding of the different terms of æsthetics. His interpretation of the meaning of realism was very different from an insistence upon the equal importance of every detail in a picture. He seems to have had a strong disapproval of the confusion between drawing and colour. German painters, for example, have insisted upon drawing, until, in a picture, they have treated the brush like a pen. As a result the German primitives were conceived as tinted cartoons, and the colour is an adjunct to the design instead of constituting, in itself, the principal of every picture. The preparation of careful drawings he seems to have left to the engravers, considering it to be their work more than his, for there is only one drawing by Greco that is known. His pupils he taught to concentrate their impressions of a subject into as condensed a form as possible. Then, laying stress upon the principal subject, and leaving out all details that impeded and interfered with the action of the picture, he made them paint their conception of the subject, without any preliminary, on to the canvas. This was a policy calculated to do away with any extraneous or alien influences in such a way that the picture could never become a mere illustration, while, at the same time, from the severity and acuteness of the image, it was unlikely that the action would be crowded with too many figures and irrelevant detail.

Before describing his work in little, let us arrive at a clear understanding of the setting in which we are likely to discover his pictures. Greco, in whom many authorities are disposed to discover one of the most typical spirits of the Baroque, and in this context even go so far as to compare him with Bernini—Greco was very far from encouraging any extravagance in architecture. Wherever any of his acknowledged work is to be found he has insisted upon the utmost simplicity and the most severe lack of detail, for he knew well that simple architecture was the best frame to an elaborate picture. His sculpture, of which very little is extant, follows the same principle of subordinating the background to the benefit of the picture or statue concerned. The church of the Escurial, as it actually remains, cannot have offended his taste by the protrusion of too much ornament: the richest marbles are used, but there is a very pleasant lack of busy detail. The most obvious fault to be found with the church is its black darkness, out of whose obscurity even an altar-piece by Greco would hardly emerge. To these principles of taste which I have ascribed to him must be added a dramatic love and knowledge of lighting, for the subordinating of architecture to the picture that it frames serves to concentrate attention upon the picture; and if, in spite of this, the latter is invisible, then the purpose of all this trouble is lost. We must not expect to find here, as one does in Neapolitan art, a competition like those described above between Luca Giordano and the workers of *Intarsiatura*.

The latest date at which the art of illumination was practised on a large scale was under Philip II. Although printing had been in use for more than a century, Philip ordered a series of huge choir-books to be illuminated for the church of the Escurial by a number of Italian and Spanish artists. Now all the introductions with which Greco was furnished on his first visit to Rome had been given him by Giulio Clovio, the greatest illuminator of the day, who, being a Dalmatian and, therefore, a colonial subject of Venice, may have considered himself a kind of fellow-countryman of the Cretan artist. It is probably the championship of Greco by Clovio that has led early books to speak of Greco as originally a miniature painter. It is, though, not improbable that Greco may have done work of this kind as a young man; and it might be reasonable to infer that he owed his commission for the big picture at the Escurial to the fact that he had already given the King a proof of his ability in the shape of illuminating some of the big miniatures in the choir-books of the Royal church. Such a specimen of his labours would have a special value inasmuch as it would bring into prominence the strong element of Byzantine tradition that really underlies the artist's apparent Baroque characteristics. The frequent use of a gold background would, in itself, carry this constituent of his art almost to the point of caricature, till his figures, against a gold background, would betray their remote origin in the same way that sham antique furniture is disproved when placed in an old room of apparently identical date. The icon-like construction and character of many of his religious pieces would be given prominence when, in a book of this nature, the very same subjects are to be seen treated in miniature fashion. But under the circumstances that I am now describing, we must assume, not that Greco painted such a book which is now lost to us, but that he and his disciples had produced a whole series of such volumes that are still existing and available for study.

As I have said, his illuminations were so successful that they secured Greco his order for the picture of *St Maurice*, and this, in its turn, met with the approval of Philip and gave him the complete direction of all the works at the Escurial,

He was able to supply each altar in the church with a picture, and we may ignore the existence of Romulò Cincinnati. There are forty altars in the church, and over each of these Greco had undisputed possession, to the extent that we might consider the whole church as a temple to his fame. The *St Maurice* was in position over the high altar, and Philip, through the window from his bedroom, at which he listened to every service, could distinguish it with a sidelong glance which compressed and perhaps still further improved the picture. In the sacristy there were more paintings and the greater part of the number of choir-books which were used at the services in the church.

As with most painters, his secular pictures were more interesting than his religious pieces, and so it is in the palace and not the church of the Escurial that we may hope to find the best examples of his hand. We may suggest, in the first place, a multiplication of the scenes that Greco painted, too rarely, from classical subjects. Instead of the *Laocoön*, the one specimen of this nature, we might imagine a whole series planned and executed, endowing the artist, on our part, with the facility of a Rubens. In his picture of *Orpheus* we can see the musician playing his lyre in the foreground in front of a sheet of water which will serve to show every marine animal in its element. On the far bank the land animals are ranged, and the more hardy of them have ventured into the depths with the object of getting as near as possible to the music. He has attempted in this picture to gather the whole elements of the music into his rendering of the water, and where there is space left over from the gleaming bodies of the animals, or from the still glassy water shaken and ringing with their movements, he has shown the gentle shadows of the trees and the slopes of the windy hills thrown back into the lake. In this way, just as you would have heard the music twice over—where Orpheus is playing and, a second or two later, where the animals are gathered on the off bank—so here you see the far hills and the drooping trees that lean over the water, and in a second breath they are seen again flickering

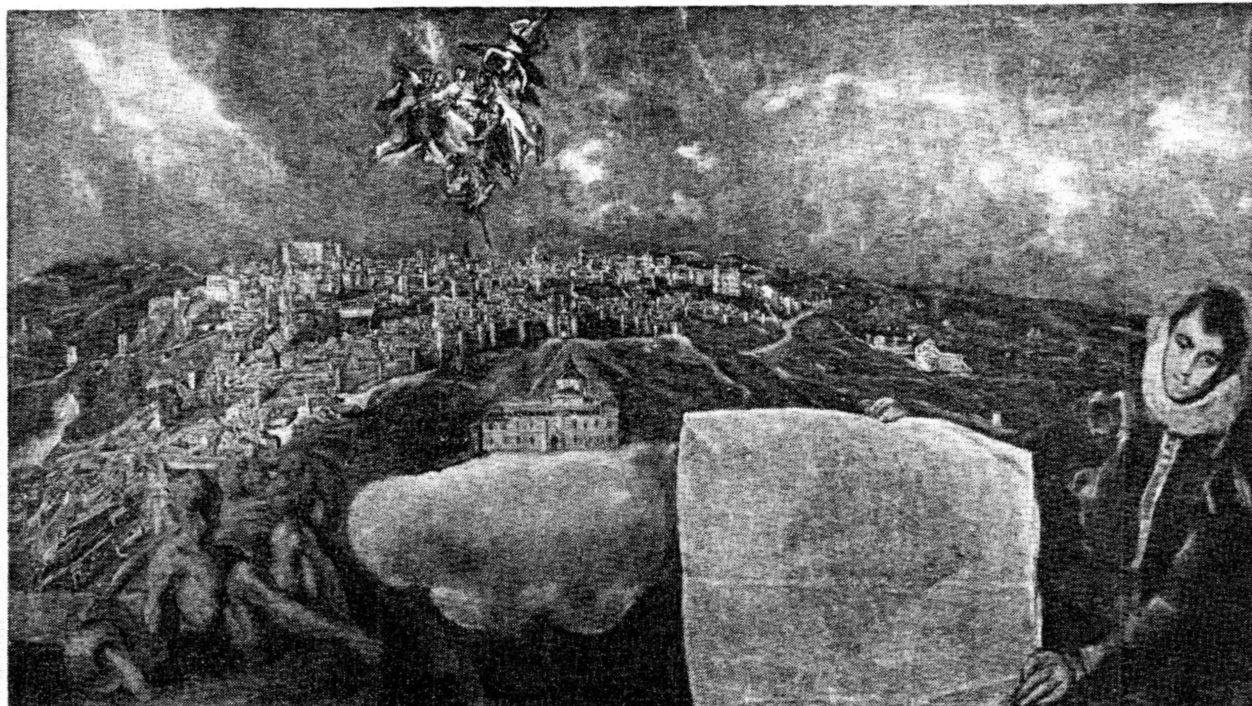

Photograph, Anderson *Museum, Toledo*

VIEW OF TOLEDO

BY EL GRECO

in this mirror and achieving a perfect balance with the music.

A second picture that you choose at random out of the series shows Perseus rescuing Andromeda. She is lying tied down against the rock, unable to offer any resistance, even to the softer assault of the waves that are making attempt upon attempt to moisten the cords through and carry her back with them down the shelving sands. Up above, Perseus, who glitters just as transparently, is fanning the air on to her in his efforts to reach ground and release her as quickly as possible. The rocks are painted just like a battered mountain of tin, taking every curious device and dint of the hammer, while the sea is not so much breaking as gathering itself together for a spring, and the whole air and Andromeda's body are covered with the last flight of snow-quilled arrows.

Over and above the *Laocoön* there were a whole set of pictures with the Trojan legend as their subject. Whatever the figures and their action, in each picture Troy appeared somewhere in the background. Sometimes it looked like an adaptation of the Escurial taken from the granite hills down to the plains beside the sea ; at other times it was a town like Venice, and the Greek fleet were fighting in the open harbour and the narrowing, shallow canals. The warships were great Spanish galleons, with as many sails as the Sierra carries snows, and when they were too close in to manœuvre with the wind they were tearing at the water with a whole armament of oars. The defenders of Troy were rendered with the wildness and ferocity that he reserved for his anchorites and which he was justified in ascribing to them after the privations of a siege of years. The Greeks, on the other hand, were lining their decks in wait for the signal to let down the gangway and get a footing on the quay. In spite of the Greek fire and all the boiling oil that was waiting for their landing they were undismayed, as if the fiery colour of their silks and armour were proof against any flame. Meanwhile their galleys had been rowed forward with utmost speed, so as to rush the enemy on their landing ; the gangways were all held ready till the moment should arrive for them to make a steep bridge from these wooden cliffs down to the quayside, and now, just a foot or two from the destination, the banks of oars were backwatering with all their strength, so as to break the force of their arrival. You could hear the hoarse shouts and the drum tapping out the time, whilst the air was cracking as if from pistol-shots with the furious whips of the overseers, and, down below, the water was seething and welling up between the ship's side and the wall as if in an attempt to escape from a boiling cauldron. Just as this flood of water was at the height of the ship's deck and ready to sweep over and submerge deck and harbour walls, with a last furious brake they managed to bring the ships in side by side with the pier. This was the moment that the painter had chosen —when the ships at the back of the picture were flapping their sails against the tall architecture of the first houses; a little nearer were the ships which had furled their sails and were racing forward with every oar toward the pier; in front of all was this vessel at the point of placing its gangways down on to the landing-stage.

Another great hall was hung with the life and the labours of Hercules. All through this series you could see the influence of the giant canon that Giovanni da Bologna had evolved from studying the Farnese Hercules; inasmuch that in each picture Hercules was of more than mortal proportion, while at the same time preserving something of the awkwardness to be expected from a god who was not thoroughly accustomed to the more confined conditions of earth. He had the strength, and its good-humoured but ignorant application, that you would expect of a giant policeman, and was built as if to go buffeting the winds or wading through a deep sea of waves. "Labours" was a misleading term for his deeds; they were more like a different form of sport for each month of the year.

These two halls, the "Trojan" and the "Hercules," were designed as banquet chambers for the Orders of Knights that Philip had instituted; beyond them and their respective ante-rooms and kitchens lay a hall for the feasting of the Knights of the Golden Fleece. On the nights of such Homeric banquetings the snow would often be lying inches deep through all the courtyards, so as to contradict and throw doubt upon the travels of these Argonauts, but the walls were thick enough to keep out the freezing cold as much as they could diminish the hot sun through the summer. Each course was carried in to the accompaniment of a flourish of trumpets, and after some time a whole band of Spanish music began playing from a gallery at one end of the hall; this was after the first drinking of toasts, and the music exercised a stimulating effect upon the talking. Every few minutes another toast would be announced by the trumpeters from the gallery at the far end, and the music would be blown far away for a moment by the fierce blasts. The long and unending melodies were back again at work, and so complete was their expression of this battle of wits that their modulations seemed to possess all the subtleties of speech. As the evening went on the band of musicians was increased, and singers and dancers made an appearance, the better part of the performers being Morisco in origin—that is to say, Moors who professed Christianity.

The music seemed so far cloaked and masked from the ordinary as to present for each person, whom one instrument personified, a whole series of variations. Every figure was preceded by a host of shadows and reflections—that is to say, all his borrowings from other personalities and the half-conscious imitations of his friends lay visible in each movement and gesture. You may often notice this tendency towards unconscious imitation on the part of a friend who has been away staying with someone else of your acquaintance. On his return you will see numberless small indications that remind you of his host. If the party has been a large one it is sometimes possible to disinter a whole graveyard of these ghosts of the people you know, and mixed with their remains there will be traces of several distinct persons whom you can separately distinguish and who are unknown to you,

This Spanish music paraded a whole company of known and unknown figures, most of whom seemed to carry the Spanish cloak on their left arms as a shield and for an additional mask to their true identity. The purpose of the music was to introduce you to these ghosts one after another with bewildering rapidity until you had reached the last of them, by which time the first to whom you had been introduced would be ready again, cloaked and disguised as someone else, and so on again through the whole series. The music was an unending narrative, moving from one topic to another with no warning, and making as many changes of scene as these flickering shadows required. It was like an endless chain of lifts, coming up to your platform from the town and the sea-front below, emptying load after load of strangers, many of whom would soon go down again to the foreshore below and come up a second time when you were too weary to remember them. But during a banquet it was not so easy to get tired with the flow of personalities, because the music only claimed attention during the lulls in feasting and talking, and therefore you never came into personal contact with any of the figures, but only remembered them as you recall a stage crowd after an evening spent at the theatre. In spite of this the music served to colour and emphasise the conversation, so that it provided, as it were, a convenient backcloth for the performance of those persons of whom you were talking or telling stories ; but all the time the other end of the hall was full of the real professional actors ; and the heroic amateurs, whose adventures were the topic, could never wholly capture your attention, which was always wandering towards that persistent drama down at the far end.

It is a misfortune for the historian that the incident of chivalry, in honour of which the Order of the Golden Fleece was formed, was not the story of Jason and the Argonauts, but had a less romantic origin in the story of the proofs to which Gideon submitted the Jewish Deity. The hint of an ulterior or worldly motive behind the gold-hunting of the Argonauts made their history distasteful as an example for

Philip the Good, the founder of the Order, to set before his knights. He retained the romantic legend while substituting a safer interpretation; but the lapse of a century and the classical fever of his age had recovered Jason from the cloud of shame which hung over his broken faith, and so the walls of the hall in which this feast was celebrated had one side painted with the history of Gideon, while the other set forth Jason's gradual perfidy as the gold glittered brighter and brighter before him through the trees.[1]

The feastings, the music and the dancing, all three of these different manners of expression were at work in this hall, on which every stimulant to adventure was portrayed upon the walls. The expedition that Philip's father had led to capture Tunis was mentioned as rival to the voyage of the Argonauts, and it was an understood thing that the labours of Hercules were no greater or more arduous than the efforts of Philip to extirpate the heretics in and outside his dominions. Very soon he was to organise an armada which was to combine the scope of the two ancient histories and their modern coincidences into one vast undertaking towards freedom from heresy, and no place more suitable for its planning could be chosen than this hall of the Golden Fleece. They were familiar, from wide experience, with the details of long sea-voyages, and the convoy of transports loaded with soldiers should not have proved a difficulty to sailors who were used to the protection of the treasure fleet, which had to be defended every year on its way from the Americas to Cadiz. Once this expedition to England was accomplished there would be little to stand against the Divine pleasure, and the Spaniards would have a free hand in their exploiting of the wealth of the New World. One must not be surprised at the Cæsarean affectation of the Hapsburgs; and no contemporary thought it ridiculous when the historians treated the Imperial campaigns like the

[1] *Jacques du Clerq*: "And this he had taken for the badge of his Order, not wishing to take the fleece which Jason won in the Isle of Colchis, because Jason broke his faith."

conquests of the Romans, and report that the massacre which the German infantry began after the capture of Tunis was stopped because the cries of the women and children offended Cæsar's ears. Such flattery was the inevitable tribute of a world to which great empires had been unknown since the half-mythical age of Charlemagne; and the fact that the Hapsburg dominions were acquired more by inheritance than by conquest sanctified and confirmed this Roman comparison by giving to it the additional strength of Divine Right and godly support.

A certain number of these Orders of Knights who combined military prowess with the practice of asceticism were always on duty at the Escurial whenever Philip was in residence there. On occasions like these annual feasts, their number was augmented by the presence of every member who was near enough to attend the ceremony. They walked in procession from the church where Mass was celebrated to the banquet chamber, and their route led through a whole series of huge rooms set apart for particular observances. There was a profusion of portraits of Philip, including Greco's celebrated picture of him as Emperor of the Indies receiving the submission of the Mexican and Peruvian kings, with a whole army of the feathered and cotton-quilted warriors in the background, who were delivering up their obsolete and barbaric weapons at his feet. They were shivering in their feathers—was it with the feverish heat, or in fear of Philip? —and their cotton padding made it look as if you could hit them as hard as you liked without their feeling it. Under no circumstances would they retaliate when close to you; only when far away they might revenge themselves by a poisoned arrow or a tiny dart from a blowpipe. When close to you they were irrepressible and did you no harm, in spite of a brave show of jade and obsidian hatchets.

The submission and conquest of England were made the occasion for another hall, the walls of which gave all the necessary evidence for the facts of the campaign. There was the fleet setting off, and the multitude of vessels seemed enough to keep the sea calm, if only by accumulated weight upon its bosom; then there were the reinforcement and the embarking of troops from the coast of Flanders, who climbed on board up steep ladders to the ships' sides, which towered far above the squat, undramatic cliffs of the Lowlands. One or two of them fell off the gangways and went spinning down into the sea, where they were quickly drowned by the heaviness of their armour. Sailors were signalling commands to the officers on shore from the tall spire-like masts, and there was a multitude of small boats tossing about that looked as if people were rowing out to the ships in their own laundry-baskets. The battle scenes, like all battle scenes, looked inconclusive; but the result was made sure of in a panel representing the triumphal entry of the Spaniards into the capital. Queen Elizabeth, humbled and led captive, was a scene into which considerable humour had crept. The grotesque elaboration of the English dress and their half-barbaric architecture were shown with an emphasis that drew additional attention to their peculiarity. The ruffs were like circular saws, with teeth pointing inwards round the neck, and it was a matter of surprise how many of her courtiers still had heads left on their shoulders. Queen Mary was rescued and restored to dignity, being allowed the permission to be present at Elizabeth's surrender of her kingdom. There was a tournament at Fotheringay, and a bull-fight before Old St Paul's.

The music, that never ceased during the feasting, was, as I have said, the best conceivable vehicle for the preparation of schemes and for every wild gallop of the imagination. There seemed to be power enough among the banqueters to carry any scheme, however fantastic, to a conclusion; no conquests and no constructions were too impossible of achievement. Confident, like every age, of their advance in civilisation, all distances seemed to be diminished; and if someone had called for volunteers to invade India, the followers of Bacchus who were present would have enrolled themselves willingly on this second expedition. The simplest course seemed to be by land, starting across the narrow strip of sea from Cadiz and beginning their march from Tangier. The line of transports from coast to coast was as solid as a bridge of boats, and their weight alone was enough to quiet down the waters. At night the waves were dazzled and spellbound by the galaxy of lamps; they looked silent and thoughtful, as if these capricious and moody animals had been bribed and cajoled to keep calm. Once the transit was accomplished they sprang out with a fury that had accumulated in the waiting; but from now the adventurers' way led, without any embarking upon the ocean, straight by the side of the Mediterranean, along through the various sultanates to Algiers, and thence across the desert to Egypt, on which they would burst like a cloud of locusts brought by the hot wind to the nearest land of plenty. The Egyptians would welcome them, the Turks would be overwhelmed, and every tomb in Egypt would yield up its treasure and, more precious than any jewels, they might find the elixir of life, by skilful combinations of the gums in which the mummies were embalmed. Leaving Egypt behind, the thirsty deserts of Arabia meant no suffering to men so confident in the leadership of Bacchus, and they could reach the plenty of Persia without disaster on the way. Here, even those among them used to the splendours of Italy were struck with the great works of the Persians; and indeed this was like the last evidence of a classical age to be found before the swamps and jungles of a mythological period were reached. It was precisely these lands, where there were to be found new subjects for poetry and for the rhapsodies of music, that the Bacchanalians had set out to subdue, and their adventures, with the accomplishments of their foes, should have provided as much material as the Golden Age for a repertory of heroic actions.

It was in Persia, the last oasis before the desert and the arid mountains which protect India, that the real gathering and equipment of the army of Bacchus was to take place. By the appointed date everyone who was expected had arrived; there was an exceptional attendance. There were great maps of India sketched out, in relief, upon the sand, and round their edges were gathered the veterans of the former campaign, with a sprinkling of those mediæval philosophers who had proceeded to an uncanny knowledge of geography with the unfair assistance of magic. They had divided India into the Greater, the Lesser, and the Middle.[1] Abyssinia—or, as they called it, Abascia—was the second or Middle India; the division termed the Greater India extended from Maabar to Kesmacoran, comprehending thirteen large kingdoms; and the Lesser India commenced at Ziampa and extended to Muvfili, comprehending eight kingdoms, exclusive of those in the islands, which are very numerous. The different sketches of these various artists were scratched side by side on the sand, and there was a continual movement of the crowd from one map to another in an attempt to compare suggestions, it being generally conceded that any feature of the country which appeared in more than one version carried the probability of truth; it was a process of identification. When some progress had been made, and it had become possible to transfer an average of these various sketches in a more portable form on to parchment, there was a general rush into the interior of these countries, until a cordon had to be drawn round the frontiers and no one admitted except the persons of extreme importance. Right out in the middle, where the rivers had flowed far enough down from the mountains to become as wide as, and fiercer than, the straits

[1] Cf. *Marco Polo*, pp. 377-380.
This division of India into the Greater, the Lesser, and the Middle does not appear to have reference either to geographical position or relative importance. By the Lesser is here understood what was termed India extra Gangem, or, more strictly, the space included between the eastern coast of the Peninsula of India and that of Cochin-China or Tsiampa. The Greater is made to comprehend the whole of Hindustan Proper and the Peninsula, as far westward as the province of Makram, or the country extending from the Ganges to the Indus inclusive. The appellation of Middle or Second India one author applies expressly to Abyssinia, but seems to intend that the coast of Arabia also, as far as the Persian Gulf, should be comprised in this division.

of sea, stood Epistemon, histrionising the dark Indians guarding their jungle-banks against attack. Then it became a competition as to who could devise the most successful feinted crossing of the river, while the main body lay hid and crossed the torrent behind the Indians' backs. Farther on there stood a line of anchorites, as gaunt and forbidding as the mountains they were posing for, and over against them, discussing a passage over their bodies, there were a group of enthusiasts sending forth a realistic firework display of gesture, till it seemed as if the least among them was hurling lightnings from his threatening hand. There were some martial-minded monks who lay down and rolled themselves like barrels, by way of illustrating how they would burst down from the mountain heights on to the unsuspecting plains below. Just beyond was Epistemon again, creeping this time on all-fours through the jungle to outwit the invaders, who were, by now, pretending to be aboard boats on the rough face of the river, whose current was sweeping them down just where Epistemon had calculated they would arrive and lay waiting for them in a cunningly contrived ambush. The Knights of the Golden Fleece stood in their companies, keeping back the crowd of spectators with linked arms, and the disciples of Hercules were ready to run out at a command and carry any message, storm any mountain, or ford any river. The best part of a day was spent in the invention and discussion of plans of invasion, and, at nightfall, even, there was no falling off in the enthusiasm of such inspiration. For two successive days after this the process was gone through again, until a real and permanent plan had been arrived at by argument and the working out and elimination of every impracticable suggestion.

At this moment there was a sudden halt in the music from the far end of the room, and during the pause somebody's speech came to a conclusion and a huge cup was passed round to drink healths from. As soon as it had started on its circuit the music began again, and Epistemon, with the vanguard, left for India upon a cloud. They were only just on board in time for the departure, and had barely settled down in comfort upon the monster's woolly back before it had risen to an astonishing height and disappeared over the desert in the direction of the mountains. This was the signal for a concerted departure, and the whole army of them began to move, concealed in the middle of a tremendous column of dust that was dense enough to act as a screen for their actions.

This huge expedition took place, as I have said, in the minds of those assembled at this inspiring feast in the Escurial, and, like all dreams, the actions of many days were crowded into a few seconds, and the whole adventure became possible in the compressed state in which it was born and died, between the drinking of toasts and the thrilling narratives of music. I have reason and precedent enough for my epic in the programme I have announced as the subject of this story, and it is in the fullest realisation of this conquest of India, and in its subsequent peaceable settlement under the invader's rule, that I can unloose the powers that were stemmed and balked by Philip, when he chose the work of insignificant Genoese artists, in the place of what might have been accomplished and added to humanity had he preferred Greco above the facile futilities of the late mannerist painters whom he employed at the Escurial. I have chosen virgin ground, where nothing of the kind was in existence before, for the scene of my experiment: the situation is unencumbered and inspiring, and the direction in which this energy was to move shows the orientation natural and only to be expected of such a gathering under such conditions. It is my desire to show the most complete fulfilment of their schemes, just as they might have realised them in a flash at this banquet.

Epistemon led off, then, on his cloud, and Bacchus was seen by more than one of his followers at the banquet advancing at the head of his army in his accustomed litter and with the usual human and animal attendants. We will not delay with the details of their advance; it is the conquest and settlement of India that interests us and not their marches through the desert. In due time, and at the date they had foreseen, they arrived without harm at the foot of the frontier mountains that protect the land they were out to subdue. They reached to this distance without difficulties and as if in a flash, and the interval in which they made their final preparations is perhaps a suitable moment in which to give a description of their forces.

There were gathered here specimens of all the varieties of human enthusiasts, whom I have described some pages back as probable starters on any crusade, whatever the object of that crusade might be. When these anchorites, these more comfortable monks, these gaunt Spanish soldiers, and all the rest of them, were joined by the two Orders of Knights whose banquet I have been describing, they made, in the aggregate, an imposing and a dangerous body of fanatics. The late hour and their state of happiness had produced Bacchus as the generalissimo of their enterprise, and his influence, running through them like an electric spark, resulted in a multiplication of their energies and powers of endurance. Nothing was impossible to them; and the vast bowl they passed round from hand to hand when each toast was drunk had the staccato movements of a piece of clockwork machinery in the process of being wound up. As the constant round after round of drinks got the better of first one and then another boldhead, it was like so many of these clockwork machines set in motion. Their sensibility was carried away suddenly with a sweep and the imagination went reeling off on its reckless course. One after another of these mechanical birds took to the air, and so there is every sign of truth for my description of Epistemon's departure upon a cloud.

The comfort and speed of his advance must not blind readers to the difficulties which lay before the main body on this enterprise, but it appeared to be the general opinion that those of their number who proceeded in the ships they had hurriedly built, from the great river-deltas down to the Persian Gulf, had an easier journey than the main body which proceeded by land. Needless to say, there was no wind strong enough to help these boats on their way, and the huge sails they had made became so much waste cargo, as heavy and as useless as the crushing loads of snow that are thrown down everywhere during the winter where there seem to be shoulders strong enough to bear them.

They are all now fairly embarked upon their voyage, or, at any rate, advanced far enough into the deserts that edge the gulf to make a return to the fat pastures of Persia as difficult as the journey that lay before them till they reached the endless plains ahead over the mountains. Meanwhile the rivers would be rolling the pearls, with which travellers always credit them, down to the sea-coast, where they are piled up high in loose, crumbling mounds, ready to rattle down at the first sound of plundering feet. At short distances along the coast, to either hand, lie the skeletons of whales that have been washed ashore by the furious waves and are stranded on the beach like ships that have been driven ashore in a gale; their bones are bleaching and the ribs falling apart, just as the timbers of a wreck become loose and fall from the body of the ship. All round, and down to where the huge herds of waves are feeding at the far end of their fields, the crackling sands, over which the waters run, lie bare and unmarked by any footfall. But the sands are not to lie untrodden for ever: there appear, crawling over the horizon, which is as marked as any garden wall, a number of slow, creeping shapes, that seem to be moving towards the shore so slowly that it is hard to realise their steady advance and growth in size. For long moments together they lie still on the sea, not stirring, and facing you with their pointed, beaked heads, looking carefully at you, as a huge insect does from a window-pane. This lasts until they suddenly loom up nearer, as if they had leapt forward in the wink of an eye. With the turn of the tide the boats were able to make an energetic attack against the shore and they lay to in shallow water, from which the tide at its highest would always float them out. Meanwhile, some half mile out to sea, the mother-ships swung slowly to and fro at anchor, and the banks of oars were drawn up out of the water and stood up against the ships' sides, with their blades in the air, just as though the whole vessel had turned upside down and was floating dead on its back, with the long line of oars holding out their helpless legs. The ships were, in fact, so many dead centipedes floating on a pond into which they had dropped from blades of grass. Everything that moved over the sea had a shadow of untiring fidelity : the clouds, as they drifted across, floated on the water as well as in the air ; the whole dome of sky was faithfully echoed as the sea spread out deeper from the shore, so that a daring swimmer who ventured far out would swim a staggering depth into space above any cloud, however high. All the boats making for land had their counterparts, and on disembarking it was more like landing upon the green tree-tops reflected there than into the actual water, knee-deep above sinking sand. As they stepped out on to the trees the whole body of leaves shook together and were blurred into one mass of green, as solidly built as a sea-wall or breakwater against the waves. Then, little by little, when the invaders had waded through this reflection and were crunching the dry sand under their feet, the water, which had been troubled by their passage, began to lie smooth once more. One by one the leaves showed out clear again from the mass ; each of them came out of the confusion, rattling and quivering like the tongue of a bell. In a moment there were thousands of these, dwindling into silence and caught up again as countless new ones rang out and died down. The sound of them built up so many towers of diminishing storeys, so that the ringing died away into a point, till the whole weight of them came down again in a huge clattering, as the walls of water and the overhanging water-eaves fell in and crashed down again on to the magical sands they were built on.

There were the same water-towers building themselves and falling back again through the leaves, all through the forests, and so near to the edge of the woods that their sound could be heard from the beginning of the great plains. The army which had come by land, keeping in touch with the seaboard by a line of outposts, was now deeply involved in the mountains, and the snow was trampled and muddy in the passes. Once these were threaded and they were safely out of the hills their way led directly down to the sea, where a meeting was to be effected with the naval expedition. The sails, which had been so much ballast during the voyage, now came into use as shelters against the sun, and sailors were to be seen dangling from the boughs as though they were furling sails on the masts of a ship. In a few hours great tents and grottos had been improvised, and a few of the high leafy trees looked as though their very altitude had trapped some of the passing clouds between their branches. The whole of these shelters were arranged near to each other, so that there was no danger of a surprise attack; and, indeed, any of the natives who might come upon this encampment would be astonished at the sight of such a wreckage of the clouds, driven, apparently, by a strong wind upon these aerial crags. The scene suggested a journey of deities whose schemes had miscarried to the extent that they found themselves ashore, wrecked, and without the flying steeds to proceed with on their journey. Trailing down from the trees, among the ropes of the awnings, there were long cords of creepers strung all over with flowers, and these could be caught and swung by the hand in the same way that you pull the ropes of a huge peal of bells. The Sun was continually dragging the woods with his gigantic nets, and there were bright flashes of fire whenever the tropical birds came out of the darkness into the light of his meshes. At nightfall all the clouds had blown away and the white shafts of light stood motionless among the trees; there was the full searchlight of a theatre instead of the plundering nets and scales. These steady beams threw a clear light upon the hornpipes that were being danced, and the stage where this took place looked particularly brightly lit, with the moonlight full on the dancers, black where the shadow of the trestles fell, and then white again just underneath them, so that they appeared floating in the air upon a black raft. They were high up, almost underneath the boughs where the awnings hung down from, and all their movements were a ceremonial setting and furling of the canvas, while, below, lay the spectators in green grottos and contrived caverns, just where the sea-gods and their servant-tritons would be resting under the shaking sea-surface. When the wind blew, ever so lightly, there was a little clatter and spin among the leaves, where a tired wave stumbled over a half-hidden rock, or a running whisper ran about overhead like the flying ripples that skim over the backs of the waves. A conch was blown while a light body glided past, parting the white air like water, and then the same horn was blown again on a branch overhead or behind a thicket of flowers. The shriller birds were like cat-calls from the gallery of a theatre, encouraging the extravagance of the acting by their inhuman exaggeration.

Beyond doubt there were a number of Indians watching what was going on through the leaves, for their eyes are accustomed to the sunless woods, and there are no screens or lattices so complicated as those which they set up between themselves and the world outside them. They are no lovers of windows or of temples open to the air, but they guard their houses and surround the objects of their worship with lattices of marble, glittering and delicate like falling water frozen before it tumbles to the ground, and they keep their temples secret and inviolate with the most forbidding of ramparts. It is their policy to lead on and entice, and then to vanish, or to turn into heartless stone. For this reason the spires and burnished eaves of their temples stand out clear from a distance, as if open and accessible to all who might wish to enter; and then, on the very threshold, a high bastion and the strongest girdles of walls absolutely preclude any approach or near view of what lies inside. It is only from the farthest point of vantage that you can obtain a full view of the deceiving towers. From the crest of a hill, over the lolling heads of the trees, you can see the tall tapering towers that they build up and string with any kind of instrument that wind or rain can clash upon or blow through ; and all these piping and clattering notes are so many bells and pipes that have been strung up for clever musicians to play upon, as they walk beneath the pergolas and arbours whence they dangle. The jugglers and conjurers are constantly running along the enclosure, testing their contrivances until it is their turn to play, like the keen wind does with the leaves and stalks of these stone flowers. Near by these towers you can see over the wall of the temple some of the high wagon-roofed buildings which accompany the tall spires and steeples, and, indeed, these are the elaborate travelling houses in which the Indians travel from place to place, halting, whenever suitable, in some waste land near a settlement. Here they pitch their tents, tie up and fasten these wagons in which they travel and sleep, and begin setting up the gate at which you pay for admission, and all the scaffolding and trestles necessary for the performance of their tricks.

This is, in fact, one way in which we may look upon and interpret the extraordinary nature of the Hindu buildings. We may regard the whole structure as one of those temporary encampments of the travelling acrobats who may be seen on any of the roads of Europe, only, as I have said, the Indians have this power of making what seems the flickering of a moment into a stone permanence that can resist the destruction of centuries. For example, the marble screens and lattices already mentioned seem to be made of frozen spray, or of the light summer boughs flashing their leaves against the sky ; their real purpose is utterly concealed by the accuracy of their convention ; so that it is a real shock to feel the cool marble with the fingers where you expected melting snow, or the soft growing leaves. In the same way, talking again of the temples, their trestle-like terraces, the tall towers waiting for lights and for the showman's tricks, give the complete presentment of a travelling theatre, while tethered near by are the great property and living wagons in which they all travel. The priests, also, by their training and tradition, are like some family of these artists, swelled by their numbers to the dimensions of a tribe ; so that all the difficult ceremonial and the hard ritualism of their service call into play the qualities which it takes many generations to produce in a family of actors, and all of it can be performed at a moment's notice with a well-rehearsed ease of execution.

The whole of one of these vast encampments is, as if by a miracle, converted from its temporary appearance into permanence ; all that was wood becomes stone. Through long waiting the great wooden wagons change into stone houses, as if by the mere duration of their stay here ; for it is a process of petrification, like that which is the property of certain wells where anything thrown into their depths is changed into stone, while preserving every detail of the original shape and substance.

The palaces of the Indians hold parallel mysteries, and seek, like their temples, to achieve permanence out of the most transitory elements. They like to grow out of the midst of a lake in the manner of some monstrous water-flower that blossoms once in a generation and then just before sundown, so that its full growth is concealed in the darkness, and by the morning there is nothing left except rotting vegetation. They can escape from their enemies into these island towers, appearing on the battlements with brandished and flashing weapons before their foes have ceased to wonder at their method of reaching this fastness without the help of a boat. The passages below the water, leading from the shelter of some undergrowth on the bank right under the lake, and ending in the rock-hewn cellars that support the towers, were a discovery of the greatest magical importance. The solution of the problem was too easy to seem possible ; just as the presence of priests inside the great stone figures of the Egyptian oracles, who manipulated their movements and supplied the words through a magnifying trumpet, was too obvious an explanation to be probable, the Divine mysteries having the habit of working by platitude.

The retreat I have described was not the King's residence during times of peace; he had a more sumptuous and a more comfortable dwelling in which to waste unprofitable days. The walls of the huge terraces on which it stood were covered from end to end with a journalistic survey of the King's actions, his wars of conquest, his inroads on the barbarians, and his distribution of the spoils of peace like a prize-giving after the term's work. These records, instead of being printed and sent out broadcast, were cut into the stone walls of the terrace so that all could see them, and, just like a newspaper, the more important news was in bigger type, all the King's appearances in person being several times larger than the figures of his subjects. The whole pile of buildings was surrounded by a moat, across which led a broad stone causeway, bordered on each side by a stone balustrade in the form of a serpent, which raised its seven hooded heads at each end of the causeway and wherever it widened during its passage over the moat to a platform. At the end of the causeway you stood at once on the first terrace, and some ten feet above this stretched the huge length of the second terrace, carved all over its surface with life-size bas-reliefs of elephants, the projecting central portion having the motive of its decoration changed to huge figures of eagle-men, winged and beaked. From this terrace (three hundred yards in length) the King watched ceremonial processions, and elephant and wild beast fights; and from the part which projected forward and was carved with the figures of the winged immortals he mounted his elephant chargers.

A little more than a mile away there lay a still older and more sacred palace, and the King varied his time, when not at war or on hunting expeditions, between these two places. The road to the more ancient building led out over the causeway through high and shady trees. Over all its length it was bordered by huge seated statues, between whom and over whose knees there curled the same gigantic stone snake, forming the most fantastic balustrade imaginable. This led to a moat above which towered a high and terrifying gate, the upper part of which was formed by four colossal human heads, smiling enigmatically to the four points of the compass. A mile farther on through this gate was the palace, rising up, terrace upon terrace. The third storey stood in the form of a cross, and in its centre supported a huge tower, which had the same four faces, only larger; growing out of the second and third storeys were fifty towers, all shaped like a long human head, with the four inscrutable faces of Brahma, each alike, and all crowned with a diadem.

We gather the look and the atmosphere of life under these conditions, and can realise that in spite of the outward splendour in the King's progresses and in the materials of his dress and the exterior of his houses, they contained nothing but small cell-like rooms. There was not even enough of the democracy to make banqueting possible on a large scale. So completely was this civilisation the result of slave labour, that those in enjoyment of its fruits were too few in number to risk their appearance together. The King was sacred and beyond the harm of sacrilege, such was the veneration of which he was the object; while all the power and all the wealth were centred in his numerous uncles, his brothers, and his sons, so that they formed a divine and superior race, living upon the credulity of slaves. There were no nobles and no rich men who were not relatives of the King, and in some measure sacred from this connection. They were absolutely different and removed from the northern free-booting races of Europe, which contained a large body of free men, who diverted themselves, when triumphing after battle, with banqueting and general intoxication. In these parts of the Indies the warriors rejoiced themselves in private, away from the obsequious slave population, and a form of theatrical entertainment, very complicated in technique and endless in duration, was evolved by them for their pleasure. The stiff and formal movements and the overclothed bodies of the dancers would have held very little entertainment for races with large appetites. Sometimes it might be necessary to impress or divert the slave population of the big towns, and it was for this purpose that the Indians organised those huge processions and combats of elephants which could take place on the level tracts of the terraces before an easily disposed audience. Their private entertainments were of a slow and formal description, giving pleasure from the exhibition of a minute and exacting technique of movement; but, in public, and to regale the minds of the great slave majorities, they devised entertainments which impressed an audience with terror, or with the sense of overwhelming power in the hands of the stage producer. Twelve elephants gleaming with jewels and drawing a gold car seemed hardly strong enough escort for the person of their King. At other times one superb animal would kneel at the foot of the terrace for the King to mount upon its back and climb into the glittering castle that it carried. Then it would bear him along, rolling a steady course down the great avenues between the seated statues, and out into the woodlands where the King liked to hunt. He was surrounded up there by several of his sons and by his chief ministers, and would sometimes doze away with the soft lulling motion till he was woken by his huntsmen at the sight of game. The falcons would be released and would whir away over the trees till they were high enough to swoop down on their quarry; and by this time the moving castle with the King and his courtiers was near at hand, waiting for the bird to fall down through the leaves. You were being carried forward on the foam of a wave, just as if you were actually part of that whirling snow, and could look up through cold windows in your turret towards the heavier masses that were waiting above until they were ready to fall. Sometimes, with the excitement of the chase, with the heavy, rocking swiftness and the unerring course between huge forest trees, the whole army of waves, of which you were, at once, a part and the whole, would spring forward, until the castle from which you were watching the game would seem as if flying swiftly above the rushing waves below, and you were thrown onward, speeding with your own volition, at the pace of the racing body, until you were ready to drop back again into the saddle and go slower now your quarry was certain. A dead bird came hurtling down, plunging through the top leaves, ricochetting off a branch or two with a terrible dead thud : it must be like this with the sea-gods when a little meteorite hits the water and goes down steeply through the black depths. When it reaches the eventual light beneath, the sea-gods stop building with their coral mortar, and wait until their breath dies in the water-flutes they are playing ; then they slowly walk towards the spot where something fell heavily on their treasure-heaps. The spaces of air below the trees through which the hunting-party are ambling on their elephants are just like the water-depths with green fronds waving down into their obscurity. There is no wind down here, but glaucous and skin-like films that are ever distending and breaking, proclaim the moving currents that are so slow and purposeful compared with our winds. They crawl along as slow as turtles, reluctant to execute the commands they have been given, but realising the necessity of obedience. There was now and again a little gust, as if a fistful of hot wind was thrown at you by an invisible hand, and this first night in the Indian jungle you were watched by a sentinel from every race of animals in the land. There were watchers from the tops of trees, as if these tall many-windowed buildings were the cliffs defending India from the seas. Lower down, the undergrowth and the low insurmountable bushes were guarded like the mountain passes. There were dark forms peering out of clumps of huge flowers, like a boat of soldiers making a black patch on the clear surface of a lake, and some of the most brilliant-plumaged trees, that rose up like one straight flame, were rushing torrents guarding the fabulous interior of the land.

But the subdual of the Indies soon began in earnest. Not the mainland only, but the seas and all the islands became so many reaped fields for the foreign invaders, and the level plains were redeemed from their flatness by the ranges of little golden hills that led the eye far away down a distorted perspective, the hills fading away so quickly into the limitless plain that its surface gave the illusion of even greater space than was the gigantic truth. Each of these small hillocks was a pile of corn, made of different bundles heaped up together into a pyramid, and the gilded heads drooped down as if each sheaf was a handful of prisoners taken out of the brakes and reeds by the corncutters, for the feathery gold hair and the water-sleek beard of each captive, now that they were tied up and held fast, were no longer the passive plants of a field, but were seen as the elusive and highly strung dwellers among the water shallows. Their gilded hair, seen just below the water as they swam, half-hid, to their feeding grounds, were so many parhelions burning among little waves, and settled there because someone has looked too daringly towards the real sun, who is the supreme ruler of the torrid Indies. Sometimes carried by the underground springs, these bearded but feeble beings are found living in deep and secure water-wells. When there has been a preternaturally hot summer and the wells are almost dried up from the drought, at the end of the day, when it is safe to drink after the great heat has died down, you may go to the well and draw, and when the water-vessel comes up again full of clouded, brackish water, there will rise up out of the steep depths one of these gilded chattering ghosts. He may seem, at first glance, just a bedraggled corn-stalk that a reaper has let tumble out of the sheaf he was carrying, while he leaned over the parapet and waited for the water to arrive up in its bucket and cool him after his terrible stooping day bowed among the flashing gold plumes, the death-dealing scythes, and the heaps of mute corpses. But one effort at understanding will show you the proud beard, for he is as patriarchal as an Arabian, and now you can easily distinguish the reedy eyebrows and his coiled metallic hair. Everything about him is fluttering in the sunset wind, and he is trying hard to breathe out some message to you before he dies. His yellow robes are flapping like a string of flags, and his eyes, so difficult to see under the flowing hair, stare intently, trying to force your attention. This brittle ghost is just about to convey his message to you when the sun suddenly disappears over the hills and the light at once dies away out of the air. Then, still in your arms, and almost before you can realise the change, all the gold fades out of his body, and he is left lying in your arms, a crumpled, lifeless straw.

We must not imagine from this that every stalk of yellow corn is a dried husk which has never yielded fruit. High up above the plain on the gentle hill-slopes there stand the houses that have been built with these riches, and it is among their hanging woods that there first rose up the Indies as you can see them on tapestries. It is a seraglio existence, but confined in a limitless garden; with innumerable retainers, but no gaolers. The blue spaces between the trees are calm enough for clouds, however full-sailed, to drift through them, and far down the horizon you can see through the leaves a whole caravan ready to start across these blue seas, once the wind is favourable. Not very far below them, so vast is the scale, you can see a stone portico like the watergate on to the great canal, and this high gateway is topped with three great urns, from which water springs up in three white plumes against the far hills and into the heart of the sky. This very water that you see sparkling up there appears next in a set of three tumbling cascades, dropping a veil of water as they overflow and flash down from one stone basin to another. But they have found their level, and cause no commotion by the time they flow into and form the body of the long sheet of water that stretches towards us. So still is its surface that you see the portico repeated again, and for the whole of its length the stone balustrade is doubled, so that you see a second row of the terra-cotta orange-pots that are like thickets of lamps to light the boats along. As you come to the near end of the water a whole family of stone dolphins appear strung up tail to tail, and spouting out water as if asking for assistance from the depths. Now that you stand on the little slope above the banks you can see away in the distance whole arcades of green architecture, great parterres like carpets too valuable to tread upon, and everywhere there is relief for its flashing white flame, a fountain spray waving a little, like a plume in the wind. On the foreground there are grouped the inhabitants of this easy paradise, sitting under cool trees near a dripping fountain. Talking to a eunuch attendant, who has brought her a casket that she had sent him for, is a woman with her back turned. The plumes in her hair are an echo of the tossing sprays of water, and she holds in one hand, balancing its base upon her knee, a twisted narwhal tusk, as if to signify that she is posing as a marine goddess, and being accustomed to the luxury of Indian life, and to its easy and splendid triumphs upon elephant-back, she must demand the nearest equivalent among marine monsters for her steed. At the other side, and a few paces from her, there is a tall and densely foliaged tree, hardly giving space between its boughs to see other trees as tall and shady belonging to the same clump. At this tree's foot, and reaching up its stem to where the boughs spring forth, there is a great group of stone horses, held back by a slave whose stone clothes flutter out with the wind from the horses' speed, as he holds them back just above the wide basin into which they are pouring water from their nostrils. Lower down there sits an old river-god in a brake of water-rushes, regulating the flow of his three streams from the jars out of which the melted snows begin running; they pour down into a troubled pool which rolls away right out of the foot of the tapestry. On a little platform of grass, edged with great stones from the frothing waters below, there sits the Sultana of this paradise, sceptre in hand, and with a crown of bright feathers. An attendant behind her is holding a bunch of flowers under the spray from one of the horse's heads to refresh the blossoms and bring out their perfume before she hands them to her mistress. At her right side is a negress, or at any rate a tropically skinned slave, with a head-dress which projects in front in the form of an elephant's trunk. In one hand she holds an exotic bird, and with the other she holds a sheaf of corn, the gold heads of which show up against the distant water that is mirroring the passing clouds above.

This is evidently but one perspective out of a whole battery of prospects, for the long straight lines of the avenues, each of them leading away in a different direction from the house, are so many huge weapons aimed down the far-off valleys as a protection to the building. In every quarter are found these immense preparations against poverty and ugliness, and they are made with the certainty of people who consider beauty can be prepared from a recipe, and is a matter of known ingredients mixed in due proportion. Given wealth, then, it is a matter of easy accomplishment, and armies of workmen can at once begin digging the defences for this siege. Like generals inspecting their work, members of the family are carried round the defences in litters, and during the long marches they can doze away in their hammocks, slung, not from the boughs of trees, but carried right up on the porter's shoulders, as though they were propped on to the edges of the clouds. On the way they pass other great nets slung upon poles and holding the fruit that has been picked and is being carried back to the house for the evening meal. Now they are right at the end of the garden, and there is a great army of workmen half sunk into the earth who are digging out a broad canal that is only lined to hold water down half its length, so that they are working underneath a dam that has been raised to stem its flow until the bed is ready for it. The trees that edge this sheet of water are still young, and they are kept in place and trained with a whole quantity of ropes tied to pegs in the ground, while their higher reaches are held up and apart with espaliers of lattice-work, so that the whole tree looks half tent and half sailing-ship, thus firmly is it held down against the depredations of a high wind. There are hundreds of these trees in line, each of them with its flaps tied down, as one might describe the lower branches that interfere with anyone walking past, and their wide sheets of leaves, that are strung on to higher ones, are furled and kept trim and neat. Each morning all the fountains are practised, to be certain that their artillery is in repair, and a guard walks the round of the walls to make sure that no breach has been made. The time between one year and the next seems no longer in passing than the passage from daylight, through darkness, to the next morning, so alike is one day to another; and so, imperceptibly, all the avenues grow in height and in density of shade, until it is no longer possible to reach their highest boughs on the rungs of a ladder, and the tenderest and most glossy leaves, that are the first to feel the rain from their exposed height, are as far out of reach as the glittering birds that can rely upon their wings and will not venture within sight of man.

Part iii

The King and the Nightingale

Part iii

The King and the Nightingale

This story, and all its action, is laid in one of those rare worlds where the children play with young nightingales as elsewhere with a kitten, and where a cruel child would pull off the nightingale's wings instead of tormenting a fly. All through the night there is a dripping, gurgling music that drifts in at every window like the spray from a tilt of waves, and its soft cadences lay an easy road into unconsciousness. Each morning this faint music has an extraordinary renewal, as if a choir of full voices were added to it, for the fountains dash up wildly into the air as soon as the water reaches their pipes, and for a few minutes they tune up and practise their throats before they are ready to take their places in the measured music. So sound is their wind that they contrive to keep up their singing all day, never letting its volume die down, however fiercely the midday sun may scald them; but just before dark the water is cut off from the top of the cascade, and one by one the water-voices die away, till their last breath has gone out and they are silent; and now the continuous soft accompaniment of dripping, gurgling music can be heard again, as if it were at the same time the background and the vital heart-beat of this small secret star. So steady is it, and so unchanging, that you cannot hear below its stir the throbbing and the whirring of the bigger world as it revolves underneath our feet. So it comes about that the secluded and stilted lives led by those inside this tract of country set apart really possess the undertones and the almost noiseless machinery that should govern a small independent universe.

The liquid songs have no sooner died away than their place is taken by still fiercer and more insistent tongues. All the dark nightingales that can be imagined in the limpid Spanish night have taken up their stations, and are singing as if they knew the King was trying his utmost to fall asleep and they considered it their duty to keep him awake with their loud declarations of homage. Many of the young birds have not yet learnt their song perfectly, and they can be heard practising their scales and trying their cadenzas over; but they suffer from no nervousness, and the more unskilled they are the louder they sing out. The trees that have the most leaves to hide among must feel their boughs pressed down beneath the drenching rain of loud voices. An indescribable lushness and sparkle are given to the night, as though the trees and everything green had been washed in the rain and now glistened wet in the light, and the hundreds of tongues singing in every direction were so many little flames burning away the dust and cleansing the air with their fire. These fabulous serenades are kept up all night, and time rolls on until the immortal and dangerous hours are reached, when all human beings are half-alive, even if awake, and there is no life showing, except in those creatures that are at perpetual war with each other and choose the dark for their working-time because of the facilities it lends to hiding or to preying. But all through these hours, when the rest of humanity sinks deeper and deeper into sleep, the King grew restless and yet more restless: he would turn first on one side and then on another. When he faced the wall he fancied he saw the menacing trees reflected in the mirror above his head, and the fiery bird-songs were now in the room and scratching the glass with their diamond tongues. In another moment he could stand them no more behind his back, and he had rolled over and was facing straight out towards the windows. This was their opportunity. They called out louder than ever, and whilst they were climbing up and down their steep spirals of song he could think of nothing else except the perilous descent and then the dangerous altitude at which each jet of song ended.

To a confused and feverish mind, as the properties that

distinguish night from day grew more exaggerated, until they reached their climax a little while before dawn, every quality and every character that would strike a foreigner who came as a child to Spain, and stayed here as King, became drawn and pulled out like strands of elastic. The wind rattling each bough was a wiry hand strumming a guitar, and any leaf that blew down, fluttering, a written message dropped from a window. There were the black and bombastic shades of Spanish captains strutting through the woods and moving between the trees from one patch of light to another, as if walking the dangerous gangway from ship to ship, or disembarking upon an undiscovered shore under flashing white sails—for the moon would sometimes light up the higher reaches of a tree, so that you could see the black webwork of boughs like the rigging against the white canvas that it held. There were so many of these white patches where the light struck the tree-tops, as the King gazed out of the window, that it looked like the Spanish treasure fleet creeping across a calm under full sail, and the bird-songs calling and answering each other through the trees were the voices underneath balconies and behind shutters when the fleet reached harbour and the money was being spent. The flood of these images, like the delirious imaginings of an invalid, at last got the better of his wakefulness and, struggling hard, as if against his will, the King slowly drifted asleep.

Every night it was the same story. In the daytime nothing could distract his mind from the melancholy into which he had fallen, and at night any noise of the very slightest description was sufficient to keep him awake. While he became ill he became more melancholy: he would sign no papers and attend to no business; he would not even allow his barber to shave him; and he reached that condition of despair in which all the senses of the body are workless but intent, and only listening for Death to knock upon the door.

He had left France as a child to learn another language, and to be lonely, in a country where he had no relatives and little sympathy. All through his life he bore two grudges, as though a pair of ghosts had made life unendurable for him : these were the spectral but different forms of Louis XIV. and of Charles II. of Spain. It was Louis who had made that ceremonious announcement to him of his accession to the throne of Spain, an hereditary prize which had previously been dangled above his head without too much explanation, like a particularly beautiful hat which would be given to him one day when he had grown tall enough, when his conduct had been good, and when the hatmaker's bill had been settled. The staccato clockwork of Louis's movements and his strangely redundant profile seemed to add to the inhumanity of the difficult rôle which had been cast for Philip. There was this terrible parade, behind which it was hopeless to look for affection, and his personal happiness was not for a moment of importance where his grandfather considered the family interest was concerned. Philip's father, the fat and unfortunate Dauphin, had the kindness and good humour which seem a part of the load of every obese person, and we may suppose that he saw the heartlessness of rigid etiquette without having the courage to defy its routine, for he had been trained to it from childhood, and he knew that behind these gestures there lay the mortal and vulnerable life of every Royal person, for they are but a conjurer's flourishes behind which he conceals the simplicity of his craft.

For Charles II., the other shade by whom he was tormented, Philip had feelings of a different kind. The death of Charles, so eagerly and so long expected by all the statesmen of Europe, came to Philip as the very opposite of a blessing. It left him heir to dominions that he would much sooner have resigned. For nearly forty years the Spanish, out of their pride, kept alive this embryo, the last male descendant of a family who had brought nothing except disaster to the races that they ruled. It was the product to be expected of their pride of race that they should seek to prolong, beyond its due limit, a life which could reflect no credit upon any human parent. For Charles belonged to that class of weaklings and of freak children whom a race with less keenness for the last word on every subject would have permitted to die at the first sign of any inclination in that direction. But the Spanish devoted every resource to keeping him alive, and they showed in their energy a conviction that he was of a different race from themselves, a being of a separate creation, who was predestined by Providence as their ruler, and to this end was differently created from ordinary mankind.

Till he was twenty he was fed on a milk diet, so weak was his frame, and it was only at about this age that Charles learnt to lisp the simple words that other children learn in as many months. His chin, the manufacturer's mark of the Hapsburg family, which was introduced into their blood by marriage with a Polish princess in the early part of the fifteenth century, and which still remains a family peculiarity for students of heredity to cherish as an example of their theories, made the act of eating almost impossible for him. It was like a cruel caricature, a dreadful enlargement of the faculties of his ancestors—as if the mediæval reverence for a strong man, the worship of physical strength as the greatest of human powers, and the leaving of mental qualities for priests to cultivate, had produced to rule over them a man they could admire at the banqueting table as much as on the battle-field. In the course of generations the effort required to produce the type had concentrated too much strength on this quality to the exclusion of any other, and an effect was arrived at in which every consideration was sacrificed as long as this sole one remained. It was under like circumstances that the Romans, who regarded sheeps' tails as a delicacy, ended by breeding sheep so confined to this one direction that their tails became too heavy for them to carry, and they had to drag them on a little two-wheeled cart wherever their browsing led them. Charles V., the great-grandfather of this Charles we are describing, is rumoured to have died in his luxurious hermitage from the impossibility of swallowing food owing to the size of his lower jaw, and this legend, doubtful in the great-grandfather, became proven in his great-grandson. Until he died Charles II. had to be dieted like an invalid child; and he could only be torn away from his religious devotions to set out on a hunting expedition, when he escaped for a little from the web-like ceremony among the folds of which he was entangled. For the Inquisition he had feelings of respect, mingled with admiration, for it provided a spectacle which he could enjoy like all bad children: and the ranks of conspirators were diminished in proportion to the Inquisitor's energy. A picture in the Prado shows Charles and his Court watching the most sanguinary of these spectacles, which had been impressively staged for a warning and a recreation by the Holy Office. Under these double enticements the Court stayed watching the *auto-da-fé* for twelve hours, and then they left the scene, not because it was finished, but because they were tired out and needed a rest.

In every respect the reign of Charles II. affords the best study to be found in modern history of the theories of absolute rule and Divine right. There is no other example of fidelity equal to the reverence of the Spaniards before this imbecile. He was the only son that survived Philip IV. and his three marriages, for the child, Don Balthasar Carlos, whose portrait Velasquez painted, died before he was ten years of age from congenital weakness, due to the inbreeding of his parents, for his mother was the niece of Philip, in addition to being his cousin. Charles was the product of a later marriage as complicated as the two previous ones, but he was lucky enough to survive—perhaps because he was the weakest and least fitted of Philip's children.

When Philip V. arrived in Spain from Versailles to take up his throne, the traditional backwardness of the Spaniards had been overlaid by the forty years of Charles's reign, in which space no kind of progress and no sign of change had crept into the country over the Pyrenees, or through the seaports along the impassable roads up to the capital. Even the periwig—most widely and typically spread of the French inventions—never reached Madrid. Charles, like Philip, his father, wore the long natural hair and the stiff starched collar which had been forgotten elsewhere for two generations. Spain seemed to the Frenchman the most barbarous of countries, and the food, final and most simple of comforts, was but another proof of the condition of savages in whose midst he was doomed to spend the remainder of his life.

No wonder he was hopeless and in despair. To make the irony of his situation more pointed, Philip was engaged in wars for the first twelve years of his reign, as though he was really bent and determined upon the conquest of a kingdom that he coveted. Truly, in his heart, Philip would have abandoned the wars and been only too pleased to return to France.

Philip's depression grew more and more marked with the passage of time, until, at the date I am speaking of, when he had reigned some thirty years over Spain, and was himself forty-seven years of age, he had reached the condition I have described in the beginning of this chapter, when he could not sleep, would not eat his food, and refused to sign any documents or even allow his barber to shave him—in fact, he had reached that critical stage when he must die—or be saved by a miracle.

I have described how the King lay, sleepless, turning from side to side, while he tried road after road and never found one that led him asleep. The air was so clamorous and noisy, so blazing with bright sound, and voices like little crackling flames, that it became an impossible task to concentrate and think of nothing, refuse to be led away by the first new voice that sang, and in this manner fall asleep in a kind of vacuum of impressions. He lay awake longing for silence to break this monotony of sound, as a modern traveller will hope against hope that his express may stop even for a second, so that he may have an opportunity of getting asleep before the din and the rattling begin again. At last, and so loud and long were the echoes and the dying noises that the change was like a great range of mountains suddenly seen far away above the edge of a limitless plain—at last, and as if with a desperate final attempt at willing it to come, the silence came creeping over the woods like a muffled heavy bank of cloud, and the King, realising it to be an attempt at chloroforming him through the open windows of the room, let himself relax slowly and sensibly until it overcame him.

His mind in its fever made him think that he had travelled a great distance, or lived through a decade of centuries, but, although he was unconscious of it, the return of daylight came in a very short hour from his falling asleep, and, some time before the sun showed up again, the gardeners had left their huts and were at work getting things ready for the day. Groping about in the half-light they had the appearance of housemaids who draw up the blinds in each room and dust every object, and in this case, as the result of their labour, you could distinctly see the mists moving away underneath their brushes. As they floated away, or dissolved into thin smoke, the smell of the flowers and the wet impalpable scent which green leaves give out under their loads of dew flowed into the air and took the place of the night mists. In a few minutes the fountains were turned on once again, and, at the moment, they showed up a steely grey against the drab sky; they gave one the idea that they were playing tricks with the steel blades of swords; they were performing very slow drill with these cold, bitter weapons, or they were themselves making a pretence of swallowing their own blades, as the steel edges of water bent at the top and slowly poured down again. In another moment or two the sun showed over the tree-tops and the slight hills, and all the drabness went at once out of the colour of everything. The fountain jets were now turned into as many harlequins leaping into the air to practise their dances and show off the new coloured suits in which they were performing to-day for the first time. So the sunlight, like beams of light from the wings, played on each jet and spray of water, changing its colour from one to another, and by turn advancing now this one, now that, into the first line of glare and prominence.

By now the trees had ceased to be flat shadows, and

became full and rounded under the glow of light. The Sun looked down first one and then another vista through the trees. Now he came to the edge of a small canal and, at once, with prodigal hand, poured so much gold into the waters that they were transmuted and lay still for him to pass over to the other bank. There fell a little hush, like the silence which precedes a great feat of strength, and the Sun, with bold strides, chose his avenue, and walked straight down it until he came to the house. The fruit trees trained upon the walls trembled and shook, making their delicate shadows dance inside the rooms they grew against. And as if to prove they were right in thinking he had come to tend and prune them, he leaned his long ladder against the wall and climbed up the rungs; but instead of staying there to look for fruit among the leaves, evidently considering he had enough breath to mount as high as he liked, he walked straight in at the King's window. He climbed easily over the sill, and his yellow mane flooded the room with light and woke up the King, who lay trembling, just as though this lion had roared.

He sat up in bed at once, seemed dazed for a moment by the suddenness, and just when his eyes should have recognised his surroundings and got back to being awake, they grew steadily more watery and nervous before this presence near him. For the bedroom seemed as if it no longer belonged to the King, and the new owner disposed things as though he had come for a long stay. So the King cowered back upon his bed, edging back as near to the wall as possible, while he left the intruder in undisturbed possession. Now he was right in the room, the Sun was in no need of ladders to retain his conquest; nor did he rely upon those sharp beams with which he searches into dark corners—the whole of the King's chamber was as if transfused with the golden light that had climbed in at the window, and everything lay spellbound and lifeless as if entranced. It seemed as though the sun had deliberately lifted up this room and set it close before his blinding eyes, so that he should never again forget where to find the King of Spain when he wanted him.

It was exactly this aspect of the affair which most annoyed the King. No sooner had he got asleep after a night of agony than this terrible revenge started on him again, and it was a retribution which had two blades, for one of them made use of all the noises of the night to torment him, and the other turned the actual substance of the day into an instrument of suffering.

The searching look, and its power to enforce obedience, was what he dreaded so much from those dire and staring eyes, for he hated to be watched and to feel that his movements held anything to distinguish him from the masses of his fellow-men among whose numbers he would have liked to hide. But there seemed to be no way by which he could escape obedience, and, to understand his personality, we should examine deeper into the reasons why he cowered down before an angry look, and we must try to explain why the King was mistrustful of being watched, and liked to live protected from peering eyes.

The lion-like glance had woken him, and now, for the rest of the day, he was tied like a captive to the Sun's chariot wheel.

He was a victim, then, of light as well as darkness; for during the day he was awake, and at night he could not sleep. In this lay the peculiar feature of his melancholy, for most invalids who dread the night-time feel at their best during the day, and are relieved, as if by good news, when the daylight first comes knocking against their shuttered windows. But Philip never felt safe, even when the light had peered into every corner, and this was because he felt frightened at every human influence. The too voluble nightingales who disturbed him after dark were so many venomous serpents; and the sunlight was like a heavy funeral pall that his enemies were waiting to throw over him. He had great wealth and high position, but Philip would use neither of these symbols to barter for the luxuries that would have soothed most men. Instead of the Sun's eyes, fierce and scorching with their yellow flame, he might have looked into smouldering fires that would have glittered again at his bidding, for no one, even if bound by religious vows, would refuse to become the mistress of the King of Spain. But his melancholy was too profound to be melted in this manner by the false heat of spring; and he was not to be moved out of this mood by glancing eyes, any more than by the songs of nightingales. In vain did the water-voices babble under green trees, for the gardeners, however skilfully they worked their fountains, only kept the King awake with this music. He could find no satisfaction either in watching the ways of Nature. It was spring, and everywhere out of the bleak winter woods the leaves were sprouting forth and allowing the winds to play gently with their soft boughs, as if to show that while the winds also were young, they had nothing to fear from their violence. The fretted shade, through which you could see little clouds sailing down the sky to take up their different posts for the summer drought, grew heavier and showed more promise of the shelter you would find under its cool roof, once the glaring summer days had begun. Everywhere at the height of a hand were fern leaves, equally good for a sword or for a fan, and serving still further to hide the dark shade in the woods. It would have been easy to pass a whole day among these green flames in a pavilion, where you could feel yourself burning one moment from two sparkling fires, and cooled the next moment by a snowy skin; but Philip would not taste this pleasure either, however sweet the fruit, and so it became evident that the miracle which alone could save him must be some mechanical wonder which could convert him again to a belief in human wisdom.

Elizabeth, his Queen, though she cherished Philip for his position and had some affection for him from long association and from the contrast of his weak nature with her own, had, up till now, spent but little time in trying to cure him of the incurable sadness into which he had fallen. She was too occupied in planning a second Armada with Cardinal Alberoni, and in securing Italian dominions for her sons, for she was determined that they should inherit kingdoms, although they had an elder brother, Ferdinand, the child of Philip's first marriage with Maria Louisa of Savoy, and his person barred them from the throne of Spain. In the year 1736, the date of which this essay treats, Elizabeth's elder son, Charles, had already been reigning for two years in Naples, where we found him in the first essay in this book, and the younger son was Duke of Parma, and possessor of the Farnese treasures of which his mother, Elizabeth, was the sole heiress. Elizabeth seems at about this date to have realised that her husband, an otherwise healthy man, was on the point of dying from melancholia, and the prospect of her stepson, Ferdinand, on the throne of Spain when her husband might still be alive, middle-aged but vigorous, determined the Queen to seek some means of restoring him to health, and give her a few more years in which to mature her plans for the future of her own children. She little knew that the same melancholy that she set out to cure in her husband would one day destroy the stepson, although it had been for some time kept under by the same process which relieved his father, and that by the stepson's death her own son, Charles, would be recalled from Naples to rule over the Spanish, and fulfil the destiny which his mother had planned for him.

Everything else had failed except music, and in this country, where the peasant music is more developed than anywhere else, and where limitless emotion can be expressed artlessly and as if without trouble, the Queen determined that she would soothe the King's troubles with the most flawless and dazzling technique that money could command.

By now, observant eyes can see the mechanical nightingale flapping in the sky on its way to sing to the King and cure his madness, and while it arrives, growing from a speck to a black glossy bird, we will describe the career and the adventures of this magician.

He was born at Naples, in the country where such a singer was most likely to be born, for Naples is one of the few towns that have been the centre of a great population right down from classical times, and singing, in this its highest form, when it expresses more than can be contained in any spoken words, you would expect to appear from one of the longest existing centres of conversation. When the huge repertory of southern gesture is added to the art of talking, and both these methods combined are not rich and varied enough to express what lies in the speaker's mind, he will take to singing as his way of self-interpretation. With such naturally endowed persons it is no more surprising than the readiness with which a duck that has never seen a pond before will take at once to the water, and float easily and safely on its surface.

Farinelli was his stage name, but Carlo Broschi was the name with which he was baptized in 1705. He must have shown peculiar genius for singing when a very small child, because the operation that all the male sopranos had to undergo and several years' training after it found him living, at the age of fifteen, as the pupil of the great Porpora. Under his guidance Farinelli made his operatic début at Rome in the opera *Eumene*, for which Porpora had composed the music. On this occasion, an important crisis in his life, Farinelli competed in a solo with a German trumpet-player, and he outdid this virtuoso in every respect, for he held his breath longer than the German could infuse life into his metal voice, and when the German sounded his most brazen, shattering note, the castrato could be heard above the horrid din as clearly as you can tell silver from copper when a handful of coins are thrown jangling on the floor. Such feats of skill made his reputation with the Italians, and he next set out to conquer Vienna, where he rested after his victory and prepared a still more dazzling set of tricks. In the intervals of exhausting work he toured Italy and was, for once, vanquished at Bologna by another singer called Bernacchi. But he profited even by defeat and persuaded his rival to give him lessons. Reinforced in this way with the wiles of his enemy, Farinelli repaired again to Vienna, where the Court of the last Holy Roman Emperor in the male line of the Hapsburgs was the most fervent supporter in Europe of this classical art that was to die in the next generation.

The Emperor Charles VI. was a patron of everything that could support the dignity of a Roman emperor. To this purpose colonnades and porticoes were indispensable, and there was no lack of able designers of these state picture-frames. Bernard Fischer von Erlach was the architect responsible for the arrangement of the stucco vistas down which, as through the wrong end of the telescope, Charles can be seen, in pictures and prints, standing in the open under a curtain, while Crown jewels and insignia lie in heaps around him like a traveller's luggage in a celestial douane. His belongings need no labels, and the passengers on these travels will recognise him at once by his chin. The geography of the background is a little difficult to follow, for a colonnade in the background might equally well belong to a summer palace outside the city, or to Charles's own additions to the Hofburg in Vienna. Between two of the pillars you can see a prancing and curveting horse, one of the Spanish race given by his cousins in Spain, and the only descendants left of the steeds upon which mail-clad knights used to ride. It is waiting there in the background for Charles to change into a field-marshal's uniform and climb into the saddle, when it will balance proudly on its hind legs while Charles can assume an attitude of command.

Of course, advice from such a personage was worth considering, and his pronouncements upon music carried the authority of knowledge on the subject. Music, like everything else, required a setting which would reflect honour on this Cæsar, and so he retained in his service a whole race of Italians, to whom he entrusted the decorations of a theatre, a procession, or a masque with the subsequent banquet. In this way a building which seemed to have the permanence of a Versailles could be put up in a few days, and by the next morning it had disappeared from the ground, as if by enchantment. The Bibbiena family of Bologna were in command of the nocturnal army. Italy at this date was too poor to retain the services of her best talent and so they were forced to seek employment abroad, and it was Vienna, more than any other town, which attracted these wandering artists, for that city was then at its greatest period of building. Only a few years before, the Turks had been driven back from its walls on their last great invasion of Eastern Europe, and the sense of security after this victory was the direct reason for the building of the great palaces of Vienna by the rich Austrian nobles. Von Erlach, a student of Bernini, did his best to foster the Emperor's Cæsarean affectation by building Vienna into the semblance of an improved Rome; meanwhile the Bibbienas and their assistants carried the scheme still further in imagination. It is as though the Italians, having matured their plans so far in earlier times, now that their imagination was unfettered and had the skill to play how it liked, found themselves without the money to realise their schemes, and so were forced to take opportunities abroad and produce in plaster and canvas that which they had planned in brick and marble.

It was out of these frail palaces that Farinelli was wont to sing, and a description of them is necessary in order that we may realise the change it was for the singer from these shaking walls, that rattled with his notes, to the more material palaces of Spain.

With many of the theatres of this date their structure formed part of the buildings of the Royal Palace in such a way that the palace gardens lay directly at the back of the stage. In such cases it was possible, on occasions of particular splendour, to take out the back of the stage and prolong the scene indefinitely into the garden behind, so that you could reinforce an avenue with a row of painted trees, and have plaster fountains playing among those of marble. During the interminable intervals, therefore, it was possible for the audience to climb on to the stage and walk straight out to the banquet under the trees.

The first scene was planned to give an effect simply of magnificence, and the best music, with the most ambitious songs, was kept for the middle scenes, when every spectator would be settled in his place, and the eye and ear had grown accustomed to the stage. Bibbiena was especially successful in these great ceremonial scenes, where the only object was to impress and beat conviction into the audience. In the middle of the stage, and to right and left, were three great colonnaded avenues down which the actors arrived, and the perspective of these routes was so skilfully exaggerated that the journey down them seemed of such length as to require a railway train to negotiate them.

In addition to this, the actors had practised the art of entrance to such a pitch that they had attained complete expression of character by the manner of their appearance on to the stage; and in this scene, where everyone playing in the piece arrived to show himself, many of the actors came as if they had just arrived from some other star, giving the air of immortals, immediately, by their carriage and entry.

A staircase of vast proportions rose up in several flights right through the roof, and the chief personages in these pagan pageants came down as if their chariots had just dropped them near the stairway for a few hours among us mortals, and were waiting to take them away again to scenes of still greater splendour.

As I have said, the opening scenes were in the form of processions, and of numberless cues for the entrance of each different star, until the whole constellation had blazed together, for one short moment, before the fall of the curtain and the alterations necessary to suit the stage for a long residence of these immortals had been brought to an end, and their palaces were perfect and ready for occupation.

The King and the Nightingale

That was the age of music in which stringed instruments were still written for in proper fashion, and as they never have been again since the death of Mozart. The composers of these pageants were not afraid of extending a long Virgilian campagna for the mind to wander across like the shadow of a cloud, and after the fashion of Gluck, one of their latest pupils, the Elysian fields may, of a sudden, be seen sparkling at a window's level, down the perspective of a colonnade, as if they were the transitory and airborn annexe to the palace, a hanging garden anchored here for the occasion. As the music drifts on, the boundaries of Elysium roll farther away, until its extent is indefinitely prolonged in every direction. It seems like the proof of the immortal condition into which the music has conveyed you that the way you choose at random out of this limitless paradise towards something with a more living and durable fertility should lead you, after long journeying, to the seashore, where those of a like mind with you are setting off in the dawn wind. The long balustrades of the palace that juts over the water are lined with rows of orange-trees in pots, and the hundreds of flaming mouths of the fruit among their dark leaves glow like the artillery of rockets which are let loose into the air to summon help from the far side of the water when there is danger. The gangways are already crowded with those boarding the ships, who walk on board, while each of them is followed across these few feet of water by his pale ghost, who treads foot by foot with his master, while both together go dryshod over the quiet waves. High up in the rigging are the sailors, who cling with their feet to the rope-ladders while they get ready to hoist the sail, and all the time their faces and hands are dashed with the dew that their busy movements shake off the overarching boughs. A moment or two more and the sails are pulled up and set in place like the clouds arranged in order for their race by the domineering wind. Then the mooring ropes are loosed, all is got ready, and shaking her wings lightly, as though to make sure of them, the ship sails away, making straight for the sun, and going quicker and quicker past the porticoes out to sea, while there is music sounding from every available window in the houses.

In another moment she would have travelled far enough over the blue plain to show far down the horizon, with no hull, but only her sails and rigging like a few white flower-petals blown by the wind into a spider's web; but before this could happen the Bibbienas sent down a long painted façade from the sky above, and this curtain gave another occasion for conversation and the killing of time.

Let us try to picture to ourselves the appearance of the heroes in whose company Farinelli lived his illusive secondary life upon the stage. They will not seem strange, let me say at once, to anyone who has looked at the engravings to an old edition of Tasso,[1] or who has seen at Greenwich the portrait of James II. as Neptune in command of the English fleet!

The exaggerated femininity, with its redoubled skill, of a castrato's singing was something that transcendentalised the voice as we recognise and hear it now. It was not like human singing at all, but like that of some strange and foreign variety of insect keeping up an incessant praise of its easy life under the help of the summer sun. His singing was like the endless and almost unconscious chirping of a cricket creaking all through the night of its satisfaction at the warm house-wall in which it lived and of the freezing winter, in contrast, outside—or still more of a caterpillar, could that creature articulate, chanting in praise of his leaf and of all the other dancing green fields of leaves above, and to every side of it, in the glancing air.

[1] Particularly the *Jerusalemme Liberata,* with engravings by Piazzetta, which was published in Venice by Albrizzi in 1745, and is the finest illustrated book of the Italian eighteenth century. The Paladins in these pages are a supererogation of Lebrun's tapestries, and they breathe that correct classical air which, at this date, only garden statues and the stage enjoyed. The original drawings by Piazzetta are still preserved, I believe, in the Royal Library at Turin.

The heroic Roman costume [1] had no strangeness for the audience, who imagined this to be the uniform of antiquity. It was not even an antiquity long past, for the heroes who went to the Crusades and fought against the paynims were, themselves also, clothed as emperors or legionaries. To the Emperor Charles it was what a review of Crimean veterans would be to us!

Pagan and Christian mythology were so many arsenals out of which artists of every description obtained their weapons of attack. There could never be lack of a subject while these arsenals were kept in order and repair. It is only because the doors have been kept open and unguarded that the supplies are now empty and these two buildings are a ruin. It is no longer possible to crystallise and turn into a convention that can sing, or move, a tree, cloud, or river. But in front of the colonnades that Bibbiena could raise in a night you would have a whole grove of trees singing to each other with their harp-like notes—a cloud might arrive like the herald of a god upon his way—or a river-god would be pouring his waters, that ran like music till the god arrived.

We can narrow the description down still further and say that we know the appearance of Farinelli and can almost hear the plaudits with which his entry is greeted, for he was anatomised by Hogarth, if flattered by Amigoni.[2] He was of disproportionate size, tall beyond the normal, and with that ample enlargement of the chest that you find in a prima donna, and that, at the same time, looked manly and truculent under the breastplate that a warrior's rôle imposed.

On this evening that he sang before the Emperor there was every opportunity and every excuse for his dazzling technique. To begin with, so realistic was the scenery that the audience might imagine they had been bidden as guests to some foreign country, where the hospitality accorded to them disarmed

[1] The statue of Mr Huskisson, the first victim of a railway train, in Chichester Cathedral, was the last to wear the classical toga.

[2] *Cf.* Hogarth's and Amigoni's portraits of Farinelli.

any criticisms they might make upon the wisdom of such conjunctions of the orders of architecture. So illusively painted were the statues that the guests half expected to be introduced to them after they had stepped down, tired out, from the pedestals on which they had been posing. There were flowering trees so tempting that you might bruise your hand upon the canvas where they were painted, and colonnades so cool that your struggles to get into them were like the assaults of a fly that sees the country outside but cannot understand the glass window that interposes between. The illusive architecture was, however, peopled by a whole army who knew their way through this maze of building and seemed to know by instinct what was painted and what was true. Just out of sight was a second army in reserve waiting to rush forth in a moment and transfigure the face of everything so completely that no one could recognise the scene again—for, indeed, within a few minutes it was no longer the same. There were new façades smiling at you, with their rows of painted windows and a different population, who appeared to live their lives entirely out of doors, for they never ventured inside and seldom climbed higher than the first few steps on the magnificent staircases. There were several of these transformations, that could only be satisfactorily explained by assuming that you were sailing on a very swift ship round the coasts of a densely populated island, travelling with an improbable speed, and halting first at one and then at the next sumptuous harbour town.

City succeeded city with an increase in splendour that ran in proportion to the distance travelled. It was obvious that the moment must come when the objective of these travels had been reached and where the music, that had up till now been eclipsed by the fascinations of the journey, must come out into a fine climax of grandeur. Only ten yards away from the audience, but hidden from them, stood the creator of all these cities, directing the instant building of this, the finest of them. The materials were ready-made but capable

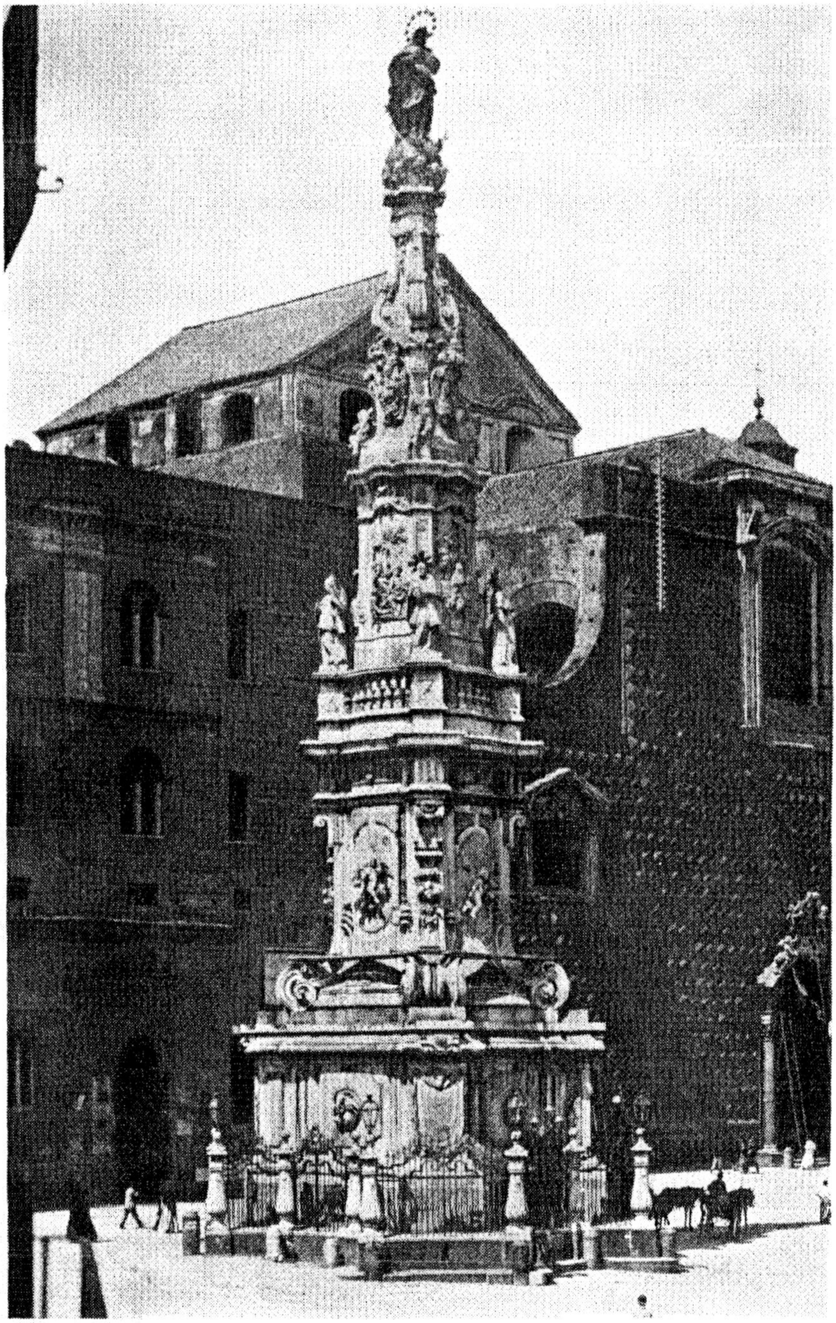

Photograph: Alinari

NAPLES

LA GUGLIA DEL GESU

of endless combination, for there were as many different changes to be rung out of these units of a pillar or the wing of a building as there are phrases to be pieced together with notes of music. Then, in the middle of the scene, in the exposed parts of the stage, where the eye could examine them closely and minutely, were the great painted screens of architecture, to be arranged among themselves in such a way that there were a like number of real and fictitious doorways and passages for the entrance of the actors upon the stage.

Round Bibbiena, like his lieutenants, stood two or three sons and nephews, while each of these sub-commanders had at his elbow two or three Bolognese assistants, for this branch of art was a speciality of Bologna. The inhabitants of this town, adepts—as doctors—in the dissection of corpses, and —as cooks—in the cutting up of fish and game, were not less skilled in a scientific examination of the parts of architecture, from which study they arrived at such a proficiency of knowledge of the art in all its details that they could diagram their fantastic combination of styles on any wall or on the largest canvas. In the painting of scenes they executed at full size the sketches of Bibbiena, while he would simply finish the most important part of the design. Thus the assistants might prepare a whole street of houses and Bibbiena would insert a fine palace in its midst; or, in greater detail, the workmen would paint a whole palace-front from Bibbiena's sketch, and, at the finish, he himself would paint the window and the balcony from which a serenade was to be answered.

Waiting behind the wings for their cues were a whole tribe of ethnographical specimens collected from the ends of the earth for study. No professor could have asked for more. They stood there in groups, talking or resting before their turn, and when they moved about, exercising care, for the floor was pitfalled with the openings of vaults, and among the machinery at the bottom there were the mechanicians, like the stokers on a great liner. Anyone careless enough to fall into one of these pits would find himself lying broken and crumpled among the sextons digging his grave.

Now the principal characters came pouring out from their dressing-rooms. The scene was almost ready, and in front of the curtain the orchestra could be heard, faintly, tuning up and trying over their parts. High up in the air some workmen were fastening the clouds from which a goddess was to sing. Beneath this the front of a huge building was still slowly travelling along toward its destination, pushed on rollers by a gang of workmen. In the clearer spaces, behind, the heavy chariots in which characters arrived were being run round to make sure their wheels were safe, and, near by, the dwellers in the air were making short experimental flights, held up by the wires fastened to their backs.

Long before anything seemed ready the curtain went up, uncovering all the crackling lights before the boxes, and the silence of the audience, who had chattered ceaselessly through every other scene, showed an air of expectancy. One or two of the most practised enthusiasts took out their watches, so as to be in readiness to time his longest sustained notes. It seemed like a queer inversion of the uses of a stopwatch, as if it were being used for a kind of Dutch horse-racing, for the stopwatch, which was invented to record distances travelled in the shortest time, had in this case a diametrically opposite purpose.

The entrance of Farinelli was most unexpected in method. Instead of gravely walking on, bowing to his reception, and then stiffly beginning a song, Farinelli adopted a more original mode of appearance. The choruses had died away and the stage was empty; even the music which had escorted all the actors as far as the passages which led to their dressing-rooms had now died down and was waiting silent for something to happen.

Down one of the corridors there came a low whispering note, like the wind beginning in the dead of night. It came a little louder, and now a shadow, closely followed by a huge figure, could be seen walking down the portico on to the boards. The voice grew louder and louder, until it reached a climax as Farinelli reached the candles and stood there in full view, shaking every ear with his sound. All the glass of the chandeliers rattled, and his voice was taken up and echoed by every bar and piece of metal in the theatre. While the handrails were still tingling and the note in the glass lights was dying away like a loud bell, Farinelli diminished the note, drawing it away again through the dying bells. Their life ebbed quickly away and his note was left, not so much dying itself also, but going away—fading further and still further from the colonnade into the landscapes beyond. No sooner had its sound completely vanished, even the echo being no longer audible, than Farinelli started off again, singing with such speed that the orchestra found it impossible to keep pace with him. Following their guide as best they could the orchestra reached the end of the journey and were landed there in safety by the middle of Farinelli's acknowledgment of the applause, but it was a world of skill and not of art, of sexless, insect-like accomplishment rather than of natural and true flowering.

The slave-like and terrible carving of the ornament required years of labour in its execution. There were designs so intricate that it seemed a miracle that any human being could find his way through them, and so deep was the undercutting that his cadenzas stood away entirely from the body of music that was to hold them.

There were no feats of conjuring, no displays of skill, of which Farinelli was incapable. He could be anywhere at any moment, or appear in several places at once, and he held the secret of that fourth dimension which enabled him to reconcile time with distance, and height with depth. He travelled with the complete equipment of the virtuoso.

His singing, as I have said, was conversation carried to a transcendental pitch, for, like Mozart, he had learnt music earlier than speech, and found it a more expressive and a more convincing weapon to his hand. He could move a crowd to tears easier than the most impassioned preacher or the most pathetic play, and the most eloquent talker there has ever been had not a more direct and overpowering attack upon the sensibilities. The most complicated passages of his singing, by incessant practice, he rendered with such facility that they were like the quickest and most delightful journeys. It is now our duty to discover where these ways led, but it was towards a very different landscape that he was to travel later on in his life.

The following list, which I transcribe from a programme of fireworks given, only two years ago, at a spa in the north of England, might be almost a catalogue of the effects of a virtuoso. It was most certainly in this direction that Farinelli was travelling at the period I am describing:—

GRAND GALA AND FIREWORKS

1. Signal aerial maroon, exploding at a great height and announcing the commencement of the display.

2. Grand prismatic illumination of the scene by large "Crystal Palace" changing colour lights.

During this illumination salvo of coloured rockets, bursting at a great altitude into many clouds of clustering stars.

3. Signal aerial maroon, announcing the Fairyland Glimpse, by the sudden and simultaneous ignition of large masses of variously coloured fire.

4. Salvo of "Celebration Rockets," filling the sky with a medley of beautiful effects new to 1920.

5. Salvo of "Golden Dawn" bombs, bursting into canopies of old gold.

6. The Transformation shell, opening out into a carpet of emerald-green, changing to a bank of roses.

7. Device: "The Magic Floral Basket."

8. The shower of glittering diamonds, produced by the ascent of rockets.

9. The fall of powdered snow. A splendid effect produced by the ascent of " Victory " rockets.

10. Grand salvo of Victory shells, emitting notable effects in rich colourings.

11. Device: "The Jewelled Tree of the Orient."

12. The radiant Emerald sprays, produced by the ascent of large rockets.

13. Salvo of coloured combination shells, emitting brilliant and novel effects.

14. Discharge of large shell—the " Empire " mystery.

15. Two devices: "The Blazing Revolving Suns."

16. Swarm of Glittering Dragonflies, produced by the ascent of large rockets.

17. The shower of White Osprey.

18. Grand salvo of " Commemoration " bombs, filling the sky with a potpourri of 1920 effects.

19. Device: "The Golden Tessela Carpet."

20. Falling Jets of Dancing Water.

21. The aerial festoons of "Empire " jewels, released from some of Brock's latest rockets.

22. Salvo of aerolite bombs, emitting some novel effects of great beauty.

23. The Mammoth Chrysanthemum shell, bursting at a great altitude into a huge golden flower.

24. Device: "The Fiery Tapestry Square."

25. Special flight of " Empire " rockets, dancing electric fire and clusters of sparkling jewels.

26. Salvo of shells, bursting at a great altitude into a cloud of National Colours.

27. The Eccentric Radiating shell, 25 inches in circumference.

28. Four devices, forming huge Electric Fountains, each flanked on either side by Emerald Aigrettes.

29. Aeroplane signal flashes, produced by the ascent of large and special rockets.

30. Grand salvo of " Empire " bombs, produced by Brock at Hyde Park for the official Peace Celebration display.

31. Special colossal spectacular device :

" *The Battle of Jutland* "

with moving ships—heavy gunfire—thrilling scenes—concluding with the sinking of the *Bismarck.*

32. Flight of Night Birds, released from some of Brock's latest whistling rockets.

33. Salvo of " Penta Pyric " shells, comprising a number of beautiful and novel effects.

34. Device : "The Niagara Falls by Moonlight."

35. The Lacework Lattice of Gold and Coloured Jewels—Roman Candles.

36. The Screen of Gleaming Pearls—Roman Candles.

37. The Curtain of Luminous Green—Roman Candles.

38. The Lattice of Jets of Dancing Water — Roman Candles.

39. The Terrace of Whirling Silver Spreaders, with clustering jewels—Roman Candles.

40. Colossal Final Device : " Good-Night."

41. Final flight of one hundred rockets, forming an aerial " Bouquet of Flowers."

Anyone who has the perseverance to read through this programme will agree with me that it reads like the catalogue of an auction sale of a virtuoso's effects, were his tricks marketable and to be bought in this manner. All these various items, numbered and described, are his assets, each one of them the result of many months of practice, and probably Farinelli, as a singer, had more of them than ever fell to the share of any other human being. Let us compare my firework programme with the actual performance given by some one of Farinelli's tribe, so that I may not be accused of exaggerating his virtuosity.

Here, then, is the programme of Paganini's last (his very last !) concert, given at Covent Garden Theatre on Friday, 3rd August 1832.

Programme

SIGNOR PAGANINI WILL PERFORM FOUR OF HIS FAVOURITE PIECES.

Part I

Grand Overture, *Der Freischutz.*—Weber. (*First Time.*)
Sonata in Mi Maggiore, in due parte:
(i) Cantabile in due voce, e
(ii) Variazione brillante sul tema, *Priache Pimpegno* nel *Amor Marinari* di Weigl.

SIGNOR PAGANINI.

Capriccio sul tema, *La ci darem la mano* di Mozart, e variazione gaie.

Part II

Grand Fantasia di Concerto (harp), in which will be introduced Mozart's air: *O dolce concerto.*

M. DIBDIN, *pupil of M. Bochsen.*

By Desire.—The celebrated Sonata Sentimentale, sulla preghiera of *Moisé in Egitto* of Rossini, followed by brilliant variations on a tema variato on one string only (the 4th).
Fandango Spagnuolo.—Variato e capriccio, in which will be introduced various imitations of: *The Farmyard.*

Conductor: Sir GEORGE SMART.

These two programmes read in a strangely similar manner, for they are both performances of the same order of invention, and the song, *Son qual nave*, from the opera *Eumene*, in which I have described Farinelli's appearance before the Emperor at Vienna, belonged, equally with these two manifestations that I have catalogued, to that cultivation of skill, to the exclusion of every other consideration, which Farinelli was so soon to renounce.

At last, as I have said, Farinelli reached the end of his roulades, and the orchestra, tumbling breathlessly after him, arrived in time to share his applause. But although they were blown and short of wind after their chase, Farinelli, as soon as the enthusiasm died down, was able to start off again in an elaborate spiral solo, unaccompanied by the orchestra, as if the stairs he was climbing were only strong enough to support one person at a time. The musicians sat there underneath, ready to catch him if he fell; but without so much as a glance beneath him, to see if they were ready to help him should difficulties occur, Farinelli climbed higher and higher, until he stood balanced on the very highest rung, and stayed there fearlessly, as though his foot were on the most ordinary doorstep. There he ended, on the highest note possible for the voice to reach, and he came so quickly and neatly down the stairs that his descent was unnoticed.

These first two songs were feats of skill, extraneous altogether to the action and plot of the opera, and merely introduced so as to give occasion for a display of his powers. But after these preliminaries Farinelli entered into the character he was to impersonate, and, for the moment, became disembodied from his virtuosity. His serenades were answered almost before you would have thought there was time to open a window: his duos were so exquisitely paired by his companion under the electrical influence of Farinelli's personality that you would think he was singing both parts himself, so impossible was it to realise that his genius, even, could rouse any other singer to such a pitch of beauty. He was at the same time more conspicuous and more subordinated than the rest of the company, for, when alone upon the stage, he was supreme in his powers, and, appearing with the other singers, he was seen in proportion with the rest, and did not try to show up their weakness with his superior skill.

The divinities among whom he was passing his life in

Eumene—these divinities and the heroes who were only not immortal by half—these figures, so dry and bleached by time as they are to us, had an appearance of freshness and green life to the audience of that time. There were, to begin with, so many statues of them in the public squares of every town, statues which stood there to serve as specimens of their race for the study of the townspeople who could see them every day, staying quite still in the blue cages that the cloud-bars made for them, or fenced in, as it were, by long railings of steel rain. Nearly every picture, again, that was not sacred—in the Christian sense—in subject, had for its story some scene out of the lives of this other omnipotent, but more reproachable, race of immortals. While there was a Saint for every virtue, there was a Pagan God for each natural object. Every star, every river, every sea, and every flower had its genealogy that could be traced; and there were no lawns without the traces of a sandalled foot, and no cloud that had not once been ridden for a steed.

After all the melting scenes in the opera, after the music that could have drawn tears from the eyes of a stone statue and was potent, in proportion, towards the soft and, as it were, feathery breasts of the audience, there is nothing to be surprised at in hearing of the frenetic enthusiasm with which Farinelli was greeted as the opera came to an end. He was called and recalled repeatedly, and was, in the end, persuaded to sing by himself again, while the whole theatre was dead silent and as if entranced.

This terrifying parade of his ability went from one end to the other of his powers. His lowest notes were like the roaring of flames imprisoned deep down inside the earth, and in the highest register his voice was a wind playing among the lolling bells of green leaves on every bough. He could travel from one extreme to the other without as much difficulty as you would have crossing from the hot glare of the sun into the deep shade beneath a tree, and yet this quick run from top to bottom of his voice was like the rain pelting down from its cloud on to the hard earth beneath. When he came to the end of his song, and all the bravura passages were sheathed and put away like a sword, the quiet level finish of the music came along, leading towards fields which were open to the sun and never frowned upon by storms. His singing died away on a wonderful sustained cantabile note, as if he were anxious for the audience to forget his skill and remember only the pathos and purity of his voice.

During the interval in which the stage was being got ready for the final ballet the Emperor sent for Farinelli, to congratulate him on his extraordinary performance. He was received in a small room leading out of the State box, which served as a dressing-room for the Royal party, and was hung with many mirrors, so that before they took their places in the box, and were exposed to public view, the Emperor and his family might have a last opportunity of appearing to the greatest advantage. This gave them a fellow-feeling with the actors as against the audience, for both parties felt they shared each other's secrets, and this may serve to explain why members of Royal families, even now, will laugh at the silliest joke when they are at the theatre.

It was, indeed, the most curious scene taking place in this little room during the interval. Before a huge gilded mirror stood the Emperor, as if confronting his own life-size photograph. He stood perfectly still in front of it, not daring to move for a minute for fear of ruffling the water and clouding over his image. Which was which? During this moment Cæsar was doubtful. Perhaps it was the other one opposite him who was to receive the actors in a few seconds! But as soon as he moved, and his empty ghost copied him exactly, he could see at once in whose direction the advantage lay, for he had all the initiative. If he moved, then the other copied him, but only thus far, no farther; for if he stood still, nothing happened. All the same, although confident in his own powers once more, the Emperor could not avoid feeling the heaviness which mirrors always produce in a room, for he could feel on his wrists and his ankles, and round every joint in his body, the invisible strings which connect you with the corresponding point on the body of your reflection, and which, without being able to help it, you are forced to pull with all the weight of your body whenever you move. Giving his wig another shake, so that it hung properly over his shoulders, the Emperor gave a last look at the mirror to see if his image had correctly followed him in all his dispositions, and seeing nothing amiss and all in order, he was now ready to receive Farinelli, and as soon as this was over, to take his place again for the ballet in the front of the box before the public eye.

Here he comes. There is a knock at the door. An attendant comes in and speaks a few words. Permission is given, and in another second or two the door opens wide and Farinelli enters and bows to the Emperor's hand, who at once raises him again, and they stand talking together, while the courtiers try to look envious of this honour paid to the singer. It was as though Farinelli had been suddenly caught up by the clouds and lifted away to be confronted with his Maker, and had, there and then, been assured of the absolute safety of his dispositions, and had been able to return to earth again, confident that he need only continue as before, and he would, in the end, have no cause to regret the purpose to which he had put his skill.

It was, of course, a very short interview, but it was, as I have hinted, the turning-point of Farinelli's career. From what passed in these few seconds of conversation he was to alter the whole sequence of his life. What the Emperor advised was no less than this: that Farinelli should throw away all the fireworks and technical tricks of his art and should adopt instead a style of absolute simplicity, under which his technique should lie hidden.

A renunciation on such a scale has very seldom been practised. Two or three centuries earlier one of the great warriors of Gothic times would give up his sword and become an anchorite, in the belief that there was still time enough for reform, even at the last moment. Such a sacrifice did not entail much hardship on an old man who had spent most of his life in hard fighting and in the rigours of campaigning and marching. But it was very nasty medicine for an artist like Farinelli to swallow when he was at the absolute zenith of his powers and scarcely thirty years of age.

The advice he had been given amounted to this: that Farinelli, who had spent all his life as a preparation to perfect virtuosity, should throw away every advantage he had gained, and rely for effect simply upon those qualities which it was in the power of any ordinary person to produce. All the effects catalogued in the two inventories given a few pages back were to be lost to him; they were to be disposed of without his having any share in the proceeds. Up to this point his whole life had been taken up in an endless study of what could be done to produce results out of darkness and night-time, and now, having learned the art of perfect illumination, he was to surrender all his secrets and appear in common daylight with ordinary mortals.

A whole tribe of painters, a school of architects, and a host of musicians, together with the whole race of actors, had been working for generations on the problems of darkness. When their services had been called in, a given space could be so emptied of the darkness that it contained in the night-time that the black threads of its texture could hardly be seen through the gilded air, so sifted by the different winds and currents of light. It was an area reclaimed from obscurity, and occupied, till next morning, by the best imitation of sunlight that man could produce. These different tribes—and Farinelli was chief of an important sept among them—were the men who produced and adorned this artificial sunlight, and this labour occupied so large a part of their energies that they lived only a very few hours of each day under the patronage of the luminary they were attempting to imitate. This deprivation gave them a double enthusiasm for the task. Then there is another thing to be remembered about them—the knowledge that the buildings

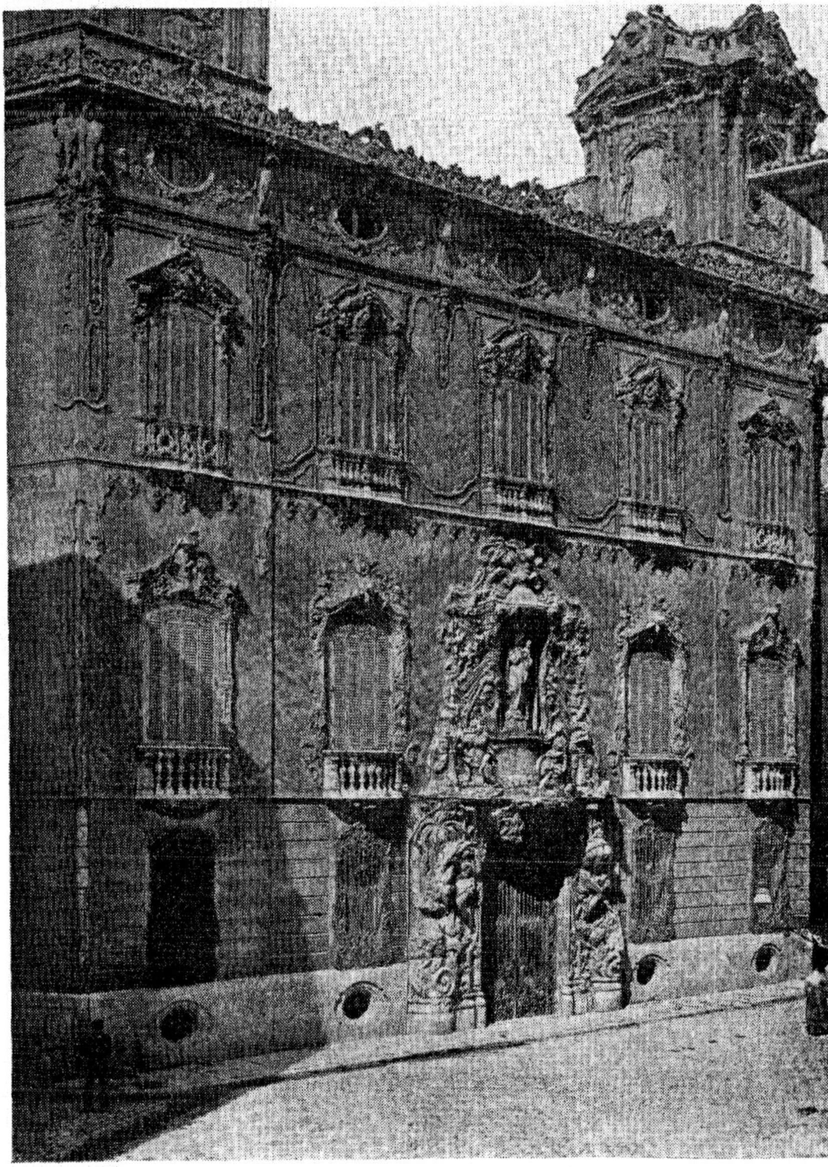

Photograph ©, August L. Mayer

VALENCIA

PALACE OF THE MARQUES DE DOS AGUAS

cf. Churriguerra, page 202

they prepared were only to last for a few nights made them concentrate on making still more mystifying the illusive and temporary character of their work. They had no time to waste on a useless permanence and solidity. In the same way a singer like Farinelli would profit by the impermanence of his song to make its ornament more prodigious than the most elaborate façade. Like Liszt, or like Paganini, he did not mind if the stone was too elaborately worked to stand a strong wind, and would collapse like a house of cards at the first sign of winter. Such a quick destruction prevented criticism, and, in the same way, the songs that Farinelli sang were finished before you could give a judgment on them, and the buildings among which he sang had grown old and were crumbled into a ruin before you could criticise them from the point of view of the architect.

Before you could arrive at a decision on one song or on one scene, another was quickly substituted before you, and this exhibition was conducted on the lines laid down by the merchants of the East, who show purchasers their poorest stuffs first, keeping the most dazzling and gorgeous materials till the last, so that their glitter is irresistible. Thus the first scene in a play should be a street scene; the piazza in front of the palace should follow; then the guard-room of the palace; the palace court, and finally the banqueting chamber, or the ball-room giving on the garden, and lying open for the curious eyes of the flowers.

I have described the manner of Farinelli's entrance and the song in which he ran from soft to loud and back again, and then sang at such a tremendous rate that the orchestra could not follow him. Softness, loudness, and speed, these may stand almost as the three normal—for I added a fourth, perhaps it should be the slow side of speed—dimensions of his art; for it was out of the different combinations and variations possible upon these ingredients that he practised and carried off all his successes. One of Farinelli's elaborate cadenzas required as much practice as the most patient of Cinquevalli's tricks, and Cinquevalli spent eight years on a trick that he performed with a billiard cue and a billiard ball. In the same way Porpora, his master, kept Farinelli twelve years on the same scale, over and over again, until he had reached perfection with it. His breathing was so admirable that he could continue without taking breath until it no longer seemed a surprising feat of skill, and it appeared simply that he must have two sets of lungs. His enunciation, again, was so good that you could hear him in recitative, in the corridor of the theatre, even if you closed your ears. Most astonishing of all things, Farinelli was entirely without the presence and braggadocio that nearly always travel with the luggage of the virtuoso. Most singers of that age, and more especially the castrati, were engaged in a ceaseless warfare of pre-eminence, and no advantage was too mean, no trick too unpleasant, for them to play upon their colleagues.

A gala night at the opera, before the curtain went up, would have made the most astounding field of study for the psychologist. These entertainments, nearly always Italian in music, in scene painting, and in the personnel of the singers, actors and dancers, were taking place at this period in every part and condition of Europe. If we take an evening where Farinelli was not singing, we may study him better in his absence, by contrast with his rivals. For example, one winter in Madrid, Charles III. engaged the singers Egiziello and Cafarelli to appear in the Opera *Achille e Sciro* of Pergolesi. To keep this contract, Cafarelli journeyed the whole way to Madrid from Poland, and Egiziello travelled from Portugal.

For Cafarelli it was a strange contrast to come from the bleak plains of Poland to the torrid heat of Madrid, even though Poland was not, at that date, the cold and persecuted monotony with which she is now inevitably associated. In those years she was part of the dominions of Augustus III. of Saxony, and the Poles must have contributed, perhaps more than they themselves realised, towards the support of their elector's regiment of three hundred and sixty-five children;

except that, as a race, the Poles have never resented a contribution towards magnificence. The Polish nobles were more extravagantly dressed than it is possible to conceive; and with their jewellery, their Oriental brocades, and their fur pelisses, they had also the peculiarity, almost alone in Europe at that date, of keeping to the old national method of headwear, so that they never appeared in the conventional wig which was the fashion in every other country. They may be seen, in exactly this style of dress, in the tapestries at the Uffizi Palace at Florence, which represent the fêtes of King Henry III. of France. These panels, six in number, were made in Brussels, after cartoons by François Quesnel about the year 1580, a century and a half earlier than the period of which I am treating. They show the arrival of the Polish ambassadors who came to France to demand that Henry should proceed as King to Poland, and the Polish nobles, who made a tremendous impression by the originality and expense of their clothes, can be seen in great contrast to the Frenchmen of that date. They sit watching the tournaments, or stand together in groups, and in every instance they have been obliging enough to turn their seal-like faces—with shaved heads and fierce-brandished moustachios—towards the spectators; for it was this particular feature in their appearance which aroused curiosity even more than their Oriental clothes. All of these scenes were at the ballet and tournament given in their honour in the year 1573, but later on, when Henry, and Catherine his wife, who had gone to Poland as rulers, seized the opportunity given them by the death of the former's brother, Charles IX., and returned, almost in flight, towards France, they broke their journey on the way at Venice, making a considerable detour in order to effect this. The Doge and Senate of Venice gave on this occasion those famous fêtes, among the most renowned in history, in order to welcome the French King on his way back to his newly inherited kingdom, and it was these which were the occasion for the introduction of Polish imitations into Venice, and, through her, into Italy and Europe generally.[1] But while other nations imitated the Poles, they themselves remained true to their national dress.

When Augustus the Strong of Saxony turned Catholic in order to secure his election as King of Poland, and after a lot of machinations gained his object and more than doubled the extent of his dominions, he brought with him to Warsaw and Cracow the first alien influence to be made visible in Poland. Cafarelli found there just the same music, the same theatre, and the same Italianised palaces of the rich nobles that were to be seen everywhere else. It was not a great transition from Bari, his birthplace, to Warsaw, as regards that part of life, for everyone concerned in the theatre in which he sang spoke Italian, and indeed the theatre and its scene were simply an Italian wood or grove of trees transferred to Poland in full leaf for this nightingale to sing from. The long stage-journey from Poland seemed to leave this oasis where he had sung far behind, and then Cafarelli passed through Dresden, the capital of the whole kingdom and the site of the grotesque Zwinger Palace, though out of its huge plan Augustus had only completed the building of the outlying pavilions. From here his journey led through Switzerland and down to the Mediterranean at Genoa, where he took ship and sailed across to Spain.

Egiziello was nearer at hand; he was no farther away than Lisbon. In this town also the opera was cultivated to an extraordinary extent, and the singers had a double rôle to perform, for they also constituted the choir in the Royal Chapel. The scenic arrangements were on an unprecedented scale of splendour, and in one ballet a whole troop of horses appeared on the stage and went through complicated manœuvres.[2] The great scenic artist and decorator, Pillement,

[1] In Venice, for years after, down to the time of Napoleon, strangers staying in the city for the Carnival, and wishing to avoid the complications induced by wearing Venetian costume, wore Polish disguise.

[2] This particular scene was the climax of the best Portuguese native opera, the *Allessandro nell' Indie* of David Perez, and this opera was dedicated to Cafarelli, who had been invited, that particular season, to sing in Lisbon.

appeared in Portugal not many years after this date, and some of his most ambitious works were produced there. The country owed all these advantages to her extravagant King, João V., who was determined to let no one else vie with him in expenditure.[1] The Palace-Convent of Mafra was the life-effort and culmination of his reign, and in sheer dimension it excels every other building in Europe. So vast is its size that every other consideration was sacrificed towards this one object, and the great walls appear to be desperately set up there just to stake the largest possible claim to some auriferous land underneath. To make this claim as far-reaching as possible each room has been extended to such an inordinate size that the four walls can barely hold up the extent of ceiling that depends upon them. The outside walls of the building are so thick and so solid that it seems as if they were planned against such an accident as a collapse, from overwork, on the part of some of the rooms inside. If this were to happen, the gigantic sides were so planned that all the building would fall inwards, littering the ground with its stones, and thus perpetuating, at any cost and for ever, this mysterious insistence upon what lay concealed below the floors.

Mafra was built, not as a rival to Versailles, but as something superior to the Escurial. This being so, the building was purposely designed to rely upon gloom and austerity as

[1] Near the town of Vendas Novas, in the Alemtejo province of Portugal, there still stands, uninhabited, but locked up ready for someone to arrive once more, the fine stone palace, with its complete equipment of furniture and comforts, which King João built in 1729 to accommodate the Court for one night only on the occasion of the double marriage of his daughter, the Infanta Maria Josepha de Braganza to Don Ferdinand, the eldest son of Philip V. of Spain, while the Spanish Infanta Marianna Vittoria de Bourbon was married to Dom Joseph, the heir-apparent of Portugal. As there was no water near the palace, it was brought, at a great expense, from a fountain made for the purpose at Pegões, where, also, the same King built another Royal quinta. The building, mostly one-storeyed, with a part of its neglected gardens, may be seen on the right of the station (*cf.* Murray's *Handbook to Portugal*, 1887 ed., p. 37).

the chief ingredient of its grandeur. The plan was drawn by a German architect, Johann Friedrich Ludwig of Ratisbon, and it was built facing the sea on, as is usual with buildings of that nature, an exposed and unsuitable site. The marbles of the church, the precious Brazilian woods of the corridors and the altar-pieces specially painted by Trevisani are the subjects of fervent praise from Beckford. But it must have been the ruinous, premature, and nearly Gothic gloom that appealed to the builder of Fonthill Abbey. As regards the King's intentions, Mafra was, as I have said, to rival and to surpass the Escurial, and João proposed to pass a month or two in each year there. He would retire for a little space from the gilded fretwork of his other palaces, and at Mafra he could make the ascetic retreat which would make null and void all his lapses in more comfortable surroundings. From Mafra he would rule, like Philip II., a great part of the world. The whole of Brazil would tremble, with its diamonds, at his word.[1] His retreat had this advantage, moreover, which Philip never could enjoy in the Escurial—the treasure fleet, on its way to the harbour of Lisbon, would sail past underneath the eyes of their possessor. The smoke from the guns, as they fired a salute towards where the palace lay, floated up into the air and hung there like so many small clouds escorting the ships, so as to make certain that they had wind enough to fill their sails, even the farthest distance away on the flat plains of sea. Then the great bells in the convent would begin ringing, and their sound went over, thrashing down the swell of the waves, towards where the ship lay, till the metallic clangor seemed to fasten its

[1] The first consignment of gold to reach Portugal from Brazil arrived in the year 1699, and the revenue to the Portuguese Crown from the King's fifth part, in spite of much fraud, was estimated at £300,000 a year. The discovery of diamonds in the newly conquered (1750) Paulist Republic of Brazil further increased the wealth of the Portuguese Crown, and in addition to the Royal right to every diamond above twenty carats weight, the King was estimated to make an income of £100,000 a year by a contract entered into with a syndicate of English diamond buyers (H. Morse Stephen, *Portugal*).

grappling-hooks on to the rigging, and the very ropes swayed in the sound more than they answered to the rolling of the ship.

The treasure fleets, unfortunately, but seldom arrived. The fortune that the King of Portugal got from his Brazilian dominions arrived more often in a prosaic form — on a paper of credit, or as a vote passed — though it was difficult for his Ministers to refuse it, since the Cortes, or Parliament, were never called till the end of the century.

This was before the great earthquake at Lisbon, and many buildings were put up by João which have long ago been shaken into dust. But the splendour with which he was surrounded may be seen, even now, by the Chapel of São João Baptista in the Cathedral of São Roque,[1] which, as an act of supplication against any further earthquakes, the King had designed and built in Rome from the designs of the architect Vanvitelli, solemnly blessed by the Pope and escorted across from Ostia to Lisbon by the Portuguese fleet. At the same time, by valuable gifts and concessions, João persuaded Pope Clement XI. to confer upon the Cardinal of Lisbon the title of Patriarch, which he shared alone with the Patriarch of Venice in the Western Church.

The collection of state carriages, like the most elaborate crystal chariots ever designed by the Elizabethan poets to be drawn by unicorns along the level golden sands of a river bank, are yet to be seen in Lisbon. They still glitter, although

[1] So large were the sums with which João was able to furnish Pope Benedict XIII. from the wealth of Brazil, that the new Patriarch of Lisbon received papal permission to officiate in vestments resembling those of the Pope, and his canons in imitation of those of the Cardinals; and finally, in the last year of his reign, the title of "Fidelissimus," or "Most Faithful," was conferred upon the Kings of Portugal, to correspond with those of "Most Christian" and "Most Catholic," attributed to the Kings of France and Spain respectively (*Portugal*, pp. 350-353. H. Morse Stephen. Fisher Unwin, "History of Nations Series." 1891).

long since empty of their load, and stand there with sparkling wheels, still and silent, each like a great sea-shell which is only waiting for the waves to reach it, when the sea-god will come back to his home again, and, released by the waves, the shell will sail out once more to sea, riding easily over the white-crested hills.

All over Portugal this was a period of great building activity,[1] and the churches and palaces which were arising in such profusion in the capital and all through the provinces belonged to that particular brand that we have recognised in Catania, in Naples, and in the Certosa of Padula. But while they belonged to the same order, the Portuguese buildings were of a subspecies in the race, and show many points of contact with, but also degrees of difference from, their neighbours. They have that mysterious kind of separation which becomes visible the moment you cross the frontier into a foreign land, and which is the more baffling and the more mysterious when it is the border between Spain and Portugal, where there are no natural features, no mountains and no rivers to separate the two countries, and yet the difference is almost more clearly marked than at any other frontier in Europe. There is, in the architecture, to begin with, less design and drawing than you find in Spain; and as if to excuse this weakness they try to make up for it by a mad profusion of ornament, the carving being of an Indian closeness and intricacy of design. There is in this complexity that trait of the southern character which a traveller always notices in the entreaties and arguments of the railway porters or the cabmen when he arrives in the south of Europe. Out of this architecture almost every trace of the classical lines laid down by the Renaissance has gone out, so far has it travelled from its centre, and it is difficult to see a pillar because it is so honeycombed with carving, or to recognise

[1] After the earthquake of 1755 Lisbon was speedily rebuilt, owing to the energies of the great Minister Pombal, and the plans of most of the fine new streets and buildings were entrusted to the famous Portuguese architect, Joaquim Machado de Castro.

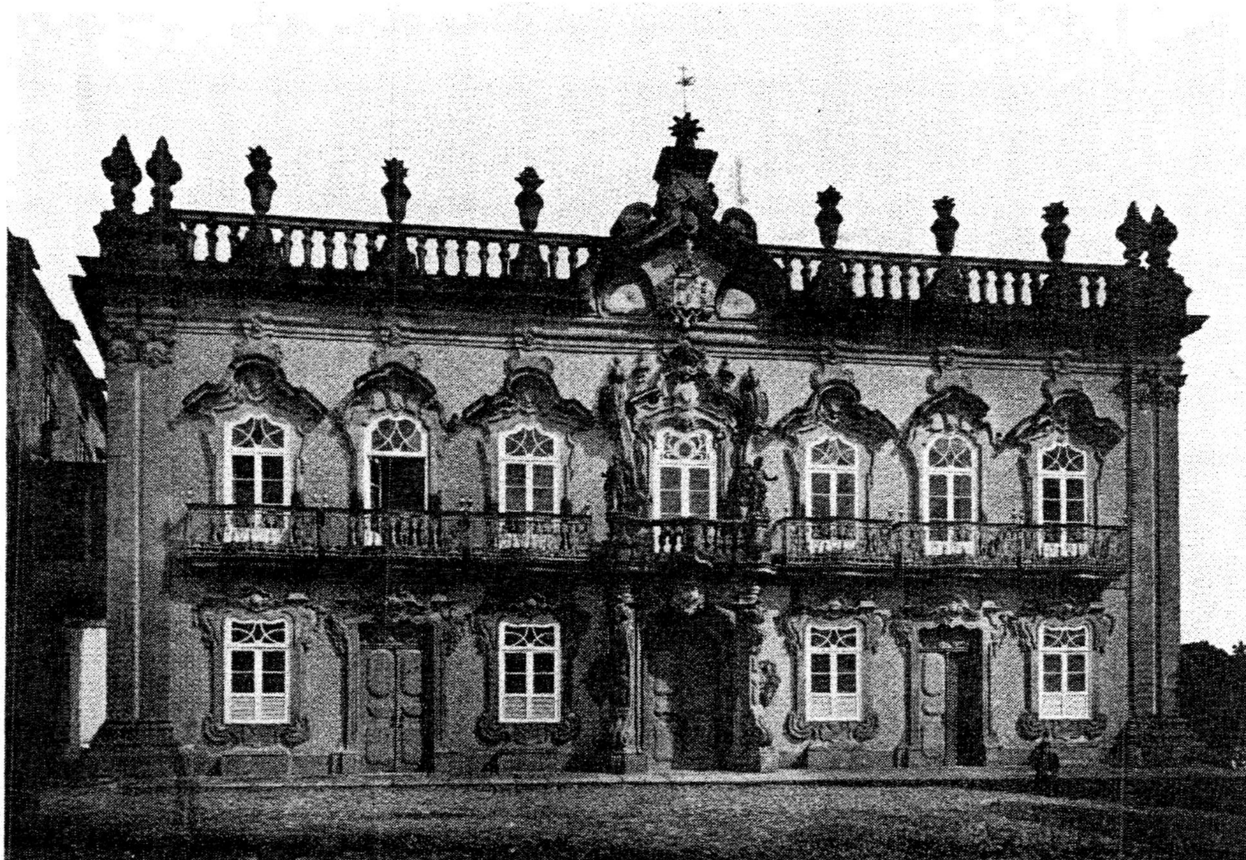

Photograph: Otto Schubert

BRAGA (NORTH PORTUGAL)

PALACIO DEL MEJICANO

an arch through the web of flowering lines with which it is overlaid. There are no straight lines along which the eye can travel; but it is recognised as a fact that in this delightful climate no hour can be wasted, and so the builders have extended time as much as they can and made each path wind as far as possible before it reaches its destination.

The Palace-Convent of Mafra, then, let it be understood, is in contrast with its severity of style to every other building of this date in Portugal. Elsewhere there is redundancy and complication of ornament. If it is possible, in a few words, to make a comparison between the Portuguese and the Spanish examples of the rococo style, one might say that in Portugal the flowing Spanish line has become cramped and coiled in upon itself; while everything that is dramatic in the Spanish sculpture has, in Portugal, hidden itself behind the curves of a manifold drapery.

The genius, or the scapegoat, at the head of this business was the architect, José Churriguerra of Salamanca. His actual performances in this manner of building were moderate and sober compared with the excesses to which his pupils ran. It is difficult to find a better judgment upon their work than is contained in the Funeral Oration which the historian and essayist, Jovellanos, delivered at the death of the rigid classical revivalist of the next generation, in which he contrasts the severity and dignity of his style with the profusion of the age that had preceded him.

The treatment of which Jovellanos complains is to be found in more places than we could enumerate in the most complex of indexes. But behind the obvious barbarity of the ornament there is to be discovered a kind of beauty to which all critics have been blind, and for which no one has been the advocate since the date, two centuries back, at which they were erected. They still remain, in their best examples, the least appreciated of all the fine buildings to be seen in Europe. The reason for this is that they present so many points of difference with the buildings of the same date to be seen elsewhere that, by their very contrast, they are judged as failures in what is considered as the general direction of ideas at that period. But it is the hypothesis that is wrong; for the Churriguerresque creations have no conceivable affinity with the Louis Quinze work of France, or with the Georgian house merging into the Adams' date in England. Churriguerra was the result of a completely different culture and course of ideas, and he is unequal by incompatibility, not by incompetence.

This is the starting-point of our travels deep into the interior of Spain once more, but towards far different places from those that we visited earlier in this book. Whilst workmen are busy in every town putting up the buildings that are to be ready by the middle of the century, the nightingale that is to arrive, then, and cure the King of his madness is hard at work also. Farinelli was still singing with the same bravura and execution that had conquered Italy and Vienna. In this interval of five years he was to make the complete reduction of England to his skill, but all the while he was practising in secret that new subjection of his virtuosity which would effect miracles and keep permanent their results. It was precisely this quality of permanence which had been absent from his dazzling victories before, and it is to compare this success by simple means, with the bravura and complication of his previous campaigns, that I am studying in such detail the works of the age by which Farinelli would find himself surrounded when he arrived in Spain. For this architecture, that is now so dead and unappreciated, had exactly the same virtuoso qualities of rapidity and brilliance that caused Farinelli to be acclaimed as a hero and a genius by his audiences. And it is not to Farinelli alone that this architecture is a parallel, but it affords a clue also to the minds of Paganini and of Liszt, and, seeing one of its best examples for the first time, you might fancy yourself present at the first performance of the Fandango Spagnuolo, or the Hungarian Rhapsodies. It is the only virtuoso architecture to be found in Europe; but whilst we are investigating its effects, all the time, somewhere in retirement, the most brilliant of all these performers is practising something that will be more successful even than his previous weapons.

There is, in a novel of Strindberg's, *The Inferno,* the description of how his impending nervous collapse became all but precipitated upon him by the insistence with which someone invisible in a near room played over and over again, so as to practise it perfectly, the most difficult passages from the Paganini-Liszt *Campanella.* The strings of notes, separated from each other and then sewed together again, came floating to him over the low garden wall one hot summer afternoon. The tinkling and feeble imitation of the church bell, as it occurs all through the first part of the piece, seemed irritating and silly beside the huge, brazen clangor of the sun, as it came beating down in a burning shower through the leaves. The piano was like the church bell in one of those absurdly needle-shaped spires of Switzerland, rung early in the brittle morning and hardly strong enough to scratch with its feeble point the ice that was lying on the little round mountain lakes. This passage was tried over and over again till the fingering was perfect, and each peal of bells rang out clearly by itself, without interfering with any of the spiked fir-trees or becoming muffled by the snow. Later on in the middle, when there comes the long tremolo for the right hand up in the high notes of the piano, a good performer will make them rattle out till the two notes together combine and sound forth like the whistle of a steam-engine. This is the signal for the feeble church peal to sound out once more, now for the last time, and after this is over the real game of acrobatics begins. Up to this moment Liszt has been hiding his strength and playing with the church bells like a cat with a mouse, but now the piece is to end with the display of all the technique of which Liszt was the master. What had been feeble before, now takes on a militant and extremely menacing tone, and the meekness of the first half of the piece has been obviously exaggerated, so as to give contrast with the magnificence of the display with which it ends. The whole range of the piano, and not only the treble register, becomes engaged in the conflict, and the sonority is such that it would seem he had the bells in every tower of Northern Europe to run among and thunder upon. The last notes end off suddenly in full force, and their echo grows even stronger before it has passed by and drifted on towards windows farther away.

This hot afternoon in Paris that Strindberg described can be paralleled in everyone's experience, though there are but few who would have felt its force so strongly as this Swede. There are few back windows in any town from which you cannot hear, at some time of day, a piano being practised, or someone singing over his scales with the help of that instrument. Sometimes it is in summer, as I have described with *Campanella,* and at other times it is in the dead of winter, when everything outside is lying so still that the stark boughs of the backyard trees are so many fragile bars before the windows. The glass in these windows is opaque, like the thin water-film of a bubble, and anyone who dared to throw them open would break this enchantment and allow the strong waters of music to flood out, snapping off the branches, till in a second the force was spent and the music dead again, fled out of the broken vacuum. On other days this incessant practising will go on through a whole daytime of rain, proclaiming that at any rate one dreary being is still alive in the sousing hours; and the same notes played over and over again sound like a catalogue of the thoughts and poor worldly belongings of the player—for the personal possession of any object is, at the same time, that which makes man different from the animals, and that which makes him more pathetic a creature than the eagle or the lion.

It is in somewhat of this manner that you hear one or more of these automata going through his practice; but it is sensation of a very different order to be yourself the cause and the giver of such music. We must imagine an altogether opposite set of images for this situation, and even then we are not finished with the difficulties, for it was not his scales alone that Farinelli was practising, but the poise of every movement, as though he were an athlete and not a singer, and the tone of each command as though he were a general and not an actor. He must be, at the same moment, quicker than Mercury and more stern than Cæsar. At one moment he would so efface himself into the music that his voice became simply the inevitable shadow that ran with the whole body of instruments, stopping with them wherever their path led, and, a few seconds later, he would leave them behind like an army in reserve, while he came forward and took all the fruits of victory single-handed. At such moments his singing was like the carrying out of a perfectly conceived plan of attack. There was not a movement, and not a note, that did not carry him a step nearer the object he was aiming at.

It was these feints, these approaches, the solos like a gladiator fighting by himself, and the choruses which he led, like a hero marching in front of his men, that Farinelli used to practise long hours each day, in whatever country might be the scene of his campaign. The appalling difficulties that he overcame in his solos were made up of sheer feats of arms and of dazzling moves to blind his opponent. There were huge tremolos that were a trial of wind and endurance ; and then there followed flashing chains of scales, and in the blinding light from these it was impossible to see, so that it was hopeless to know at what point his cadenza would end and the measured music of the air begin again.

Exactly the same practice was in progress at this season of year behind blue windows among the glancing boughs. Whilst Farinelli was preparing for Spain, the Spanish nightingales were getting ready for the summer. They were making the best use of the dwindling spring evenings to practise their virtuoso-music. They began with the first moment that the labourers had left their work in the fields and were walking back, at so many tangents from the trees, towards their cottages. The corn had grown to such a high hedge of green swords within the last few days that the gleaming blades left no spaces between themselves through which the labourers could be seen toiling homeward. It was only when their path led them over the slope of a low hill in the corn-land, that they came suddenly into sight out of the green depths they had been wading through. There was always wind on this high ground, because it was on a level with the lowest storeys of leaves, and so, on reaching the crest of this little billow, they appeared to be jostled together and almost flung over the back of the wave. Then they sank back and were seen no more until they were shaken up again, in time to be swung over the next chain of waves.

As soon as the look-outs on the tree-tops could see these different groups taking the crest of the hill, they knew that the cornfields were empty and safe of enemies. Until next morning, when colour and light would be born again in each blade and leaf, they had the whole of their world to themselves, with only those enemies whom they were accustomed to, and no creatures alive except those others that used night-time as a curtain to their actions.

But, like the musicians I have described, the time has not yet come for the nightingales to do anything except practise those effects they want for the long summer nights that are, themselves, nearly perfected. Each evening has been a little shorter, a little more concentrated in its purity from too many clouds, so that there should be no unnecessary shadow thrown upon the hills, that are already dark enough with corn, and with the massed trees that have stretched out their hands as far as limbs can carry them so as to catch the cool water of rain, and the yellow bread of sunlight that is given them to feed upon.

It is only practice and not performance, and therefore you must not expect to hear those long-sustained melodies, like a whole love-story told in one breath, that are poured out later in the year. Just at present they are at work upon short phrases, very sharp and poignant like an invocation. There are a hundred voices trying over this passage, but they are none of them alike in the interpretation that they give. It is the same sentence, terrible and imperious in meaning, that is repeated over and over again in a hundred different languages. Each version is apart from any other, and yet they all of them carry this same message, so that one being could understand all these strange tongues speaking at once. In another place they are practising the opening that must come before the burden of the song. It is like a call to arms. They begin with so soaring a flight of notes that it is surprising how the structure of their music can stand such a frightful elevation with so thin walls. Then there come the tremolos of a vibrating sweetness, as though having reached this height they have to whir and thrash their wings to keep themselves steady to sing, and prevent their falling down headlong to be crumpled on the ground.

The whole night through they are sitting still on the boughs. They practise every one of these effects till it is perfect, as they stay safely under the leaves; for not until absolutely sure of its perfection do the nightingales venture out into the shadowless dark over the fields. At this time they are still uncertain of their skill, and, so as to test its strength, you can hear them trying over the most difficult evolutions, purposely setting themselves the hardest problems to solve. They will set out on a spiral climb so steep that it does not seem possible for them to reach its summit, or they will turn about in such desperate fashion that it would seem hopeless for them to preserve their balance. Their control is without a flaw; so that the simplest turn of the wing is calculated, and there is not an inch of error in their reckoning as they fly from one end to another of the scale.

Everything is nearly ready now. It requires only another week of still nights, and they will all be able to launch their skiffs and push off over the deepest pools of darkness, where their skill will make it safe for them, however perilous the depths, and no matter how strongly the wind may work to blow their song aside. They can float swiftly over the most turgid chasms, and can hover with their wings before a window, in any wind, not minding its breath any more than the still star who sings every night above such and such a quiverful of leaves.

All this time, as I have indicated, the workmen were labouring, even at night, on the buildings which are still to be seen in Spain, but now only seem like the burnt-out framework holding the illuminations that once made night brighter than day. Since all the processions have rolled away, they seem empty like a shell without an echo. Spanish sculptors had produced among themselves a special race who prepared the statues that were carried round the town on the days of religious festivals. José Zarcillo, who was born and worked all his life in Murcia, but was of Neapolitan descent, had the reputation of being the most skilful of all these image-makers. I mention these artists immediately in this connection, because, by the very nature of their commissions, they were bound to produce statues for some particular festival at the shortest possible notice. They must often have worked all through the night to produce that host of saints and of " walkers-on " in the sacred drama with which they peopled the whole reaches of a procession.

Zarcillo I mention, while omitting Montanes, Juan Martinez, Pedro Roldan, Alonso Cano, and the rest of them, because he represents, at the same time, the zenith of realism, and the highest pitch of fantasy to which these sculptors attained. He had the greatest technical accomplishment among them all, and in his best work there is something transcendental that rises above the conceptions of the other decadent sculptors of his date who were content to carve the face and hands of their figures while the head was concealed with an artificial wig; and the most skilful embroiderers in each town vied with one another in the elaboration with which they could work the real clothes that the figure was to wear. There is a tensity about the expression with which he invests each figure, as though these wooden statues were revealed to you in a flash of lightning, from whose sharp surprise they are suffering. They seem to stagger back, dazed and dazzled by the light, while they keep every muscle taut, and are rigid and motionless with the force of catalepsy.

Most especially are these qualities to be seen in Zarcillo's greatest and most famous work, the group of the Last Supper in the Ermita de Jesus at Murcia. This group offers a most interesting comparison with those pictures of the Last Supper which El Greco painted, in a series which are dispersed almost too widely for it to be possible to compare them together. The Last Supper has exactly those qualities which make this picture by El Greco so unexpected and dramatic in treatment. He gives individuality to each disciple, more by investing him with a whole repertory of gesture than by the usual method of distinguishing a figure by its dress, and by the portrait features of its head. All the disciples belong to the ordinary race of models : they were fishermen, porters, or lazzaroni ; but, on top of this family resemblance, Zarcillo has superimposed a racial diversity, so that while all the figures start from the same point, they reach widely different objectives. They have every extravagance of gesture that it is possible to conceive, and you would think from their long thin hands that, like the people of Greco's mind, they talked with their fingers, finding there ten tongues more voluble than the one poor instrument of speech. The manipulation of these life-size figures is most strange when it is taken into account that they are not built up, but carved down—that is to say, each figure began out of a rough tree trunk, which Zarcillo whittled down into the shape he required, turning these trees into the strangest of dryads. In the whole of his career he is estimated to have brought some four thousand of these monsters into existence, and this family of them represent the most life-giving features which he was able to particularise among them.

The importance of Zarcillo's work consists in this. He represents the full maturity of that fertile invention which we are noticing all over Southern Europe at this date ; and his genius has something rough and vigorous about its force that is infinitely removed from the sophistication of France or England. Zarcillo, who was the last of the race of sculptors, possessed this progenitiveness to the full, as I have indicated, and he has also the interest that in his work, more than in that of any sculptor who preceded him, can be traced some distant descent from El Greco, whose progeny I have attempted to establish in the last chapter.

It must not be imagined that Zarcillo was alone in his work. There were architects and sculptors all over Spain who were working in the same taste. The buildings of Churriguerra, the most moderate of his school, belong to the same extinct family. His dramatic façade for the Provincial Hospital at Madrid gives a fair example of what powers he possessed. This is a façade which was intended and designed to be seen under every variety of strong light. It was prepared for the even and searching glare of the sun, as well as the fitful, but dazzling, starlight. Therefore, at all times, it must help towards its own quick comprehension, and to get his effects Churriguerra relied upon the deep undercutting, and the emphatic shadows, which he must always expect for his treatment from the Spanish climate. He made use of the piercing light to show up an intricacy of ornament which could never be followed by the eye in a more northern climate, except when the white glaring snow shows every detail with a painful emphasis. Here, in Madrid, Churriguerra had not the same degree of darkness to guard against, for in the day his building showed up in the sun with the white glare of the moon, and at night his façade was honeyed and golden like the sunlight.

He shows the same character in other buildings which are still defiled by his name, according to the guide-books. The great piazza at Salamanca, his native city, designed by him especially for the unrolling of the scrolls of a great procession, shows a consummate mastery of stage effect, for it is like an Italian set-scene erected in permanent stone, and here he has made durable and lasting that which, with its frail elaboration, seemed only to have life enough for one night. The sacristy in the Cartuja of Granada has, again, just these same qualities, for the faceted and spangled pilasters are what you can see in any one of Ferdinando Galli da Bibbiena's sets for a Royal marriage at the Austrian or the Saxon-

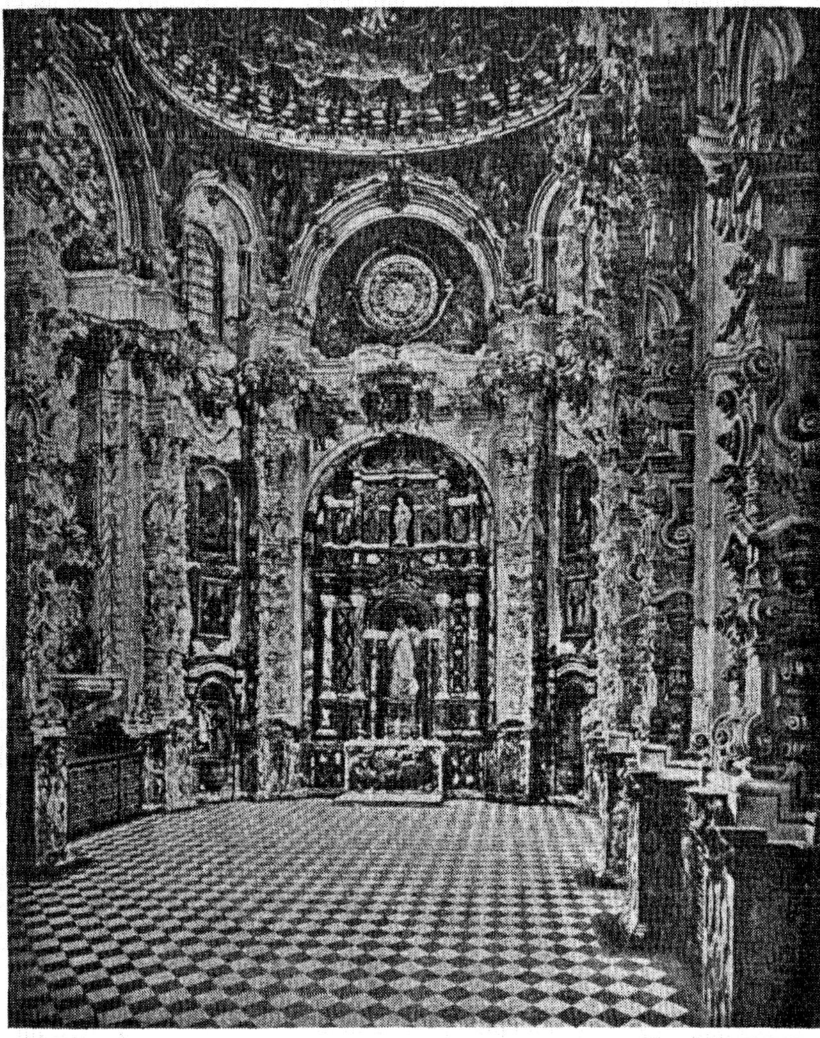

Photograph: Otto Schubert

GRANADA

SACRISTY OF THE CARTUJA

Polish court. Here, in Granada, what was the temporary and short-lived annexe to a palace has turned into the permanent wardrobe in which the Carthusians keep everything that is necessary for service in the tremendous, but now unhappily demolished, church.

We have read of these elaborations in the funeral oration by Jovellanos. Those faceted and fretted pillars were the admiration and the marvel of an age. The wildest of all the followers of Churriguerra, Don Pedro de Ribera, was praised and extolled for his pillars, faceted like the diamonds of Golconda, from out of which the light came gleaming and darting as though they were the actual pillars of the temple. Churriguerra had a whole army of assistants, who took the law into their own hands and became, first of all, pupils, and then the masters of other disciples. Here, in Spain, they were as far away as geography will allow from any of the Arcadian fashions of the rest of Europe. They were as safe, also, from the effects precipitated upon taste by the discovery of Pompeii. There was in Spain, then, a school of architects who had arisen to supply the demands of a community that could still throw away much money on building. They were free from academical control, and there were no bounds to their performance, except the laws of mechanical impossibility.

We shall see this movement, in the next chapter, floating across, guided by skilful hands, towards Mexico, its second home, where it grew to immense proportions under the imperious commands of a great and unappreciated genius of native Indian blood, the architect Tresguerras ; and we shall establish that this fleet sailed simultaneously towards Mexico from two harbours, one in Southern Spain, and the other in the southern extreme of Italy.

Only a very few years later than the period of which I am treating, Charles III. proposed seriously to move the capital of Spain from Madrid, where it was unsuitably situated from every point of view, to Seville, the centre of the richest and most fertile district of Spain. Had this transference taken place we should have seen, before the classical revival came in and straightened every line, the most perfect maturing of the rococo spirit, for Charles had the intelligence to employ the best artists of any race he could procure, and under this double stimulus of patronage to native workmen, and the importation of foreign artists of talent, architecture would have run into the deepest channels of development.

Just in the actual years that I am speaking of, Charles was still employed, as I have described him in the first chapter of this book, in converting Naples into the capital of a kingdom once again, which position it was to occupy as the richest and most populous town of Italy. His short reign at Naples has already begun, and it will not be many years before he will be called back to Spain to pension off the nightingale that had preserved his father's reason. Charles, himself, realised the danger of melancholia to which he was hereditarily inclined. It was to keep this menace away that he started on such prolonged and energetic hunting expeditions. He would start off early and stay in the hills all day, not minding what extremities of heat or cold he might be exposed to; nor had he any objection to offer to the wettest of weathers, for, as he would very justly remark, " rain does not break bones."

He knew that the holiday which these expeditions gave him from State affairs, and the extreme fatigue which they induced, constituted together the safest guard against the melancholia to which he realised he was predisposed. All of his family had this same enthusiasm for shooting. Very many years after, and when he was an old man, his sister, the Infanta Marianna Vittoria of Portugal, who had been separated from him since her marriage twenty years before, returned to Spain on the death of her husband, and Charles came out a long journey to meet her, for the brother and sister were extremely devoted to each other; but even the most loyal and affectionate among the courtiers, so we are told by contemporary writers, could hardly restrain their amusement at the sight of this aquiline and untidy old

Infanta shooting from horseback with her brother, and appearing unmoved by the most strenuous exertion.

Charles's return to Spain was a duty and not an act of choice. He had been accustomed, ever since he left home, to take up the Duchy of Parma, at the age of sixteen, to the climate and the arts and luxuries of Italy, and the depression of his family at their return to Spain draws a contrast between the comforts of their former life, and the semi-barbarity of their new conditions. Soon after their arrival in Madrid, his wife, Maria Amalia of Saxony, writes to a Neapolitan friend of hers: "Imagine my sufferings in this horrid climate. Picture to yourself that there are not even any of those little strawberries we used to like so much at Naples." Most certainly Charles did his best to remedy these deficiencies, for he built, from the plans of the Turin architect, Sacchetti, the present Royal palace of Madrid, and he employed Tiepolo to fresco the roof of the finest hall—the throne-room—of the palace; while before his death he had discovered Goya and made him Court painter. If Charles was so thorough as this in great works, we may feel sure that he did not leave details unaccomplished, and we may expect that the Queen's complaints were listened to and redressed.

The rebuilding of the Royal palace was made necessary by a fire which had destroyed and gutted the former one, but, from Charles's haste to rebuild, it would be unwise to conclude that comfort was at such a minimum in Spain. The walls against which his father, Philip, butted his head were more softly padded with tapestry than the most luxurious cell. He hardly came to the capital, owing to the condition of his health, but stayed in the country palaces round Madrid, and more particularly at Aranjuez, within sound of the fountains that we heard at the start of this chapter. It was under their spray that we left him, and now we rejoin him, still bound by those crystal chains.

His condition had grown from bad to hopeless, and he was now, to all outward appearance, in an incurable condition of lunacy. He had that exaggerated and staccato walk which is one of the most fearful outward signs of insanity. He would travel with an incredible speed up and down one of the garden paths, shooting out his arms and legs as though it was the use of all four limbs that propelled him through the air; for, in his own mind, it was not the gravel that he walked upon, but a peculiarly brittle and crumbling air above the path, and on this medium he slipped back as much as he went forward, so that it called for all his energy to keep him going. All this while he was fighting for life; for if he were once to stop, he would die like the travellers who are rash enough to fall asleep in the snow, never to wake again. It was better, though, out here in the open, than to be imprisoned in one of those black box-like rooms of the palace. After a time there came a consolation even in walking, for you could forget your sufferings and imagine yourself a piece of machinery driven round, not disagreeably, but without being able to resist against the force that drove you on. He found it easy to turn into a clock; for this piece of machinery was an especial toy that his family collected in Spain to an absurd degree for several generations; while in France members of the family even turned their skill into making these instruments. If he was a clock he should move his limbs but stand still, and so Philip would run back into the house and sit for hours on a low stool, imitating the steady and exhausting heart-beat of these bloodless creatures.

At other moments he was troubled by quite different incarnations. He would shout out loudly when any of his family or attendants spoke to him, roaring in a more and still more menacing manner, until he drowned the voices he heard speaking, so that he should not understand the unpleasant messages they were carrying to him. Then the voices turned into the screams of tortured people, whose cries he was shouting down, and an insufferable odour of burnt flesh came into the room, as though he were responsible for every *auto-da-fé* that had taken place, and was having the guilt brought home to him in this fashion. The horrible reeking fume went down his lungs and choked him; his eyes smarted with it, and the whole room became so dark and confused that he dared not move, for fear of the phantoms that were waiting for him behind each pillar of smoke. Then, just as he expected would happen, some figures came looming out of the dark, and his food was brought to him by the servants, who would insist on every dish being covered so that its contents were invisible. They were set down before him with an exaggerated and sinister politeness, and the covers were lifted off to show him the roasted flesh which would poison him, in vengeance, were he to eat it. Blinded and choked with these horrors he would shudder and stagger back into the farthest corner of the room, where he had at any rate two angles of the wall behind him. But even here he was safe only for a moment; they were watching him, as in the prisons of the Inquisition, through invisible slits in the wall, and in a few seconds they had moved round behind him and come to just the spot where he was crouching. He could see the flash of their eyes, now in one place and now in another, wherever he looked, and could feel their breath on his cold nervous neck, so that his corner of the room was more dangerous than the middle. He would crawl out from the wall towards the centre of the room, and would lie there crouching upon the carpet, exposed on every quarter and without protection. So hideous was the suspense, in front of all these dangers, that he even shut his eyes and pretended to himself he was asleep; but then he woke again in a moment, terrified by this real nightmare, and more awake than before. Just as it all seemed quiet again, somebody moved in the darkness down at the end of the room, and in a moment the whole place was alive with enemies. But this time the dangers were too great for his reason, and his memory crumbled like a handful of snow which melted and ran away till he lay unconscious.

On other days he would reverse the rôle by a metamorphosis in which he became the persecutor, from his hereditary right as King. He would remember his position, like an impecunious lady in a provincial town, and would lay the most elaborate traps to expose one of the flaws in the etiquette with which he was surrounded. No trouble was too great towards this end, and a discovery of the slightest description repaid him for the labour of days. These exposures, indeed, constituted his only relaxation; and while every other thing harassed and depressed him, a victory of the flimsiest nature in this campaign he waged, renewed the life in his slow veins.

This particular morning found him once more as he was when we left him early in the previous summer at Aranjuez. He had been kept awake all night by the nightingales until, in the accumulation of fatigue from all the previous nights, he had dropped asleep just as the drab dawn came up. But it was into a very limited paradise that he had travelled, because in a few minutes more, as the light grew stronger, he was to be woken up again by the very strength of the change he had been waiting for. The Sun, as I have described, came straight down the avenue to the house, put his ladder against the wall, and climbed straight in at the King's window. He climbed easily over the sill, and his yellow mane flooded the room with light and woke up the King, who lay trembling, just as though this lion had roared. He sat up in bed at once, rubbing his eyes, that grew steadily more watery and smarting before the new presence in the room. But while the King cowered and crouched back in a corner of his bed, the Sun played happily like a lion in its native haunts. The white walls of the room were fretted and slashed with shadows from the leaves outside, and the Sun ran in and out among them, now hiding behind a wall of leaves and then, of a sudden, making a lion-spring out from the shadow into the open room where the King's bedstead stood.

Meanwhile, outside in the garden, one of the summer mornings had begun again. For all the difference that it made to the song-birds, it was only as though they had, up till this minute, been practising in a semi-darkness upon the stage, and the sudden coming of the Sun was but the transformation when every light is thrown on, and the stage appears glowing in the concentrated and searching rays that are directed upon it. Now there is nothing that can be hidden, and every singer and each glittering dress has to be judged on its own merits. There is the very faintest early wind for the leaves to shake off their dew, and these millions of hands make a murmur as they meet together like the soft, distant hum of applause. But it is still subdued, for the songs are to die down before long, and nothing must break in to prevent the music living on to its natural end.

The Sun, who was a moment ago tormenting the King, making him cower back each time that he gave one of his proud leaps, was, at the same time, feeling the ripened skins of all the fruit, and pouring out the day's measure of gold for the corn to gild itself and get dried in the warmth, so that the colour remained. But his great work lay up above in air, for the whole of space was still full of the elaborate machinery with which the mysteries of the night are worked. There were castles hundreds of storeys high, and with their battlements, almost to an absurd degree, beyond the reach of an enemy. Lower down were whole inland lakes of the deepest blue, that were cliffed and cased by ranges of chalk-white hills. Out and beyond these continents, the sea of space was crowded with an archipelago of islands, no two of them alike in colour or shape. So as to secure daylight the Sun must utterly burn out every trace of this elaborate paraphernalia of darkness. To this purpose the lower reaches of sky were already lit with huge braziers and grids; while their bars became in a few minutes white or red with heat. All the litter and every piece of plunder from the fight were to be burnt on these pyres until they dissolved into smoke, and when this had drifted away the whole of space would be free for the Sun to work his miracles.

Down below, under the double strength of the Sun's rays, and the beams from all the fires that it had kindled, the trees had a fresh and vivid quality of light that they would never show again in the more thorough and glaring strength of midday. The sheaths of green leaves were, in fact, like so many green flames, for they had exactly the flickering and soaring qualities that are the property of tongues of fire. The flowers among these leaves stayed there, just at this hour of morning, as you can only see them elsewhere when collected by the most pyrotechnical of Oriental artists. Each blossom stays on its branch like a captive rocket—a firework tied down so securely that it cannot leave the ground, but burns with redoubled force because it is restrained. Lower still, where you can see the cornfield against a background of white cloud, or the dark flank of a hill, each corn-sheaf is about to burst forth into a veritable cannonade that will begin just at the moment the Sun looks down at them over the high trees in front. But he is still earthbound, and throwing light on to the lowest storeys of leaves, that are only very seldom to be peered through in this way.

Just as the Sun placed a fiery paw on top of a range of hills, so as to climb above them and come into the open, the gardeners began collecting for their work, and in a few minutes more the fountains were playing once again. This was the signal for a redoubled effort from the birds, for it was now as if they were accompanied in their song by a full orchestra, which would drown their efforts if they did not sing out at their loudest.

The King, in his bedroom, heard this reinforced singing with alarm, for it meant that the day had now irrevocably begun, and there was not even any of the grey light of dawn left for him to steal a little sleep in. Sometimes the Sun would climb into his room early, but would find the shadows of the leaves on the wall too dense to hunt among, and would climb down again and busy himself elsewhere. On those mornings, after he had been gone a few minutes, the grey light would steal back and the King would go to sleep in this second sham dawn, lulled by the low music of the rain that sang to him, keeping away the tongues of the nightingales and the voices of the fountains.

But to-day it was too late. The Sun had come to stay, and the birds were singing his praises to the loud accompaniment of the waters. Therefore sleep was hopeless; and so he got out of bed and himself put on a few necessary clothes, so as to avoid the tiresome attention of his servants when they should arrive. Then he sat down, drawing his chair near a mirror, so that he could see his reflection, and, at the same time, watch what was going on behind. He could catch anybody who came into the room without their knowing that he could see them, and, down below in the garden, he would know at once if anybody stood still to watch him, for some of the gardeners were suspiciously curious.

He sat still there for a long time. He thought he was ready for them to come and call him—dressed and in no need of their attentions; yet there was an hour or two before he need expect them, and during this while, there was nothing for him to do except listen. And every moment, as he waited, and kept a look-out for signs of anyone coming to disturb him, new voices came in and swelled the sound that was rising, almost like steam, from off the leaves. It seemed as though, to pay homage to the heat in which they thrived, the trees were sending up a continual mist from the fumes of the dew that was being melted away. But the noise of this eternal smoke of sacrifice came, not from the haze rising up, but from the incessant and continual chorus of bird-songs and water-voices.

How hopeless it seemed that he should ever find human beings with such a subtlety of expression as these different voices; and yet here they were, out of counting in numbers, but all of them without that power of answering which is one of the few sympathetic traits in a human character. For the sounds that kept him awake every night could postulate—they could frame a speech or utter a declaration; but they had no way to answer any question put to them, and one had to accept their statements without an explanation.

For this reason their songs only preyed on his melancholy, for it became equivalent to handing him the elixir he wanted, but without the statement of how it was to be used, so that all the healing power in this music was wasted.

As soon as he heard them begin he was attacked again by this feeling of utter melancholy. It was just exactly the impossibility of understanding them, or getting an answer to one's questions, that made their songs into simply a show of useless technique. Once they were seen in this way it seemed to impoverish and tarnish everything about them. Their coats were no longer glossy or flashing with colour; they became, instead, moulting, or the fading colours ran into each other as though rain-soaked. Under this shrunken motley their bodies became wasted and ravaged by fever. In sorrow for their sufferings the King's melancholy grew worse in time with his galloping fancy, for the longer he stayed awake, the quicker did his mind run from one grief to another. Gradually the thought of so much unhappiness made him long to cry out, and thus he would reach that desperate state of misery that I have described, when he would fall asleep solely from the excess of the heavy load on his shoulders.

The mirror depths showed him nothing new. Outside there was apparently not a leaf out of its place, not a fountain jet that was not playing at its settled height. There was not even enough wind off the leaves, or from the wings of birds, to bring the music a little more into focus—make it sound a few steps nearer his window. Everyone, players and singers included, was in his appointed place, and the music was running straight along without a break, like the most carefully rehearsed play.

But, unbeknown to the King, while he sat there listening for an alarm, and, were it possible, steeling himself against another of these nightmare days, his Queen was preparing a potion for him. She was already mixing the elixir, and she was no farther away than the next room to that he was waiting in.

She had procured, in the last resource, and at a wholly fabulous price, the services of that mechanical nightingale whom we have seen incessantly practising from the moment Cæsar gave him counsel. He had come at her bidding from England.

The Queen, with a courtier or two, the King's doctors, and Farinelli, crept silently into this room next the King's bedroom. Through the door they could hear him moving nervously now and again and every moment sighing deeply. They must not be heard making the very slightest sound before Farinelli started singing, otherwise the spell would be broken.

He began with that same song he had conquered with in Vienna. The crescendo, like a terrifying hurricane, made the King tremble. But Farinelli sank his voice back to a whisper, as if to show that every mood was in his control and that he could attract affection as well as command obedience. The King sat spellbound in front of his glass, unable to believe that this singing came from an invisible source, for there were no signs of its origin that he could see collected in his glass from the widespreading area of the garden. Then some peculiar quality in the way the sound reached his ears, suggested that the voice was somewhere near, perhaps hidden directly underneath the window, and too steeply down to be reflected. So he got up and walked cautiously to the pane.

No! It did not come up to him from below. It was somehow floating to him from his own level, over the rounded backs of the pillars between the windows, just like a stone that ricochets over the humped backs of waves. Now it had stopped, and everything was silent while the magician in charge of this creature got it ready for a second song. Perhaps it was only capable of this one ravishment; but, before he could have hoped for it, a second song had begun, as beautiful but of entirely different character.

This time he had decided it must come from a window only a few feet along the façade, but hidden by its pompous architectural counterpoint; and by now the King had recognised that he was listening to what could only be a human genius of the highest order, one who could work miracles, or charm wild animals with his skill. While he stood in the window listening to the voice's dying fall, as the song came to an end the door opened, and in walked his wife, with the doctors, the chief Ministers and, last of all, Farinelli, so that he should see familiar figures till the last entered the room, and he could have no doubt as to the author of this music.

He felt soothed and enchanted, as though the effort of remembering this magical music effaced from his memory every single unhappiness that had been his lot. He was as if renewed by some miracle of rebirth; and while his own body felt new limbs and a fresh life-power, outside, by the dissipation of his mood, the fountains were dancing in new colours which the sun gave them as he came out at last into free and boundless space, having disencumbered himself of all his foes.

When Philip, in the rhapsody of his new sanity, asked what reward he could give Farinelli, the nightingale showed that he was without a mercenary character, for he replied that all he required was that the King would consent to have himself shaved, and to benefit his people once more by attending to the requests of his Ministers.

That evening, after a happy day spent in looking at all the beauties of art and nature by which he was surrounded—for it was as if the King had come back here for the first time after his absence, without hope of return, for many years—there was a fête to which all the Court staying in this summer retreat was invited. The Knights of the Golden Fleece came, as though a new treasure had been discovered hung up behind the trees; and they were almost right, for it had been a miracle effected by such music as you can never hear approached, except by the voices that drift down through the thousands of windows between the leaves. They marched in a solemn procession down the great staircase, and then the guests collected on the widespreading lawns. This was to be the last public appearance of Farinelli, and, at the same time, the first night on which the nightingales of San Ildefonso heard their rival.

Never again after that night did Farinelli sing in public, for he was bound by a strict contract to sing only for the King and for no one else. One day Elizabeth Farnese even kept him to his contract by a refusal to allow the Prince of Asturias and his wife, the heirs to the throne, to hear him sing. He was to perform for no one else except the King, and he soothed Philip's disordered mind every night for ten years with the same four songs, which he must have repeated altogether some three thousand six hundred times. Later on, when Philip died, he performed the same service, to the same purpose, for his son, King Ferdinand VI., and it was only the accession of Ferdinand's half-brother, Charles III., who had other methods against melancholia, which brought about Farinelli's pensioning and his retirement to Bologna.

For nearly twenty years he lived in Spain. He became Philip's Prime Minister, and was created a Knight of the Order of Calatrava, one of the greatest dignities that he could be offered. During all that time, in spite of the favours he received, he never became an object of jealousy or complaint to the Spaniards, but gave wise advice and conciliated quarrels. He was an oracle-giver as well as a miracle-worker.

Every evening these four songs were sung to the audience of the King and Queen alone. It was a cure by seraphic influence, for by no other agency could such beauty be extracted out of the rugged Doric, or too sugary soft Lydian languages of music. There is also the Æolian mode. But if I say that three out of four of Farinelli's songs were rendered in one of these three tongues, I must concede that the fourth song may have been in the actual speech of the seraphim, for there can be no other explanation of their potency.

Part iv

Mexico

Part iv

Mexico

Our Conquistadores are upon the point of starting. The masts are flapping under every conceivable piece of bunting and the whole ship is held back on its cable only with difficulty. Don Antonio Gonzalez is in command once more, with his old charge Luca Giordano on board, and the latter's pupil, Solimena. They are bound for Mexico.

The provisions are already below, part of the ship's ballast consisting in bales of canvas, so determined are these artists to find material ready to their hands on landing, for with the help of their gang of assistants they can paint at the rate a spider spins its yarn.

The port, of course, is Cadiz—beyond the Pillars of Hercules—and it wanted only a few minutes' sailing to get out of sight of these lintels to the Mediterranean. So narrow is this water-gate, that it is unbelievable that ships sailing back from the Indies can arrive in front of this open arch at the first attempt; it is more likely they will be driven in and battered on the rocks of Africa, which should be red as the coals in a fire from the torrid heat, so that the water hisses up in steam as it reaches them.

Very different is the objective for their expedition. They must crowd on all the sail they can, to get them across the deathly calm of the Sargasso sea, so that they may arrive in its midst with as loud a flourish of trumpets as possible. If dramatic and piercing enough, one of the sleepy winds, waiting like a sentry or a porter, will be stirred out of his slumber to come to their rescue, and pull the ship out to the far side of the calm, where the gales are at their usual work again. If this does not happen, they must trust to the lazy currents to drift them out; but this is the slowest of progresses, as though drawn by the huge turtles that are crawling over the sea-floor. Once out of the Sargasso, they can sail again under the same Trades they started with from Spain, so that the cause of this sudden calm lay only in the distance between the centre of the ocean and the nearest mountains; for out in the midst here the winds are far away from their nests and breeding-grounds in the crags. The expanse of sea is too great for them to manage, and the centre lies too far to be reached from either side. It is true that the Sargasso sea is only half the distance from Mexico that it lies from the cliffs of Europe; but, while too far away for the gales from the East to interfere, equally it is undisturbed because the Mexican breezes are enervated and weak from the tropical conditions of their life; they are powerless to interfere. There is no narrow and defined point, like the Pillars of Hercules, for their ship to aim at. They may strike anywhere on the huge length of coast, and then, having found their position, move south or north towards Vera Cruz, the port of Mexico.

The coast lay far down, with no cliffs and a great extent of sea apparently sloping towards it; an effect which made the journey half round the world more realistic, as though part of the unavoidable terrestrial curve of this straight voyage was visible, inclining down gently from the heights of mid-ocean. They came near to shore and lowered a boat to make inquiries, and rowing off, the boat-crew quickly found a village of half-breed turtle-fishers living in arbours made from leaves. It was low down in the Gulf of Mexico, near the island of Cozumel, along the huge coast of Yucatan, that they had arrived, with a long coast voyage before them until they reached the port of landing. They stayed for an hour or two at this small settlement, to take supplies of water and fresh fruit and vegetables on board. Meantime, some of the important passengers who had been landed to get an early impression of the new continent took a walk along the beach, to while away the time of waiting.

Along the shore, at no great distance, was a funeral-pile

of the carcasses of turtles, half-burned and covered with countless millions of flies, actually heaving and moving as if alive; and near this hideous mound, as if to draw a contrast in beauty and deformity, was a tree covered to its topmost branches with the white ibis, its green foliage appearing like an ornamental framework to their snowy plumage. Some fishermen near-by, dragged across the beach two large turtles, and leaving the carcasses to swell the funeral-pile brought down to their arbour strings of eggs, and the parts that served for food or oil, and hung them quivering in the sun along a fence. Walking farther along towards the end of a sandy beach, was a projecting point, on a line with which they noticed on the water what seemed to be a red cloud of singular brilliancy and, at the same time, delicacy of colour, that, on drawing nearer, they found to be a flat covered with flamingos.

High overhead, on a solitary cliff-like piece of hill which broke down into the water with a precipice edge, was a ruined tower or temple; one of those ruins which the Spanish sailors who first came to this shore describe every few miles along the immense Yucatan coast. In their day the ruins were still inhabited, with the altars smoking and with the weapons of the warriors leaning against walls that are now the hiding-place of snakes and every kind of venomous reptile. The hill was not so high as to be inaccessible, and it afforded the widest view to be got over this wild and unknown region of the Indies. Near the mouth of a creek, on their way to the foot of this hill, a flock of roseate spoonbills flew overhead.

They climbed up, hacking their way through a dense jungle of creepers, looking carefully where they trod for fear of snakes.

At last they came to the first of the fallen stones, lying moss-covered in the damp undergrowth, and, following along the line of wall, looked out upon the boundless ocean. There, below them, deep in the clear water at the foot of the cliff, they could see, gliding quietly by, a great fish, eight or ten feet long. Inside the walls, in a dark, cell-like room, were many carvings in hard stone of human figures, all of them crowned with immense plumed head-dresses. But before there was time to investigate these bird-men, they were signalled to by the boat-crew below, and had to climb down as hurriedly as possible, for it was time to be off. As they came back along the shore, the snowy plumage of the white ibis still appeared among the green of the trees, and a heron stood like a statue in a river pool, just where the creek reached the sea, turning his long neck almost imperceptibly to look at them.

In the coast voyage, sailing slowly along, the same experiences were repeated over and over again. Every few miles they passed below one of these white gleaming ruins, which shone out so mysteriously at sunrise or sunset when the beams of light came towards them at their own level. They were so many signal-towers to warn the Indian cities, far inside, of the presence of enemies, for it was impossible to believe that they had been deserted by their sentries for many years, and that the thriving and teeming cities they were guarding were no longer anything but a metropolis for snakes. This island of Cozumel had been the last centre of Indian civilisation to be taken by the Spaniards, and the centre of Yucatan has remained unexplored down to our own generation, so that in the days of Luca Giordano there was more than a possibility of the existence of great Indian towns hidden away in the interior.[1] It was this that gave a peculiar danger and excitement to the coast voyage, for at any moment the sands might be covered with a horde of feathered warriors, plumed and winged for battle. They were quilted with their cotton armour to the extent that you could hit as hard as you liked without hurting them ; and from their hiding-places among

[1] The island of *Pelen,* with the town of *Itzen,* was only subdued by the Spaniards under Don Martin de Ursua in an expedition that sailed from Campeachy in the year 1697 (cf. *A History of the Conquest of Itzen,* by Don Juan Villagutierres, a native of Yucatan, Madrid, 1701).

the trees, where their bright colours were indistinguishable from the leaves and flowers, they made the best use of poisoned darts from bows and blow-pipes. They were an enemy dangerous, not so much from strength as from skilful defence, for fighting the Indians was like an attempt to gather the fruit from a prickly tropical plant, which infects you with poison every time you are scratched by its thorns. It was only the sight of a horse which reduced the Indians to obedience, and the landing of a specimen was a difficult undertaking on so surfy a shore.

As soon as Yucatan was left behind, the coast grew flatter and more sandy, and the chance of meeting a buccaneer became the only offset to the monotony of the view. The beach was more and more monotonous to look at, while the sea, as if to enhance the dullness of land, put on every variety of colour. The ship sailed in to shore like a horse galloping over the fields. Vera Cruz appeared depressing in the extreme. The town had been founded by the Viceroy, Count de Monterey, at the end of the seventeenth century, in front of the small and heavily fortified island of San Juan de Alloa, on the same shore on which Fernando Cortez landed; and the parched and arid desert, so different from the green West Indian islands, was no encouragement to march inland. All round the town were low reddish sandhills which had been heaped up, and were gradually blown from place to place by the north wind, which still blew cold after its handling of the icebergs far away in the Arctic Seas. The houses of the town were as if blackened by fire, and the long straight streets were always full of wind and blinding dust. Hordes of sopilotes, the huge black "police" birds, were flapping heavily along, or hovering over some carcass on the road outside the town. They had black feathers, with grey heads, beaks and feet, and always flew about in troops searching for their prey, while at night they perched, still in their regiments, upon the trees.

Only a few miles through this Arabian desert the country blossoms into a magnificent and almost eternal paradise.

The fruit and the flowers seem in themselves sufficient to sustain human life without the carrion diet which a less favoured climate imposes, but there are other aspects to be considered before we can make a map of the paradise and describe its towns and gardens.

In Mexico, and there alone, is to be found the most perfected flowering of the architecture we have traced through the kingdom of Naples, and growing from a separate and independent centre in Spain and Portugal. Here, in Mexico, where more money was at its command, the style reached to its fullest expression. The city of Mexico itself I am not proposing to examine in close detail, because its fine buildings are, for the most part, the work of architects imported from Spain, and they have a certain dignity and sobriety suitable to the capital, but dividing them apart from the class of buildings that we have come here to examine. Nowhere else in the world, except in Austria, at this period were convents being built on the same tremendous scale that made the mediæval monasteries as powerful as a small principality. On the higher reaches of the Danube, at Melk,[1] at Göttweig

[1] The Benedictine Abbey of Melk, or Mölk, stands on a high rock two hundred feet above the River Danube. It was founded in the eleventh century, and almost entirely rebuilt by the architect Prandauer between the years 1702 and 1736. There is an immense domed church with two towers, the interior of which is lined with rare marbles. There are magnificent refectories, a library, and a picture gallery in the abbot's palace; looking on to the river is a walled garden with a colonnade.

Farther down the Danube towards Vienna, three miles from the bank, on a hill nearly nine hundred feet above the river, stands the Benedictine Abbey of Göttweig. This also had been founded in the eleventh, and was restored in the eighteenth, century. The buildings form a vast square which covers the whole plateau of the hill. There is a ceremonial staircase of superb size, a library, and enormous refectories and corridors.

Klosterneuberg is some twelve miles from Vienna. The abbey of Augustinian monks is the most ancient and the wealthiest in Austria. An Italian architect, Felice Donato d'Allio, rebuilt the abbey buildings between 1730 and 1750. On the west dome is a huge gilded Imperial crown, and over the east dome an archducal hat, in wrought

and at Klosterneuberg, near Vienna, the last Roman emperors employed the best Italian or Italian-trained German architects on buildings that were hardly finished before the reforming spirit of Joseph II., their descendant, caused them to be emptied and to lie desolate. Out in Mexico the size and magnificence of these last of Imperial works were far outdone, and the classical, if flowery, lines of the Italian façades were changed and transmitted into something more suitable to the extraordinary concourse dwelling inside their walls.

Added to all the influences that I have traced in the former chapters, there were at work on the buildings of Mexico two strains which are found only in that country. In the first place, obvious traces remain of the ancient Aztec work, because the architectural details were carried out by Indians, who had been hurriedly converted to Christianity and could not forget their ancient temples or the figures from their own mythology. They could not avoid, for no other method of expression was familiar to them, the treatment in Aztec fashion of the Christian legends upon which they were at work.

It must be remembered that the great time for emigration from Spain to the New World took place in the generations immediately succeeding its conquest by the Spaniards, for, in the seventeenth and eighteenth centuries, Spain was poverty-stricken and falling into disrepute as a military power because of the drain of emigration from the peasant and soldier-producing classes. The Moriscoes (Moors converted to Christianity after the conquest of the Caliphate in 1492) were not driven out from Spain till the year 1609 by a decree of King Philip III. A large proportion, therefore, of the emigrants to Mexico and other Spanish states of America were of Moorish, and perhaps also of Jewish, blood, for the most useful trades and occupations in Spain

iron; for this insignia, which was used at the ceremony of swearing allegiance, is in the keeping of the monks. The present buildings represent only a part of the original plan: it was the intention of the Emperor Charles VI. to build an Imperial residence attached to the monastery.

were in the hands of the Moors and the Jews, and these classes were the most likely to be called upon for emigration. In Mexico there are very patent signs of Moorish influence, and, indeed, there are as striking examples of the Mudejar [1] style in Mexico as there are in Spain. These two facts, the Aztec and the Moorish influence, taken together explain why the Mexican buildings are unlike any others in the world.

The native craftsmen, living contentedly in an easy slavery to the Church, were content to spend a whole lifetime carving the retable of an altar or inlaying the presses of a sacristy. Their labours were directed by an Indian or Creole architect, who, in most cases, could not write and was not draughtsman enough to draw a plan. It is related of one Indian architect, whose extremely interesting work will be described later on, that he used to scratch his plans with a pointed stick upon the sand, while the workmen gathered round him or could look down on his plan from the scaffolding above. The sand below acted like a mirror to their labours, for the actual and the intended states could be examined together; and when they were in need of a detailed instruction, the information they wanted was sketched out in the same scale on the sand.

The dress of the Indians is to this day well calculated to enhance the effect of their architecture. The women can be seen at work, or on their way to and fro, carrying the youngest child slung upon their back; while the pointed Mexican hats with their immense brims make a fine finish to

[1] The Mudejar influence is especially noticeable in the polychrome tile-work decorations upon the buildings of Puebla. Travellers have always remarked upon the resemblance between the district of Puebla and Andalusia, both as regards the architecture and the character and appearance of the population. All the Spanish settlers in this province were of Andalusian origin, with, of course, a strong element of Moorish blood in them, and the situation of Puebla between the coast and the city of Mexico made communication easy with Seville and the ports of Southern Spain.

Another example of the Mudejar style is the Casa de los Azulejos, or the House of Tiles, in Mexico city. The Capilla del Pocito, or the Chapel of the Sacred Well, at Guadeloupe, is also a first-rate example of this manner.

the white pantaloon clothes of the men. Market-day is like a parliament of the birds, so far removed do the scene and its characters seem from ordinary human activities. But this scene we must describe in its proper setting under the shadow of the great church at Tasco.

Each province shows differences in its architecture. For example, the buildings round and in Puebla have domes covered with glazed tiles, which are arranged in formal patterns after the fashion of the domes to the mosques in Persia, and the roofs can be seen gleaming far away, their visibility from a distance being very much increased by the bold and lavish colour upon them. Then, again, there are the buildings in quite a separate manner at the rich mining towns of Tasco and Cuernavaca; while Celaya and Queretaro have the finest work of the great Creole architect, Tresguerras.

The place-names of Mexico, whether Spanish or Indian in origin, never betray the souls committed to their charge, for the remotest and most fever-haunted village has a name magnificent enough for a dynasty to call itself by. They have very often an effect of onomatopœia, as though, in an obvious instance, imitating the perpetual prospect of a volcanic eruption. In less known and more remote examples the name is still better, and distance and inaccessibility are balanced by the sonority of the word. The names are a skilful imitation of the sounds that nature makes: the heavy rain tumbling clumsily from leaf to leaf till it booms down upon the sodden soil; the sawing noises that the jagged-edged cactuses make upon the wind; and high up, but always in sight, the snow biting into hard rock.[1]

[1] Wherever the Aztec tongue is in use, the letter R is unknown, while in the Otomi dialect it occurs in nearly every word. Thus, Popocatapetl, Istaccahuatl, Tenochtitlan are Aztec names, while Ocambaro, Puruundiro, Litacuaro and Cinapecuaro, in the province of Valladolid, are Otomi in origin. Humboldt quotes, as a record in impossibility of utterance, the word meaning "venerable priest whom I cherish as a father," which runs as follows:—"Notlazomahuizteopixcatatzin." But is this more frightening to a neutral observer than:

"VenerablepriestwhomIcherishasafather"?

We will begin our survey with the greatest name among Mexican architects, Francisco Eduardo Tresguerras. The bearer of this curiously militant surname was born in Celaya on the 13th May 1745, and, let me add at once, he died at the mature age of eighty-eight, on 3rd August 1833, of fever, so that it was not old age that removed him. He was a Creole—that is to say, a Mexican of Spanish blood—and at various moments was sculptor, painter, etcher, engraver on wood, musician and poet—as well as architect. He worked entirely in the district immediately surrounding his birthplace—in the Bajio, that extensive, low-lying plain in the midst of the central tableland of Mexico, at Celaya, Queretaro, Irapuato, Guanajuato and San Luis Potosi ; and now we may examine his work without the statement of any more leading facts.

We will take, first of all—because it was his earliest work—the buildings for which he was responsible at Queretaro, beginning with the church and convent of S. Rosa di Viterbo. Here and at the convent of S. Clara in the same town Tresguerras produced the most perfect and complete examples of the Churriguerresque to be found anywhere in the world. An enormous sum of money, realised from the merchandise seized from *contrabandistas*, had been placed at the disposal of the convent of S. Rosa di Viterbo. In both churches the choir screens and the screened balconies for the Mother Superior show the most extraordinary development of this, one of the strangest devices of monasticism. They are of wrought ironwork and are designed, not for themselves alone, but so as to form a decorative composition with the rest of the architecture. In that of S. Rosa the balcony for the Mother Superior has its elaborate golden base supported by the carved retable of an altar, and in S. Clara it stands like a bridge over a richly carved doorway below. The confessionals of S. Rosa are designed in keeping with some of the rest of the colour scheme, so that their gilding is sharpened with shrill touches of metallic lustre, an effect which is obtained, in the mediæval fashion, by mixing the colours with a transparent varnish medium applied over a ground of gold-leaf. In this way ruby and emerald-green effects of great violence and brilliancy are procured. His use of colour is seen all over the building, and, for example, the reredos of the altar of S. José has its picture by Miguel Cabrera (the greatest Mexican artist and master of Tresguerras) framed with garlanded lines that are treated in emerald in the process I have described, making a beautiful contrast with the rich gold masses about them. The pulpit of S. Rosa is a superb piece of inlay in ivory, tortoise-shell and mother-of-pearl, the tortoise-shell being underlaid with thick gold-leaf.

S. Clara has a fine example of the tiled domes which Tresguerras brought to perfection. It has a pattern of blue on a yellow ground, like the smaller dome of the lantern; while the base is of white and blue. The lowest belt of the tower has a pattern of blue and white on yellow and light green; the two middle belts are blue, yellow and white below, and blue and white above, the dome of the tower being blue and white over a belt of yellow and white.

Of the convent of S. Clara it is, unfortunately, only the church that now remains, but the convent covered with its buildings alone several acres of ground, and was the home of as many as eight thousand nuns. The whole of this huge building had been designed by Tresguerras, who was responsible for all the details, and supplied rough sketches, even, from which the best of his band of sculptors, Mariano Arce and Mariano Perusquia, carved their figures.

In S. Rosa there is a great deal of decorative painting by Miguel Cabrera, and in the sacristy there is the famous performance of Tresguerras, the *Hortus conclusus*, a huge painting, as a background to wooden polychrome figures, which shows the nuns of the convent and their pupils at work in the garden. This picture has, unfortunately, some of the woolly softness that characterises Murillo's work, but in every other respect it is a most extraordinary proof of the varied powers of this Mexican genius, who had the ability to make successful every scheme to which his exuberant imagination directed him.

This convent, as I have stated, was the home of some eight thousand nuns before the dissolution of the monasteries, out of whose number only a small proportion can have been of pure Spanish blood. A large detachment was permanently engaged upon the embroidery of all the vestments that the splendour of the church required, but large numbers of them found work in the convent sugar plantations and upon the fields. The bombardment of wild flowers in the early spring was something from which a stranger might recoil in fear, and the saw-blade of the cactus was as dangerous as an armed sentry; but under all these alarms the nuns kept up their daily routine. In the course of the year enough cloth of gold and silver was woven to clothe every one of them with a rippling gown that would make a better mirror than any water-film, but all this splendour was denied by them and kept only for the pompous ceremonial of the church.

They were hidden from view during the service behind the huge flying metal lattices that I have described. It was like looking through the meshes of a fan down into the body of the church below, and all round, lining the whole wall of the church, were more of these boxes full of nuns. Higher up still, where she could see into every box and observe every corner of the building, was the Mother Superior, waited upon and guarded like a queen bee; behind her was a group of servants, waiting like aides-de-camp to take her orders. The highest lattice of all sprang right up, starting almost from the ground, and, spreading out its wings to protect the balcony full of nuns, mounted still higher and burst in a kind of golden spray upon the roof. There was a full military band, mainly of Indians, joining in the service down in the aisle below, and the heroic players were prevented from any view of the Creole beauties above by the contrapuntal intermixture and flow of metal screens. Some of the nuns were in boxes facing straight down at right angles to the nave of the church, and the lattice that guarded them was like a palisade of sun rays, for their strength of defence lay in

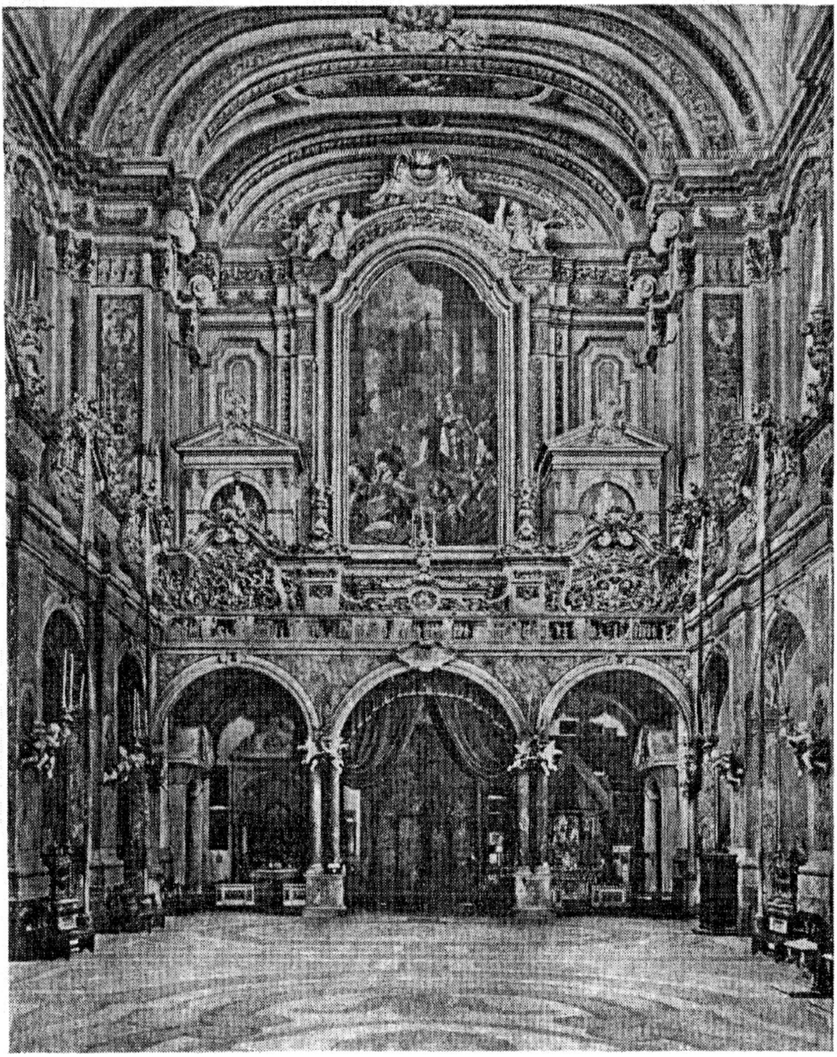

Photograph: Alinari

NAPLES

INTERIOR OF S. CHIARI

blinding light. So brilliant was the gold-leaf laid over this metal work that, after looking at it for a few seconds, the different rails and bars did actually seem to move and drift into and among each other, like intermingling sunbeams. Above the heads of the nuns in this balcony was the organ, and the angels that leaned out blowing their trumpets were actually sounding out of the lattice, in special places where room had been designed for them, so that they were crying out shrilly from the very heart of this splendour, and were no nearer to heaven than this, when sounding their fanfare out of the actual sun rays, as they dart into space over a cloud-edge. The balconies along the side walls were more difficult to examine because of the steep and neck-craning angle up to their height. They were so many boats riding a sharp sea and hidden in the spray they cut out of the waves, for the lattice in front of them had the flung-up and curving line of foam.

After mass was over the nuns left their boxes and made for the door in the organ-loft that led from the church into their sequestered life behind. Their bare feet sounded from below, as they walked along the narrow gangways leading from balcony to balcony, like a flock of birds, a tribe of pigeons, half-walking and half-flapping along to their dove-cots. The refectory where they were eating their evening meal was throbbing with music again from another band which had taken up its station in the musicians' balcony. The Indian servants came in carrying huge platters piled up with fruit, while others went round pouring out water or wine from a hollowed-out gourd. The band now playing consisted entirely of the nuns, and there were none of the heroic brass or percussion instruments that give character to a military band. There were, instead, the long and sliding measures of a string band, to which the abbess of the convent came in with her retinue, and they dined off the produce of lands that belonged to, and had been mostly worked by, the nuns, while the pastoral music suggested a landscape in which there was no human violence.

The entire and splendid isolation which these two convents afforded their regiments of nuns, the demands even that these two small universes made upon the invention of Tresguerras represent only one-half of his output of work; since Celaya, his birthplace, four leagues from Queretaro, is the scene of his other great labours. The huge five-spanned bridge, as you come near the outskirts of Celaya, over the River Laja, is to the design of Tresguerras, and has splendidly rolling send-offs in the form of four great stone finials at each end of the bridge on either baluster. The whole four of them roll in the direction of the centre of the bridge, so that whichever way you are crossing there is a demonstrative farewell. On the centre of the bridge, before you have got to the entrance into the town, you can see the dome of the Church of Carmen, the greatest triumph of the architect.

The main plaza of the town is an example of his garden-planning: in the centre there is a fine column from his design as a celebration of Mexican independence, and he felt this change in the national life to the extent of writing a long patriotic hymn in its praise and winning the reputation of having been mentally affected by the news; while all round the square there are secular buildings planned by Tresguerras, including two splendid private palaces. The churches, like the plaza, are the late work of Tresguerras. He had built, in the Church of S. Rosa, the finest example of the Churriguerresque, while S. Clara showed him working in a more directly rococo manner; and now, in the Church of Carmen, at Celaya, Tresguerras changed into the classical mode that was then spreading all over Europe, but, instead of the pseudo-Greek, he adopted a classical Renaissance manner. The date of this church (1803-1807) seems anomalous beside the huge classical line of this building, for which Wren might have been responsible. The famous dome, covered with glazed tiles that alternate from yellow to green, he might have copied from a mosque in Persia, so perfectly does the brilliant colour suit the rounded lines of its architecture. Inside the church the sculpture and the mural paintings are his work, and there are three large frescoes (the only works in pure fresco that he ever executed) in the Chapel of the Juicio. Here also are two medallion-shaped portrait frescoes of himself at the ages of thirty-five and sixty-three.

There are many other buildings at Celaya of which he was the architect. The tower and Church of S. Agustin are his work, and in the parochial church of S. Francesco his tomb lies in a little mortuary chapel that he built against the side of the church. Inside it he painted a frieze of the Twelve Apostles, and there is his own portrait again to the left of the entrance. Various poems by him in manuscript and signed with his name hang in frames upon the walls, and a door leads into a small room in which there is a shrine, over which hangs a crucifix carved by his hand.

This little chapel sounds a depressing end to the gorgeous and exuberant life of Tresguerras. He died just at the worst period of art, and had he lived a few years longer we might have had to describe a Mexican rival to Pugin. It was, as I have hinted, only a putrid fever that prevented this. He had lived, if we really search for the truth about him, some forty or forty-five years too long, and though he had the ability to change with the times, his real work lay in the eighteenth and not in the nineteenth century. In spite of this he considered Mexican independence, which was proclaimed when he was over seventy-five years of age, as a culmination in the history of his country, which he was lucky to have lived to see; and yet, within ten years, it was to lay waste and leave empty the convents that were his lifework. It is a very remarkable feature about his buildings that there is no trace of provinciality about them; they are not second-rate, and there is no feeling that they would have been better if nearer a capital. How a completely uneducated Creole can have attained to the degree of mechanical knowledge necessary for this work is in itself difficult to understand until it is realised that, from the very first, the Spaniards had embellished their colonies with the most magnificent churches that money could produce, and there was, therefore, in Mexico a tradition of magnificence that even in the early life of Tresguerras was two centuries old.

It is not the work of Tresguerras alone that makes these two cities of Celaya and Queretaro so interesting to study, for there are in both places other and earlier traces of this tradition of building which explain the apparent miraculous endowment of talent upon him. At Queretaro there is a famous aqueduct spanning the valley, like the work of the Romans, in one flight of seventy-four arches, and two-thirds of the cost of this huge work was contributed by the local nobleman, the Marqués de la Villa del Villar de la Aguila, whose share alone came to one hundred thousand Mexican dollars. The palace of this grandee in the chief plaza of Queretaro is as fine a building as any in Naples or Seville, with its frieze of glazed tiles and the splendidly wrought iron balconies; and the descendants of this public benefactor are still in possession of the property, ruling the town like one of the lesser principalities of Italy.

The monastery of S. Agustin, built in the middle of the eighteenth century by the two Augustinian monks, Luis Martinez Lucio and Carlos Benito de Butron Moxica, is so remarkable in style that it is impossible to suggest a date for its construction without definite knowledge of its history, for the building has the appearance of being earlier than its real date by at least two centuries. There is, to begin with, the unfinished and extraordinary-looking tower. This rises up above the body of the church, carved elaborately in a kind of flat bas-relief, in which the figures have the still but complicated pose of the Aztec and Maya carvings, and then suddenly, just as the tower is collecting itself for the final leap up above the roofs of the church, it stops short, where even the Mexican gold and silver mines were unequal to the strain put upon them. So the tower ends just above the knees of the huge statues at each corner, and it is as though these archangels had their feet upon the earth, but were yet, as far as the rest of their bodies was concerned, in a kind of lambent invisibility. They can be seen to the knees, and up to this point they show the strained and leaping muscle of a dancer who relaxes as soon as he stands still for a moment; and these four dancers have the strong light thrown upon them so far as this, but all the rest of them is cut off and hidden in the darkness of the theatre, while everything round them is burning in a white heat of sunlight. At any minute they will shift their position and walk round carefully like dancers, to take up a new position for the music to begin. Then they will, all at once, emerge into the dazzling light, which will show up the rainbow feathers on their heads, and their breastplates shooting out gold and silver rays. Farther off, at the side of the dome, there is a seated archangel waiting for his turn and clothed in the full heroic costume, in a breastplate and with a profusely feathered hat. At each corner of the dome there stand the more than life-size figures of angels, who wear enormous plumes on their heads and are like the statues of Indian caciques executing a pagan dance.

At the side of the church the convent encloses a cloister of large dimensions, and it is upon this that the two monk-architects have engaged their strongest powers of ingenuity. Between each pair of arches the pillar that acts as the separating bar between them has been changed from its ordinary business as a pillar into a caryatid. The cloister has two storeys and, in consequence, two tiers of caryatides, those in the upper tier being allowed the greater freedom of expression. Each caryatid represents a different individual in this strange race: some are bearded like a patriarch, some have the aquiline warrior features of the Indians, while others are fauns laughing over the frightening effect their appearance always exerts on mankind. They are holding their giant hands, with the fingers outstretched, to the full height above their heads, in order to support the arch for which each hand is responsible. All this time they are talking to each other in the deaf and dumb alphabet, for each one of them is spelling out different words with his fingers, and at the appointed moment they will throw down the loads they are carrying and let fall the whole mass of building, to crush those walking in the cloister beneath. Their faces are actually carved with the derisive and cynical smile that is ready for this signal, and till that comes they call across to each other in their disconcerting, quiet fashion.

The two convents at Queretaro, the churches at Celaya and the other buildings in both towns that I have described, may serve to give some idea of the huge mass of material that is still waiting in Mexico to be investigated by someone in sympathy with this class of building, and who is, at the same time, well enough informed of the contemporary work in the Spanish Peninsula and in Southern Italy to be able to present the one in relation to the other. In the villages round these two towns there are numerous large churches possessed of the same characteristics as those of which a description has been given, and even in the two towns themselves there are many smaller remains just as interesting in their detail. Nor has the complete work of Tresguerras been described. There is, not far away from this district, in the mining town of San Luis Potosi, a great theatre, the Teatro Alárcon, which was designed by him, and for the performances at which he doubtless on many occasions designed the scenery. In Queretaro itself there is the Palacio del Estado, or State Palace of the Province, where the governmental offices and the governor's residence are situated, and this palace is a superb example of the more restrained Churriguerresque. Its gleaming white façade can be seen, as if bathed in a diurnal moonlight, through the shafts and broad-bladed leaves of the palms that grow in the public square, and it affords at once a most interesting comparison with the Town Hall in the chief plaza of Salamanca, which is one of the most successful of those buildings for which Churriguerra gave the designs. It is extremely difficult, owing to the bad repute in which this architecture is still held, to discover writers who have been conscientious enough to describe and investigate what they know will not interest readers of the class who buy such works, and, in consequence, there are many contradictory points to be solved before the work of Churriguerra can be disentangled from that of the plethora of architects working at the same time and involved in the general confusion and disgrace. But Salamanca was the birthplace of Churriguerra; and should this argument not carry weight there is, in the building that he designed, his actual model for it—a fact which must be allowed to dispose of the problem once and for all. The palace, then, at Queretaro may be compared with a building of exactly the same character and built for the same purpose in Spain itself, and this analysis will reveal to what a wonderful degree this architecture is elastic in scheme; for, while preserving all those characteristics that contribute its point and give it the bad name, it has, at the same time, transmuted itself from being the one point of elaboration in a stern and rock-laden Spanish landscape into the only quiet but consistent relief in this country, where the sun is a scorching fire and the vegetation a cannonade.

There is now time to examine for a short space the scenes by which these buildings are surrounded, so as to arrive at some estimate of their suitability to the country they are situated in. The convent of S. Clara, at Queretaro, with its army of eight thousand nuns, is a sufficient proof of the enormous and plutocratic scale of things. There was such a concatenation of influences, that something transcendental in its effect was inevitable, if only the various factors could be fused together so that their result was not wasted on each other, and this cancellation into one movement was achieved by the power of the Church, which, in Mexico, was preternaturally endowed with wealth. So skilful were their dispositions that, within fifty years of the Conquest, all the great monastic orders were established in Mexico on the most permanent of scales, and the Jesuits, as we shall see later on, in discussing their work down in the wildernesses of Southern America, were training and employing the Indians in those particular directions to which their racial ability was most suited. In a climate so enervating, and where the labour of agricultural work is reduced to an absolute minimum of trouble, it may at first seem a surprise that the native workmen and carvers should have attacked their material with so much energy. The carvings and ornaments are all executed in the very hardest of wood or stone and with the most simple of instruments, so that the thoroughness and elaboration of the work is a topic of endless surprise. But the answer to this question is that, far from these ornaments being a test of disconcerting energy from the Indians, they are, on the contrary, a tribute to their slow and contented laziness; for, like patient beasts of toil, once secure in the prospect of the little food and the shade rather than the shelter that they require, they were content to while away the whole of their lives over the carving of a panel or the inlay of a cupboard. No one admires the beasts of the field because of the amount of grass they eat in a year, by patient and long-continued labour; nor should the Indian, who sits year after year working gently, be a subject for astonishment. He works to while away the time, and probably even the cow would complain were everything else except sleep forbidden to it.

The three zones of Mexico, disposed like as many terraces, add enormously to the peculiar character of the country. The big landlords, by skilful preparation, could procure tropical summer foods during winter from the low-lying *tierra caliente*, and, in the most torrid of weathers, could cool themselves on early summer fruits from the highest tableland of all, the *tierra fria*. There was a year's climate in all its different stages within a day or two's travelling, and when you reached the point where one zone melted into another, within the space of a few yards, there was an intermingling of tropical and European vegetation, for on the slopes of the low hills there would be woods of fir and oak and in the plain below plantations of sugar-cane, divided by woods of bananas and orange-trees. A river came tumbling down, falling in small cascades among the rocks on its way to fertilise the plain with snow-water from the mountain heights above.

"The parasitic plants of the tropics are exchanged at a very early period for the evergreen oak, and the deadly atmosphere of Vera Cruz for the sweet mild air of Jalapa. A little farther the oak gives place to the fir, the air becomes more piercing, the sun, though it scorches, has no longer the same deleterious effect upon the human frame, and nature assumes a new and peculiar aspect. With a cloudless sky and a brilliantly pure atmosphere there is a great want of moisture and little luxuriance of vegetation; vast plains follow each other in endless succession, each separated from the rest by a little ridge of hills, which intersect the country at regular intervals and appear to have formed, at some distant period, the basins of an immense chain of lakes. Such, with some slight variations, is the character of the tableland from Mexico to Chihuahua.

"The transition is sometimes extremely sudden, for a ravine or cañada is sufficient to occasion it. Thus, in the cañada of Queretaro and in the famous barranca of Regla, at Real del Monte (both of which places are situated in the middle of the central tableland of Mexico), a few hundred yards change the face of Nature entirely. The luxuriance of tropical vegetation replaces the stunted growth peculiar to the central plateau; the birds assume a more variegated plumage; the inhabitants a more relaxed and indolent expression; and the whole scene the characteristics of another world."[1]

The music in the villages was of a character in keeping with the country. Each tune had the long termination which the Arabs brought with them to Spain, and the drawn-out close of the melody was accentuated by the clashing of little bells and any metallic shaking sound which could be contrived,

[1] Such is the description given by H. G. Ward in his book, *Mexico in 1827*; and, in further proof of the diversity of climate, Humboldt mentions the valley of Rio Verde, where sugar is raised with success at nearly four thousand feet above the degree of elevation which previous experiments had induced him to fix as productive of the minimum of heat requisite for its cultivation.

as if the precious metals of Mexico were playing their share in the music. The stringed instruments, far from being taut and flat in their sound, as they are in Spain, produced an effect as if the actual strings were of a different material and were made out of the longest quills that could be plucked from the tropical birds. The liquid sounds were more gurgling, and the loud passages far more fiery in their speed.

The big towns celebrated their religious *festas* with an even more fervent enthusiasm than the Spaniards. A love of flowers is the most permanent quality of the Indians, and they took part in these processions wearing long garlands that they had hunted for through the woods the previous evening, as they attached a peculiar significance to their choice of flowers. When the evening service was over they spent the rest of the night dancing and playing their instruments. Farther south, in Yucatan, a great feast-day of this character would be celebrated for as long as three days and nights, with a fair, and huge arrangements for gambling to add to the entertainment.

These were the conditions of life in the mild and rather sleepy market-towns of the countryside, where the peasants got their livelihood from working on the *haciendas*, or large estates of the landed proprietors. To the Spaniards it was nearer to the pastoral life than anything to be found in Spain, except in those southern provinces to which the Moors clung with a desperate tenacity, knowing them to be more alluring and fertile than the burnt wastes or the over-stocked oases of their native Africa. The *haciendas*, seldom visited by the owners, who lived in the capital or passed a month at most on their country property, were under the direction of an overseer, whom we may imagine cracking his whip like any driver of a galley team. But his charges were large-eyed and gentle, unlike the savages who were shipped from the coasts of Africa to Northern America and the West Indian Islands. Every traveller records the submissive way in which they accepted punishment, and they always showed an astonishing resistance to pain, so that an Indian seriously injured in a fight or by some accident, bore his sufferings with a stoicism which seemed to argue his belief in one recipe or other of philosophy. This insensibility to pain holds true of the Indians in every part of the continent, for in the north there are the tribes of Indians, whom the cinema has made the heroes of a Homeric campaign of skirmish and outrage, while in the south the death of Guatemozin proves the truth of this generalisation as regards Peru.

The Spaniards, once they had built their cities, treated the Indians as though they were a race of mild antelopes or gazelles. They must be broken in, but after that they might be allowed a certain amount of freedom and a few of the rights of Christians. They had been given away with the land to the Spaniards by a Deity still grateful to them for their expulsion of the Moors, and it was the triumph of a Spaniard or two, here and there, over the flower-like multitudes of Indians that inspired many a Captain Fracasse to give the Italian comedians those models of the Spanish captains, who strutted up and down the trestles that they set up on feast-days all over Europe.

The religion to which the Indians found themselves converted became, under the hands of the Jesuits and the monastic orders, the purveyor of more general and better regulated pleasures than had fallen to the share of the natives as a reward for attentions to their own pagan deities. The numerous Church *festas* were organised by the priests in such a way that the Indians found their own simple and childish delight in music, in bright colour and in flowers changed from an amiable weakness into a religious duty. These very safe indulgences were not likely to find a recusant, for returning to the old pagan times meant worship combined with danger, and the fires of the *auto-da-fé* confined themselves in Mexico to those Indians of the far backwoods who were too stupid to seize at the bargain that the Jesuits dangled before their eyes.

Let us examine, as an example of their powers, one of those districts in which the Indians form almost the entire population ; for in such circumstances they are taught the method, but themselves provide the style, and the buildings they put up are, in consequence, a real expression of how the new civilisation mixes itself with the ancient traditions. Tlaxcala is a case in point. It is to this day almost wholly Indian, and we may be certain that at the date the churches were built, European influence came simply from two or three priests who could train their workmen in the process of carving or carpentry, but had to leave them to themselves over the detail. We may let the churches of the town go undescribed, as the example we want to discuss is a pilgrimage church, the Santuario de Ocotlan, which stands on a high hill some three miles outside the town. It is in this church in particular that there occurs the theatre-like arrangement of the whole space between the end of the aisles and the altar, that I have mentioned a little way back. There are huge retables and carved wooden panels reaching right up to the ceiling, and the golden glitter and droop of their ornament makes this open space like a grotto, at the back of which, through a huge open proscenium, the high altar appears like the stage beyond these effective footlights. When hundreds of lamps were strung from every corner and point and the great crystal chandeliers hung down scintillating, with their candles burning again like sparks in the water-like fronds and leaves of crystal, the ordinary daylight glamour of this grotto was transmuted into a darkness more played upon and pierced through with artificial light than any stage. The priests were moving slowly from altar to altar, lighting fresh candles, and they were followed and waited upon during the service by barefooted Indian servants, who moved about through the fields of light like birds treading golden lawns.

The whole of this grotto, with its carved walls, the drooping stalactites among the figures of saints, and the roof inlaid with precious woods, was the work of a pure-blooded Indian, Francisco Miguel, who spent twenty-five years of his life on this work. Leading out of this part of the church is the *camarin*, a word for which it is difficult to find the counter-

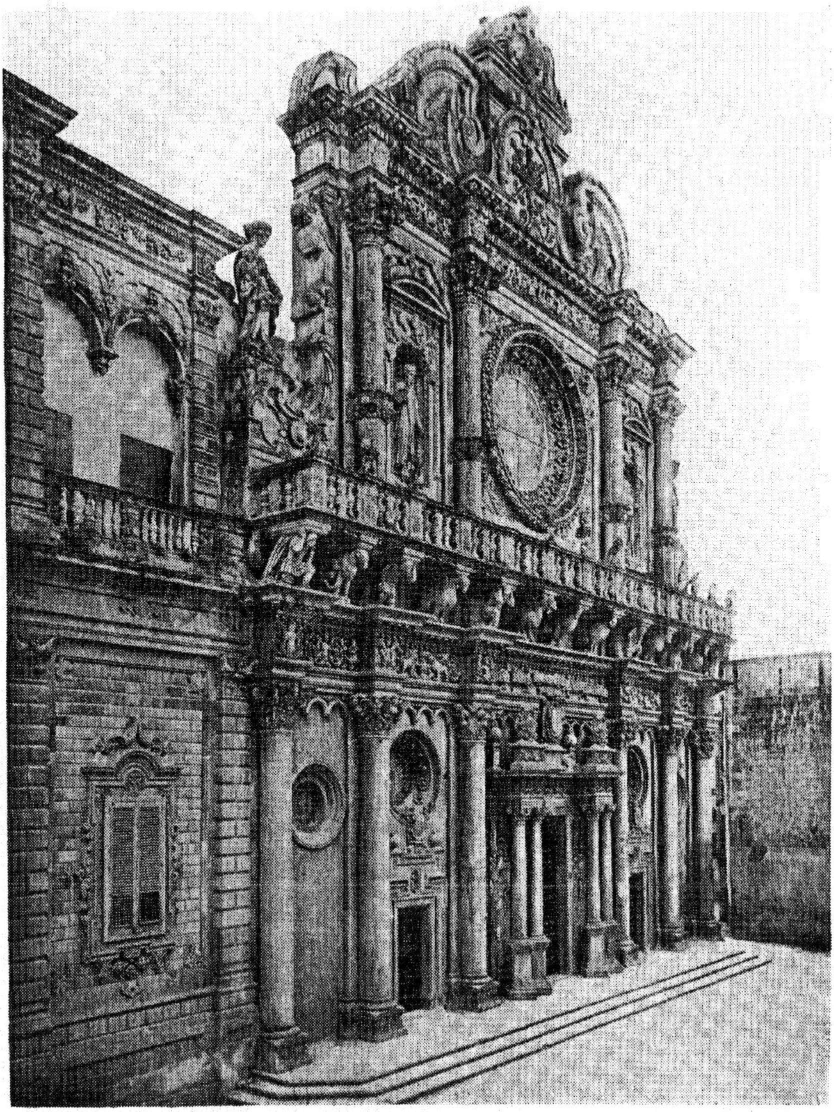

Photograph: Alinari

LECCE

CHURCH OF S. CROCE

part in English. These rooms are to be found only in Mexico, and are really a kind of boudoir in which the vestments for the image of the Virgin are kept, and where the image is dressed with an elaborate ceremony. On this *camarin* Francisco Miguel spent the remainder of his years, and, to judge from the work it contains, his life must have been healthy and protracted. The decoration is gold and green on white, with other brilliant colours used as accent. The dome has a blue ground, with a circle of gold on scarlet. A circle of polychrome apostles stands round a blue ground in the act of receiving tongues of flame from the Holy Spirit, here symbolised by a white dove in the centre. The feet of the apostles stand on a white and gold cloud. The altar beneath the dome is silver and the figure of the Virgin is of pure gold, while round the walls, the doors, the cupboards and the presses, are carved and inlaid by this Indian. The floor, of inlaid marbles, is covered with a piece of ancient Mexican figured tapestry.

Immediately after this, so that comment may be made upon these two churches together, I will describe a rather similar group of buildings at Tepozotlan. In this case, again, they are situated outside the town, about an hour's drive away from the station, and on this occasion it is not a pilgrimage church but a Jesuit seminary that I am describing. The Seminario de San Martin was built as early as 1584, but it was very largely rebuilt again in mid-eighteenth century, and the work of this latter date is, in some respects, the finest example of the Churriguerresque to be found in Mexico. The convent was, naturally, dissolved eighty years ago, at the time of the confiscation of all the monasteries; but being Jesuit and not strictly monastic it is now once more in the hands of that Order, and in consequence the church is still splendidly kept up, unlike nearly every other institution in the country. There is an elaborate façade, so fabulously intricate in design that one may imagine the most staring of Suns might blink his eyes for a moment before he looked down to investigate the detail. The floors of all the chapels are in glazed tiles of yellow, blue, and white, and above this chequered field rise the huge carved altars, like knights and castles ready to move at the right moment, however heavy their clanking armour. The *camarin* built on to this church is the most splendid example of its class, far surpassing even that described at Tlaxcala. It has, to begin with, a domed ceiling lighted by a triple lantern. These following colours flash out, one after another—gold, scarlet, blue, light and dark green, and silver, all of them obtained out of this metallic lustre. As each new colour meets the eye it is as if the one before had been extinguished, and the whole room thrown suddenly into darkness, for the force of every one of them blinds the eye for a moment, and the whole lot of them together flare out, one after the other, like the beam in a lighthouse, which owes part of its strength to the darkness between each flash. For the rest, the *camarin* has the usual inlay on doors and presses ; there are huge panels of wood-carving, big groups of polychrome sculpture, and great oil-paintings framed in panels.

Tlaxcala and Tepozotlan, taken together, show that the line, which even a photograph of these buildings will show, has colour to support it ; so that, when standing actually in front of one of them, it is difficult to say whether it is the colour or the drawing that gives the better effect. They are both there in equal proportion. No feather tapestry could be more gorgeous and flashing, and not one of those sea-shells that are washed up like a magical castle on the sands is more delicate and touching in its design. The imagination of Gracian or Gongora would be satisfied with these transcendental qualities built into and over the mortal fabric of stone, for they realise in the most permanent form those superstructures that these authors had attempted out of ordinary words, above the printed line and the cut page of a book.

We will amplify and fulfil this remark. The lantern to the dome of the *camarin* of Tepozotlan is in three storeys. From each of the two lower storeys, heads of cherubs, angels, and saints, lean out sculptured in relief, looking down almost as though they were all the stars of the universe concentrating their gaze upon this one miserable globe. The light from the windows in these two storeys is modified by screens, but from the third and highest floor the full illumination is admitted, so that the emblem of the *Espiritu Santo*, the white dove upon a ground of azure, sculptured up there, seems to be floating upon a veritable sea of light. It is such a gloria as no words and no music can convey, for speech is dwarfed by the symbols in which it has to be written, and music is dead as soon as ever the instruments and the voices have stopped.

I will now give, in rapid succession, nearly the whole remainder of the buildings that must be described, so that when their account is safely finished there may be no data wanting in the discussion of the whole. By this method we may, first of all, state the facts and then prove the case, while for final evidence South America can be searched and I can keep, for my peroration, the finest example in the whole of the repertory of Mexico.

There is Oaxaca,[1] the most southerly town of any interest in Mexico; and it may please American statisticians to know they live on the same continent as the Church of San Domingo in this town, upon the building of which twelve million dollars were spent. The ceiling of this church, now largely in ruins, has such an elaborate system of inlaid coffering that this sum of money might well have been spent on this piece of work alone. To the side of the church is an immense convent, and consideration of the whole affair induces the opinion that labour here must have been as cheap as in China,

[1] The palace in Mexico city of the Marqués of the Valley of Oaxaca is the finest example of Churriguerresque domestic architecture in the country. This gentleman, of an obviously geographical import, died in the year 1771, leaving the palace unfinished, in spite of the huge sums he had lavished upon it. The architect was Francisco Guerrero y Torres, and the palace is called by the people the Casa de los Mascarones, because of the huge grinning masks with which its four façades are adorned.

so that work of the same proportion in Europe would have been perhaps a hundred times more expensive.

Almost at the other end of the country is the town of Zacatecas, in which the church was continuously building for a space of one hundred and thirty years—from 1612 till 1742. Here, again, the traces of purely Indian workmanship are to be seen at the first glance. Before the confiscation of Church property the interior decoration was rich beyond belief. I will mention the font, which was of solid silver; so that every child baptized in Zacatecas may be said to have been born with his head in a silver spoon; but I refuse to divulge at what figure this piece of metal has been valued.

Then there is Morelia, the capital of the state of Michoacan, with an early sixteenth-century church of Plateresque design. And there is Tzintzuntzan (how the Mexicans like the letter *z*!), on the lake of Patzcuaro, with a picture sent over from Spain by Charles V. and reputed to be by Titian. The church was built at the expense of the famous lawyer, Quiroga, for a town which contained at that date not less than forty thousand inhabitants, while it has now shrunk into an insignificant hamlet, with only one priest left in charge of the church.

There is quite a distinct difference in style between any of the buildings already indicated and the churches in a group of mining towns I shall now describe. One of the finest of this class is the Church of San Cayetano, in the town of Guanajuato. This was built for the miners of the Valenciana silver mine by the proprietor, the Conde de Rul. During the years of its productivity the output of this mine was eight hundred million dollars; now it is worked out, and the town, like Tzintzuntzan, has shrunk back into a miserable hamlet, with but a handful of population. Here, again, the church is in the charge of one lonely priest; while, in the days of its plenty, the scale of extravagance on which it was built can be indicated by the elaborate temporary ornament that was provided for the ceremony of dedication when the church was opened on 7th August 1788, for the tissue that entered into its composition cost three hundred Mexican dollars a yard.

At Cuernavaca, in the state of Morelos, besides the church and what ruins there are left of the castle that the Conquistador Cortez built here for himself, there are the remains of what is most unusual in Mexico—a great formal garden. This was made by the millionaire mine-owner, José de la Borda, whose work at Tasco we shall describe at the end of this book. There are terraces now overgrown, statues lying in the undergrowth, and pavilions upon islands that are inaccessible for want of a boat. The man who built it came as a young boy, penniless, from Bordeaux, his native town, at the very beginning of the eighteenth century, and made a colossal fortune out of the mines of Tasco, with the proceeds from which he built the church there, and the palace and gardens in which he spent his old age at Cuernavaca. The palace is in ruins and the garden desolate and snake-haunted. All round the garden stretches an immense sugar plantation, which was established by Cortez and now belongs to his descendant, the Sicilian Duke of Monteleone; but he is not allowed to enjoy the revenues, which go, by the will of Cortez, to support the Hospital de Jesus in Mexico city. The Marquis de la Borda lived, as I say, with his garden entirely surrounded by the property that was conferred on Cortez, but this oasis was laid out by him in a way that utilised every slope of the ground for a terrace and every hollow for a tank of water, just as though he had to defend his ground against the sugar-canes. Their hollow, reedy music, when the wind blew through them, was like a perpetual sighing that came from behind every tree and through each spray of water.

After this group of mining towns, in which the dust and the darkness of work in the mines is compensated for by an intensity of colour not obtained anywhere else in the country, there remains to be discussed the work of an extremely interesting architect of pure Indian blood who was working in the seventies and eighties of the last century, and who is very probably still alive at this date. He worked entirely in his remote native province of Guanajuato, and chiefly at San Miguel de Allende, a town which already possessed some interesting buildings for a local architect to found his studies upon. There is, for instance, the oratorio of San Filippo Neri, a building in the richest of Jesuit styles; and near to it is the chapel of the Santa Casa di Loreto, built in 1735 by Don Manuel Tomas de la Canal and his wife, Dona Maria Herras de Flores; its superposed dome is very like that described of the *camarin* at Tepozotlan.[1] This is quite sufficient to show that there was already a tradition for Ceferino Gutierrez to work in. He did, in fact, rebuild the dome, in a drum of two storeys, of the convent church of La Concepcion in the town of Guanajuato, not far from San Miguel de Allende, in a pure Renaissance style that he may be said to have refined out of the later and more elaborate work of his native town. The two markets, with their deep-shadowed colonnades, are his work, but his distinctive originality appears in the new façade and tower that he added to the Church of San Miguel, the parochial temple of the city. Gutierrez had never in his life seen any building in the Gothic style, but he had arrived at some idea of what it must look like from studying the early Victorian steel engravings of the cathedrals of Northern Europe. It was he who, as we have said, could not even draw a plan, but used to scratch out on the sand, with a pointed stick, a huge sketch of what he intended his building to look like, and from their perches high up on the scaffolding his workmen would look down and follow his suggestions. In this way the building was finished piecemeal, until, on the day when the church was finished and ready for service, the whole town was dominated by this barbaric and tropical interpretation of the icy pinnacles and dripping grottos of the North.

[1] There is also an extremely fine private house at the corner of the Plaza Mayor, the Casa de la Canal, with balconies, and the most elaborate of carved doors.

With the work of Tresguerras and Gutierrez we arrive at so recent a period that, in the case of the former architect, tradition is still in existence about him, and with the latter, many of the workmen, and very probably the architect himself, are still alive. The Indians, far from being reduced by the Spaniards to that abject submission and impassivity in which they are usually depicted, have produced, as we have seen, as many great works of architecture after, as before, the Spanish Conquest. The churches are bigger than the ancient temples, better planned, and show a more successful expression of exactly those emotions that they tried to give shape to in their pagan temples. It was because life was more secure under the Spaniards that the Indians, in the three centuries of Spanish rule, were able to finish more great works than their ancestors had achieved during a much greater lapse of time. The ruined Indian cities, with their traces of a huge population before the Conquest, can be paralleled by the mining towns like Oaxaca, Zacatecas, and Guanajuato, that once held a population of forty or fifty thousand in their times of prosperity, when the mines were working, and have now shrunk back again into hamlets and a collection of tumbling hovels. The mixture of strange blood among the inhabitants is exactly what is wanted to produce those conditions in which a vigorous tradition of art may flourish. Now that the emigration of Japanese to Mexico has reached such a scale, there is an even stronger probability of the rebirth of a great barbaric art, for none has existed in the modern world since the collapse of every Mohammedan power, and the Westernisation of Japan. The Japanese artists, so unlike the Chinese who love repose, find their subjects in the violent exploding curves of vegetation, and in flowers that open wide, as though detonated by the first touch of sun. The dizzy perspective, the volcanoes, the tropical flowers and birds, the huge cactuses with their saw-like leaves and the tiny flower, so seldom in blossom, at the top of an inaccessible ivory tower rising out of the heart of the guarding saw-blades—all these ingredients of the noisy and melodramatic Japanese art are present in Mexico. If only Japan should ever conquer and occupy Mexico, the third religious state to which the Indians would be converted should produce more rhapsodies in all the arts than ever music has given birth to in itself.

Now that the country is in a state of transition, in order to realise how it looked in a period of productivity, we need carry ourselves back only eighty years, to that decade after the separation from Spain, before the Republic and the revolutions had ruined the work of three centuries. It is of this period that the diary in Mexico of Madame Calderon de la Barca treats,[1] when the waltz had just reached to those far shores and the romantic operas of Donizetti and Bellini were played by a military band in the gardens of the chief plaza. All the balconies were hung with tapestry, the church doors were open; and glittering brightly in the darkness down at the end of the church, the jewelled cups, the relics, and the vestments of the priests could be made out like some fiery creature moving slowly in the mud at the bottom of a pool.

With an appalling rumble a great gilded coach would lurch along, while the postilions cracked their whips as though to disperse the evening mists and restore the air. The horses had broken into a wild gallop in their attempts to get free from the coach they were dragging, which had the appearance of being about to topple over, at any moment, on to the horses' backs. Behind the windows the residents in this glass palace were glittering with such a steady fire from their jewels, that to see them through the window as they passed was like leaning over the side of a boat to watch the stars reflected in the sea below; for however much the water shook and trembled, the stars were still there a moment later, blazing away through the glassy depths. At other times, when the roads were too difficult for a coach,

[1] Cf. *Life in Mexico during a Residence of Two Years in that Country*, by Madame Calderon de la Barca. First published (with a Preface by W. H. Prescott, the historian), London, 1843.

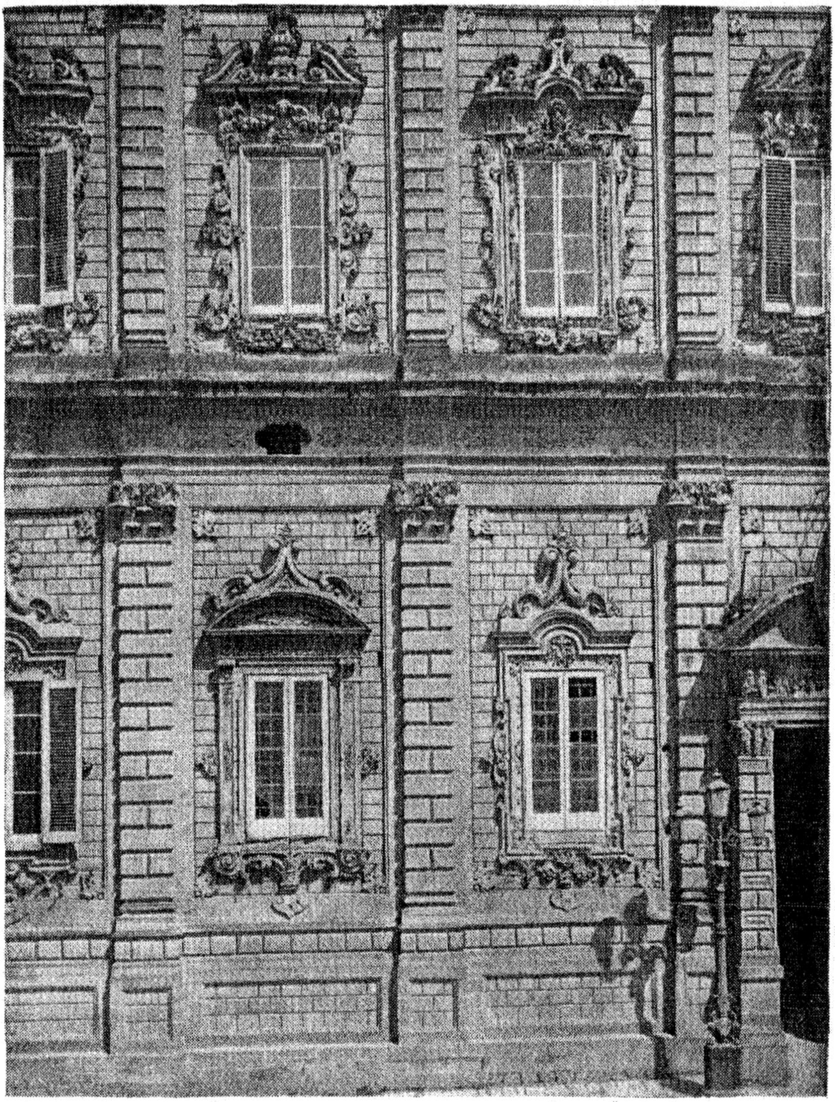

Photograph Alinari

LECCE

DETAIL OF THE PREFETTURA

a person of great importance would come riding along in a cluster of mounted attendants, and their huge Mexican saddles were one mass of jewels, with gold and silver fastenings to the harness. It may be imagined, if such was the appearance of an ordinary country landowner, to what a far greater degree of splendour the progress of the Viceroy was carried. He would appear in the plaza of a town in the middle of a tragic blare of trumpets announcing his arrival. The Corregidor and his Alguacils, the attendants of office, were waiting there to receive him, standing perfectly still at attention, as though in terror at his coming. The crowd, also, was still, with the words hardly dead yet from their mouths, like a wind that dies down suddenly before the leaves have time to hush their low voices.

Travelling over the countryside you were continually meeting with these traces of the peculiar terror with which Spaniards have always contrived to invest their public ceremonies. In every big town, and all along the chief roads, you met companies of travelling matadors, like a small army in perpetual readiness for a campaign; for the chief matador had his officers with him and the rank and file, all of them in condition for battle. They rode along on the miserable cheap horses they bought in each town to carry them through to the next, where these steeds would die as an offering to the bulls. Their fine clothes they kept for the fight, and, except in the case of the one or two chief matadors, the bull-fighters rode past in ragged, blood-stained clothes, that were a witness to the hard lives led by their wearers. A day or two later you might meet with very different travelling companions, like the experience of an English traveller of the period, who complains that, by he knows not what accident, the whole country was covered with a deluge of monks, who took up all the easy carriages, so that it was impossible for him to travel any farther in one of the Mexican mule-carts, but had to ride the rest of the way on a slow and famished-looking horse. This deluge, spread over the countryside like the rain you may read of in Australia, which comes down and covers the country with millions of frogs or small fishes, was a section of the inmates of some such monastery as those I have described a few pages back, who were on their way to one of the monastic *haciendas*, where, by rotation, and a certain proportion at a time, they went to pass the heats of summer, moving in this way from the *tierra caliente* to the thicker shades of the *tierra fria*. Nearer the central tableland, where most of the big towns are situated, you met the companies of travelling Italian opera-singers on their way to convert, for a few nights, the stage in one of these bare Spanish theatres into the shadow beneath a Neapolitan balcony, or into one of those shuttered but still fiercely lit rooms in which the Italian women are secluded, while, as though borne in on the yellow bars of sunlight that are creeping between the black lines of the shutters, you can hear the rattling nasal voices singing outside in the street, and now and again the church bells, that give the only indication of flying Time, who, in this easy climate, seems to have no divisions to mark his progress.

The Cardinal of Mexico was a greater, because a rarer, figure than the Viceroy. He moved about as though protected and hedged round by the fires of the *auto-da-fé*; and to the superstitious Indians the ease with which the Inquisition could commit its victims to the flames bespoke the Cardinal's authority, and made him not less dangerous than their pagan high-priests, who, before the Conquest, arranged for the sacrifice of human victims to placate their bloodthirsty gods; while the form of sacrifice was no more awful in the latter than in the former state. The Church found an audience of Indians as enthusiastic and impressionable as a congregation of Italians or Spaniards; so that the love of splendour, which was part of the doctrine and most of the instrument of the counter-Reformation, found itself with full occasion for use, and with no Calvinist criticism as a set-back against its employment. The extraordinary mineral wealth of the country made this lavish expenditure easier than anywhere else in the world, and the gold and silver of Mexico found its first application, on being recovered from the mines, in the service of the Church. As an example of the methods of this direct utilisation of wealth from the mines, I will give the Church of San Cayetano, which I have already mentioned, as having been built in the town of Guanajuato by the Conde de Rul, for the use of the miners of La Valenciana silver mine. For the use of this church, every one of the thousands of miners employed was compelled to give, each week, a piece of ore called a "*piedra de mano*," a stone the size of the hand, or of a size that could just be held in the palm of the hand. This produced a sum of fifty thousand dollars a year, and in addition to this there were the customary church-tithes and the revenues derived from the huge estates which the mine-owner, the Conde de Rul, had handed over for the endowment of the church. From endowments and revenues of this nature a huge army of priests was supported, and the works of carving and building were maintained on the generous and apparently permanent scale that I have indicated. Vast sums were expended on vestments and jewellery, and the church *festas* were organised with their fireworks and triumphal decorations, so that every inhabitant could play his part in them and feel that the entertainment had been devised for his own especial benefit.

The lake, in the centre of which the Indian city of Mexico stood till the Conquest, had dried up, until nothing was left to show where it had been except a few areas of plain, which shone out like beds of snow under the incrustation of salt which the waters had left behind them when they sank back again into the depths of the earth. Over these plains, and some ten or twenty feet above their present level, the Indians had glided along in canoes over the mirror-face of the water, just at the height of the best leaves of a tree above where you can stand now, crunching the soft salt with your feet. The little waves overlapped and broke upon each other just like the feathers, which melt from one colour into another, on a bird's breast and wings ; while the canoe itself glided along like a bird sweeping down from the heights of air with just a stroke of the wings now and again to change its direction on the stream of speed which is rushing by, for it is always the air that is moving and not the bird or the aeroplane, and the canoe itself is filled with a crew of Indians, plumed and feathered as though born into the world with these sails and rudders. As though their appearance was not ornithological enough, the Indians kept the feathers of one or two particularly rare races of birds for the insignia of Royal blood, while, in drawing or carving the human figure, they imparted a fluttering air to each being, so that he looked as if just caught for the moment on the ground beneath the flowers, trees, and clouds, among which his occupation lay. These transmutations of the human physique they carried still further in their feather tapestries, the most supreme of all Indian arts. These were made of the most delicate and brilliantly coloured feathers obtainable, and more especially of the soft downy breast of the picaflores, the humming-birds, called by the Indians huitzitzlin. Each of these tapestries, according to the description of Madame Calderon de la Barca, was the work of many different hands. Each person finished his part and then all the different pieces were sewn together to form the whole. After the sketch had been made the feathers were first taken up with some soft substance with the greatest care, and fastened with a glutinous matter upon a piece of stuff; then the different parts, being reunited, were placed on a plate of copper and gently polished, till the surface became quite equal. The nuns were still making these tapestries at Pascuaro, the chief centre of manufacture, in the days of Madame Calderon de la Barca's visit to them, but they imitated, in a poor fashion, the original art, which had become extinct only some twenty years before, with the death of the last real artist of this nature. Unfortunately, for some two or three generations before its extinction a century ago, these tapestries, though preserving the original method of manufacture, had fallen upon evil days, for, as subject, they reproduced sacred pictures by

Murillo or Sassoferrato, and these timid performances gave no indication of what the Indians had produced by this method before, and for a generation or two after, the Spanish Conquest. With the exception of one or two pieces in Spain, and a cope and mitre of this material in the treasury of Milan Cathedral, there would appear to be no specimens existing now of the Indian work, for the colour was not permanent for more than the space of a century, and, if exposed to strong sunlight, all the feathers crumbled into dust, and the whole design disappeared as rapidly as the Indian civilisation before the Spaniards.

Besides the Spaniards and the Indians there were a large population of half-castes of different degrees; for some were the compound of the two races named, while others were half Spanish and half negro, or else negro and Indian mixed. It was from these mongrel races that the soldiers and the men of violent lives—matadors and bull-fighters of every rank—were drawn. These half-breeds were, in fact, more energetic than the Indians, and not so disdainful of trade, or any work except fighting, as were the Spaniards. It is also established beyond contradiction that it is the Creoles who have a love of music, for the Indian music is monotonous and depressing almost beyond endurance. In Mexico it is the Creoles who both compose and perform the native tunes, and the beautiful Brazilian dance-music is produced by the same race. It is sometimes a Spaniard, more often a Creole, but seldom an Indian, who discovers the secrets of this new music that will one day improve upon and drive out the negroid tunes of North America in its appeal to the popular sentiments in every country.

In the same way that it is difficult to arrive at any just perspective of the ancient Mexican civilisation, that has no parallel in any other continent of the world, without some knowledge of its sister culture in Peru, so is it impossible to see the results of Spanish settlement in Mexico, without some small acquaintance with the fruits of Spanish rule in other parts of the American continent. Such a reconnaissance is a continual journey towards the south, for the mission settlements started by the Jesuits and Spanish monks in Texas or California are not large enough to repay a close investigation.

Leaving Oaxaca, the most southern town of Mexico that has any architectural pretensions, you come to the Republic of Guatemala. It is in the jungle to the east coast of this state, and bordering on its frontier with Yucatan, that the ancient Maya civilisation flourished, producing more works of art in sculpture than any of which traces can be found in Mexico or Peru. Yucatan, to this present day, is still the property of some three or four great landowners whose estates are worked, almost exclusively, by slave-labour; and their *haciendas* are on a scale of size and strength that is only to be compared with the colonial villas of the rich Roman patricians in Africa or Syria, and with the castles that the Normans built wherever there was a subject race to hold in check. Each one of these gigantic properties has been developed with the completeness of an Italian principality, for religion, education, health, the printing of books, and the teaching of every skilled trade are entirely dependent upon the munificence and liberality of the landowner. There are the remains of big Indian cities still lost in the jungle and waiting for the explorer's spade some two or three days' journey inside the impenetrable wilderness; while nearer at hand are found ruined monasteries still more imposing in their remains, and lying desolate for only a century past, but overgrown by the jungle as luxuriantly as the ruins of three centuries ago. It is the island of Pelen, with the Indian town of Itzen, lying off this coast, that the Spaniards subdued as late as the year 1697, when it was still inhabited by myriads of Indians, as the Mexican towns had been nearly two centuries before this date, at the time that Cortez first marched inland from Vera Cruz.

The remaining states of Central America have, all of them, many traces of the first conversion of their natives to Christianity, but we can pass through Panama, and Colombia, where the purest Castilian is still spoken, before we come to the first signs of civilisation on a settled scale once more, at the frontier of Ecuador. It was in the big indenture on the Ecuador coast—the Gulf of Guayaquil—that Pizarro and his sailors first caught sight of the Indian boats moving slowly across the bay towards their journey's end; for this gulf was the farthest north to which their voyages reached, and its Indian harbour was the port for Quito, one of the two capital cities of ancient Peru, which lay a long distance inland from this harbour, to the north. The ancient empire of the Incas included the whole of the modern Ecuador and Peru; the northern capital, Quito, was in what is now Ecuador; while the southern, Cuzco, lay in what is, at this day, called Peru. These two cities, Cuzco and Quito, contain many ancient Spanish buildings; they have convents and monasteries in a number quite out of proportion with their population, and at Cuzco there is a monastery built on the site, and actually made out of the cyclopean stones with which the Incas had built their convent for the Sacred Virgins of the Sun. To the south of Cuzco, towards the Pacific coast, the town of Arequipa stands, which has great Spanish buildings in a style of architecture quite unlike that in use at Quito and Cuzco, for the stone is much softer and requires an altogether different architectural treatment. In all of these places mentioned, the carving inside the churches was carried out by the Indian population, and reaches to a degree of delicacy and invention that had died out in Europe many generations before this, when the Gothic art drank itself to death on such occasions as Brou in Burgundy, and Louviers in Normandy. The Jesuits built their churches in situations that have only become accessible again in the last half-century with the aid of railways and river-steamers; for even a settlement so remote as Putumayo, the place of torture for the Indian rubber-gathering population, on a river which is one of the most distant tributaries of the Amazon, hundreds of miles inland over the snow-mountains from the Pacific, and literally some thousands of miles from the Atlantic, where the Amazon flows into it, has a Jesuit church of beautifully worked stone, the most elaborate internal carving, and a pharmacy and refectory, to the finishing of which many Indians must have devoted their lifework.

Lima was the residence of the Viceroy, and his palace still stands there with the portraits of the Incas, whose aquiline features are so different from those of their placid and complacent descendants. There are also many faded family palaces and a great deal of that splendour, as regards the churches, which one would expect to find in the port at which the Spaniards first landed after leaving their harbour of Cadiz and rounding the dangerous Horn. But in the whole of this region under discussion, although the Spaniards produced many great buildings, there is nothing comparable to the Mexican remains; for there is nothing Andalusian about the high stony deserts and the violent precipice edges of Peru. The snowy mountains can be seen, as you come near the coast in your ship, until they loom like forbidding cliffs straight out at the water's edge; and there is none of that gradual accommodation to the climate, so that you may try one terrace after another till your taste is suited, which helped the Spaniards to adapt themselves to the Mexican atmosphere. Peru is a sterner and more forbidding land; and there is a monstrous distortion, like the human disease of acromegaly, about the very bones of the country, for the stony ridges, alike with the high snow-capped mountain ranges, are swollen out of all perspective and proportion. The animals of the country—the llama and the vicuña—are uncouth and clumsily contrived, while the Indians bear out, in their distinctive appearance, the modern theory of a separate human creation for the ancestors of the Indian races of America. They seem, like the Jews, to be a parallel to the rest of humanity, but no part of it; they are human beings like the rest of us, in everything except fact. It is from their understanding of this, perhaps, that the Spaniards, in this region of South America, so seldom intermarried with the Indians; and the two races remain apart as rulers and conquered, in quite different circumstances from those prevailing in Mexico. All the provincial towns are purely Indian in population, and the Spaniards form the bulk of the big towns and the harbours, and in the country are only landowners or officials. It is only in the Republic of Colombia, for some peculiar reason, that you find a village population of pure Spanish blood.

We now move across the Andes to the Atlantic seaboard of South America, and before we come to the Portuguese settlements of Brazil there remain to be described the Jesuit settlements in Paraguay, that were the most southerly of all Spanish works, and, indeed, farther to the south of the world than any other works of Catholic activity. The Jesuits landed in this part of South America towards the end of the sixteenth century, and they marched far inland on their missionary enterprise till they came to the huge rolling pampas plains of the interior. These districts were inhabited by the Guarani Indians, a race of absolute savages, who, now that the Jesuits have left them, are back again, once more, in their primitive condition. The Jesuits set about the immediate conversion of these natives, and within twenty-five years of their first arrival in the country the Guaranis had altered their mode of life, and were living peaceably in the Misiones, or settlements designed for them by the Jesuits. These villages were uniformly alike in arrangement; the church, with its monastery, was in the plaza, and the long tenement houses of the natives lay along the roads radiating from this centre. The houses were built on a fixed plan, and the Indians wore a costume which the Jesuits had designed for them. There were altogether thirty settlements of this description, eight of them being in the modern Paraguay, and the rest of them in Brazil, and in the Argentine provinces of Entre Rios, Corrientes and Misiones.

This territory, which was ruled like a republic by the Jesuits, lay far concealed, some one thousand or fifteen hundred miles up country from the Gulf of La Plata. The

Guarani language was studied and written down, and the Indians themselves taught to print books, or where this was impossible, to copy, with a pen, the printed letters of a book in so close a fashion that the forgery could not be told from the original. The great missionary, Ruiz de la Montoya, who travelled for some thirty years through the wilderness among the savage Indians, was the author of the first book on the Guarani language, while the Bible was soon after this translated and printed in Guarani, and there is a book of sermons in this language by the Indian Jesuit, Nicholas Yaparaguey. These books, which are some of the most valuable of bibliographical rarities, were printed and finished entirely by the Indian workmen, and they bear the imprint of the various settlements, principally that of the Misione di S. Loreto.[1]

The Indians were taught, also, every art connected with the science of building; they carved the statues and painted the altar-pictures. Many of these churches were of very great size, sometimes with as many as five aisles, for the Jesuits were very rich from their cattle-ranches and from the various objects that they exported, on a fleet of their manufacture, down the La Plata river to Montevideo and the great ports at its mouth. Maté, the South American tea, coffee, and sugar were part of the sources of their wealth; while some of the medicines—as, for example, quinine—that they extracted from the herbs and flowers of this region were held in such value that the Jesuits were directed to send every year a quantity of their balsam of the Misiones for the use of the pharmacy in the palace of Madrid. They supported an army of Indian troops, and on more than one occasion drove back the marauders, who had come eight hundred miles through the wilderness to attack them—from

[1] *Manuale ad usum Patrum Societatis Jesu qui in Reductionibus Paraquariæ Versantur, ex Rituale Romano et Toletano descriptum* (Misione di S. Loreto). And for a description, with maps, of this region, *La descripcion geografica del Gran Chaco*. Padre Pedro Lozano. Cordoba, 1733.

the robber state of San Paolo di Piritinanga, the so-called Paulist Republic, a colony of all the desperadoes who could reach it from every country.

It was their wealth and military strength which brought about the downfall and expulsion of the Jesuits, against whom charges of cruelty and extortion to the Indians were raised by their jealous neighbours. It is well established that these charges were unjustified; but so great was their wealth at the time of their expulsion, in 1767, that in cattle alone their possessions reached the following figures:—cattle, 719,761; horses, 27,204; sheep, 138,827, and oxen, 44,183. As soon as the Jesuits were removed (there were apparently only some four hundred of them among a population of as many hundred thousand Indians), the whole region fell back again into barbarism; the churches and settlements were lost in the jungle, the Indians forgot everything they had been taught and became savages again, while so complete was the ruin that it is only within the last twenty years that settlements have sprung up again in the neighbourhood of these towns, where the Jesuits once lived in peace among their Indian dependants for the space of a century and a half.

The scene of their labours was of extreme beauty, hundreds of miles removed from snow-mountains or dangerous volcanoes; and apparently so far away from human interference that war or pestilence did not enter into the calculations of those who built these colonies. There are huge rolling plains, with blue or red hills far away, perhaps one hundred or one hundred and fifty miles into the distance; and to describe the flowers and trees with which they were familiar, I can only quote a paragraph from Mr Cunninghame Graham, one of the few travellers who have visited this remote region[1]: "The Croton Succirubrus (from which a resin known as the sangre-de-drago is extracted), the Sumaha (bombax—the fruit of which yields a fine vegetable silk), the Erythroxylon or coca of Paraguay, the

[1] *A Vanished Arcadia.* Cunninghame Graham.

Incienso, or incense-tree of the Jesuits, are some of the most remarkable of the myriad shrubs. But if the shrubs are myriad, the flowers are past the power of man to count. Lianas, with their yellow and red and purple clusters of blossoms, like enormous bunches of grapes, hang from the forest trees. In the open glades upon the Trandubays, the Algarrotos, and the Espinillos, hang various orchidaceæ, called by the natives "*flores de aire*," covering the trees with their aerial roots, their hanging bolssoms, and their foliage of tender green. The Labiatæ, Compositæ, Daturæ, Umbelliferæ, Convolvulaceæ, and many other species cover the ground in spring, or run up trees and bushes after the fashion of our honeysuckle and the traveller's joy." [1]

Like all the aborigines of the American continent, the Indians had a very highly developed cult for these flowers, in connection with which they believed in many pagan traditions as to the origin or the different uses of each blossom. On particular feast days they would decorate the whole interior of the church with flowers, and used to build up triumphal arches of them along the roads leading to the church door, while even the very trees by the roadside would be hung with flowers in such profusion that the branches seemed to be festooned with different coloured snows. The uniforms worn by the Indian notabilities on such occasions as this were of a gorgeousness in keeping with the colours of nature. " All the militia of the town "—I quote again from Mr Cunninghame Graham—" were in attendance, mounted on their best horses, and armed with lances, bolas, lazos, and a few with guns. The officers of the Indians rode at their head, dressed out in gorgeous clothes, and troops of Indians, at stated intervals, performed a sort of pyrrhic dance between the squadrons of cavalry. In front of all, on a white horse, rode the Alferez Real, dressed in a doublet of blue velvet richly laced with gold, a waistcoat of brocade, and with short velvet breeches gartered with silver lace; upon his

[1] For a study of the flora, see Vasconcellos, *On the Flora of Brazil*; and the works of Montenegro, Sigismund Ansperger, and Lozano.

feet shoes decked with silver buckles, and the whole scheme completed by a gold-laced cocked hat. In his right hand he held the Royal Standard, fastened to a long cane which ended in a silver knob. Behind him came the Corregidor, arrayed in yellow satin, with a silk waistcoat and gold buttons, breeches of yellow velvet, and a magnificent hat. Other officials—the Commissario, the Maestro de Campo, and the Sargente Major—were in scarlet coats, with crimson damask waistcoasts trimmed with silver lace, red breeches, and black hats adorned with heavy lace."

All of these settlements are now a melancholy ruin, and the very stones of the building are covered under such a growth of tropical jungle that it is almost impossible to discover their whereabouts. There are a few carved stones, and one or two mutilated and broken statues, but, except for these, every sign of ornamental work has disappeared many years ago, for, after the expulsion of the Order, every object of value was removed, and those that were too heavy were broken up and thrown out to rot away in the wet woods; while the very natives, as I have said, relapsed again into barbarism, until, at this day, the Guarani Indians are among the most savage of the aborigines of South America.

In Brazil, as we leave the Misiones and make for the Atlantic, the race of conquerors changes from Spanish to Portuguese. I have described, in an earlier part of this book, the sources from which so much wealth was drawn by the Braganza family early in the eighteenth century, and without enumerating these again it is enough to say that the riches of Brazil drew away from Portugal huge numbers of the peasant classes, and many of those younger sons of the nobles who would be likely to depend upon war and adventure for their livelihood. The emigration from Portugal grew, in fact, to so serious a pitch in the Algarve (the part of Portugal lying south of Lisbon and the River Tagus), that negro labour had to be imported from Africa, by which expedient the Portuguese living in this part of the country are now very negroid by race and appearance. Meanwhile the most energetic of their countrymen had sailed across the Atlantic to Brazil, where they founded great cities and started valuable industries. Earthquakes, fires, many revolutions, and a century of desolation have nearly destroyed the buildings with which the Portuguese colonists adorned their towns, and it is only safe to surmise their activities by drawing a parallel with the remains of the days of Portuguese colonial supremacy elsewhere. Macao, an ancient Portuguese city on the Canton river, some forty miles from Hong-Kong, has huge churches and decaying palaces that testify to her former importance; but it is at Goa, on the west coast of India, south of Bombay, that these energies can be seen working to their fullest extent. Old Goa, which is some five miles from New Goa, to which the Viceroy removed in 1790, had, at one time, a population of some two hundred thousand; while in the year 1890 there were only eighty-six fever-haunted inhabitants remaining.

There are, in this ruined town, four or five churches of great splendour. The Church of Bom Jesus, built in 1594, contains the body of S. Francis Xavier, and is the principal building of the place. Its high and complicated façade runs straight on into that of another huge building with lofty halls and immense corridors, the Convent of Jesuits, which was finished in 1590, some forty years after the death of S. Francis. This was the college from which so many missionaries were sent forth to India, China and Japan; but the Jesuits were expelled by Pombal in 1759, and their property confiscated by the Government. The other monastic orders were driven out in 1835; but the endowments of the churches have never been forfeited, and so the archbishop and secular clergy of Goa still receive large allowances from the Government. The Church of Bom Jesus is entered by a side door from the Jesuits' College, through the sacristy, a huge room with wardrobes filled with embroidered vestments. The tomb and shrine of S. Francis occupy a side chapel; and his monument consists of three tiers of sarcophagi made of jasper and marble, and given, in the year

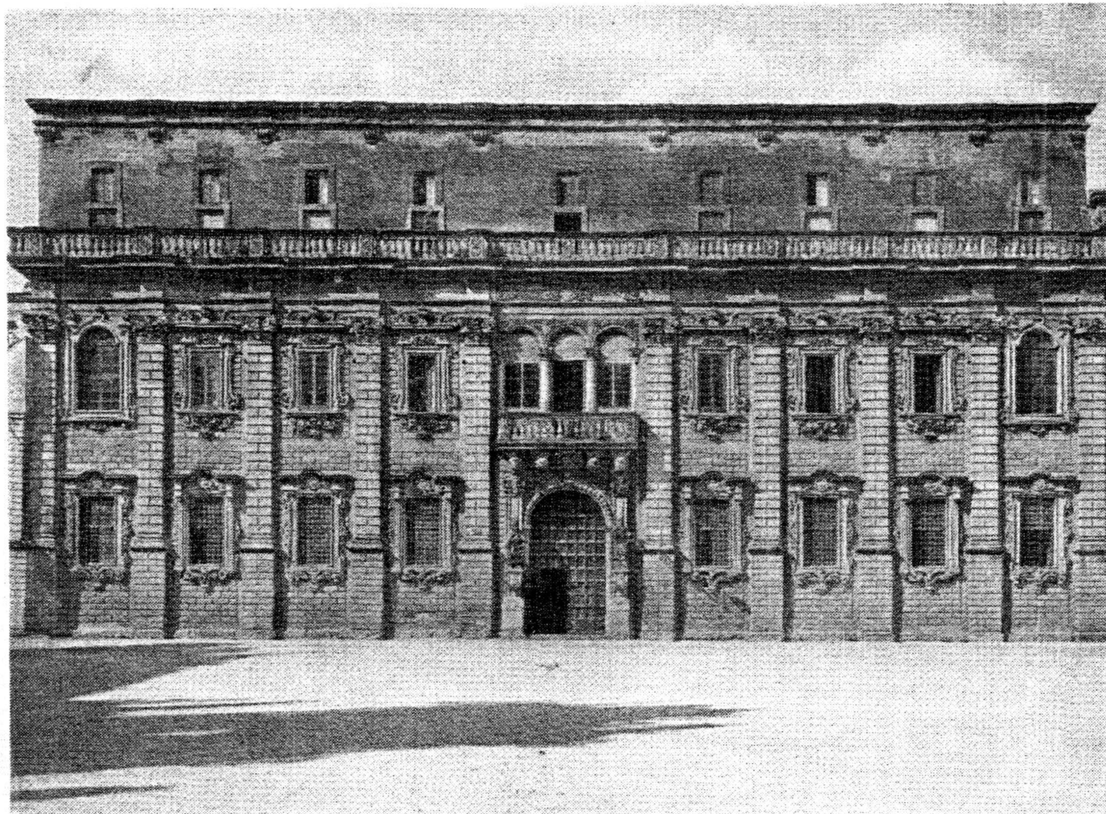

Photograph Alinari

LECCE

THE SEMINARIO

1696, by the Grand Duke Cosmo III. of Tuscany. The upper tier is decorated with inlaid panels in Florentine mosaic, representing scenes in the life of the saint, and on the top of this is his body in an enormous silver coffin ; while on the altar is a life-size statue in solid silver of the saint, which was given by Queen Maria of Portugal late in the eighteenth century.

A little distance away is the Sé Primaçial, the Cathedral of S. Catherine, built between 1562 and 1623, which still has a staff of twenty-eight canons, who live in the archbishop's palace, a magnificent building next door ; the archbishop yet, on occasions, lives here, while the Viceroy, on his periodical visits, stops in the neighbouring monastery. In front of the cathedral the Palace of the Inquisition used to stand ; and it was in this square that the terrible *autos-da-fé* were held at which, so typical of a religious controversy, the Nestorians, the primitive Christians of India, suffered so much more than the Hindus. At the other corner of this huge square were the buildings of the Misericordia which enclosed the Church of Nossa Senhora de Serra, a building made in fulfilment of a vow taken on one of his sea-voyages by Albuquerque, and in which he was originally buried.[1] The palace of the viceroys is nearly a complete ruin, but it still shows traces of its once famous windows, in which the panes were made not of glass, but out of sheets of mother-of-pearl. Beyond this there lie the Great Bazaar, the vast domed and double-towered Church of San Cajetano, the convents of the Dominicans and Carmelites, and the renowned missionary College of S. Paul, or Santa Fé.[2]

These details of Goa may give some idea of the extent to which colonisation was in those days associated and connected with building, for Goa was intended as the metropolis of a Christianised India. In the absence of any good

[1] The body of Albuquerque, who died near Ormuz in 1515, now lies in the Church of Nossa Senhora da Graça at Lisbon.

[2] Goa, about the year 1700, is said to have contained as many as thirty thousand priests, monks and nuns in its population.

photographs it is almost impossible, without a personal visit, to describe the nature and appearance of the churches and palaces that the Portuguese erected; but their activities in India were not on a greater scale than their South American adventure. The settlements of Brazil were, of necessity, strongly fortified, for the Dutch had a powerful colony on the same coast, and there were, in addition, huge bands of mamelukes, as they were called, and marauders from the robber republic of San Paolo de Piritinanga [1] to be reckoned with.

A little later than this, by the time that the Paulist Republic had been subdued, and the Spanish and Portuguese had expelled and absorbed the wealth of the Jesuit Misiones, Brazil received an additional dignity by the presence of the Braganza family at Rio de Janeiro, who had fled there on a British man-of-war, before the victorious French under Junot, in the year 1808. Ten years later, when the Braganzas were compelled by public opinion to return from Brazil, that they preferred, to Lisbon, the elder son of the King of Portugal was proclaimed Emperor of Brazil under the title of Dom Pedro the First. His son, Dom Pedro II., who was only expelled by the revolution of 1889, was a suitor for the hand of Queen Victoria; and the writer of a recent book of memoirs, who was a diplomatist at Rio de Janeiro in the days of the last Emperor, tells a curious and fascinating story of the peculiar etiquette with which his Court was conducted. It appears that the natives of Rio de Janeiro were under the necessity of leaving early each day, by train, for the suburb in which all the business houses are situated. It was Dom Pedro's custom to attend every day the departure and arrival of the business men's train. At six-thirty each morning it started, and Dom Pedro appeared at this ceremony

[1] *Histoire de Nicolas Neenguirui (Nicholas I.), Roy de Paraguai et Empereur des Mamelucs.* San Paolo (de Piritinanga), 1756. This book, according to Mr Cunninghame Graham, was, if really printed in Piritinanga, the only specimen known from any printing press in that region.

in top hat and evening clothes; there was a brass band always in attendance, playing to the Emperor, who stood in the waiting-room. It was a moment of tense excitement for all concerned when the train drew out of the station, with the band at full blast, and the Emperor on the platform surrounded by his staff and the foreign diplomatists. The evening train, that brought the business men back to their homes and suppers, was equally an excuse for ceremonial on the part of this really democratic monarch. On days of particular splendour—a national fête or a religious *festa*—he would appear, less soberly dressed, in his Imperial mantle of the pink and scarlet feathers of the toucan, providing in his person a parallel with those plumed and feathered kings whom I have mentioned earlier in this book, when they could direct their cotton-quilted warriors under no menace from Spanish aggression.

The Emperor has been gone more than thirty years, and most of the business men ride to their work now in motor cars, so that the suburban railway also is out of use; but Rio de Janeiro still lies there, sheltered between the two rocky hills at each corner of its wide-spreading bay, and there is still the avenue of trees, one hundred and twenty feet high, that flower like gigantic roses, leading up to the palace where the Emperor used to live, for it is a town better suited than any other to be the culmination of a huge empire. Brazil is nearly double the size of India, and contains more possibilities of new and strong developments in human history than any other country in the world; for, like all the other Latin republics of America, it was colonised from Europe in the days of the greatest fertility of European culture, and once this immense land has become peopled to the extent of the United States, she will far surpass the Northern Republic in her influence upon the decaying European civilisation.

The other great cities of Brazil, towns that are simply names to all who have not visited them — Bahia and Pernambuco on the Atlantic coast, and Para, the gigantic settlement at the mouth of the River Amazon, where that river at last flows out into the Atlantic, attacking its tumbling waves on a perpetual battle front of some three hundred miles—these three towns will one day become provincial centres for a culture, that, while it shows a strong unity, will allow as much diversity in its different parts as you may find between Hindu and Mohammedan in India. Bahia is, for example, already a centre for music, and the Brazilian dance-music is more continual and complicated than anywhere else in the continent: it is there that they invent the most languorous and the most fiery of measures, which, indeed, is only natural, as they have bands playing dances in their streets all day long, from one early morning to the next. Between these dawns that they contrive, by this method, to telescope into each other, hoping, perhaps, that the collision will flare up into a brighter conflagration, they discover the beat and the rhythm that are caught and handed on from one band of music to the next, like a sacred fire that is never allowed to die out. At Para, where the millionaires outnumber the beggars, and the rubber that has been collected all over the interior of the continent enriches all the hands it passes through, the perpetual drift of life is so quickened by the flow of fortunes and the endless motion of the river, that is like a huge sea moving uniformly in one and the same direction, that you seem to grow old almost before you have had time to draw the Brazilian air into your lungs; it is alternately fierily white, and then tropically dark, like the alternating squares of a chessboard; the air scorches, and then freezes as though the sky has as many icy shafts and pinnacles glittering there as it has soaring flames; time, flying with strong wings, or rolling its wheels lazily along—these two conditions are simply a brake or a higher speed at work on the continual flow of the waters: they laugh out loud or whisper softly like young leaves in the wind: it is a steady flame or a whorl of sparks . . . golden lawn or black chasm . . . fire or ice . . . eagle or tortoise . . . the lion or the crooning turtle . . . staring sun or drooping, heavy eyes . . . sleep, out of which we were born, and into which we die . . . till once in each life it is a dream, and we can wake again and find ourselves in the great plaza of Tasco; from its high tower I now deliver my peroration.

The house where we slept was in the street of the Flamingo, built of stone and in one storey, with a big sala covering most of the space, and a courtyard behind with the kitchens, where a great flame was used to temper the strange steely fruits of the land, for their core underneath this armour is cool and refreshing; while the fire has also to draw out the golden ore from the sugar-canes, where it is hidden behind glass walls, and the brittle music that the wind makes when it sighs through these golden groves. The sugar-cane was imported from the Canary Islands to Santo Domingo, whence quickly it passed to Cuba, and was introduced by Cortez into Mexico. The descendant of the Conquistador, the Sicilian Duke of Monteleone, as heir of Cortez, and Marqués of the Valley of Oaxaca, still holds these sugar plantations, especially in the neighbourhood of Cuernavaca, where they still produced a rental of thirty thousand arrobas of silver,[1] and these sugar-orchards fill all the valleys towards Tasco, which is high on the mountain slopes, five thousand feet above the sea. The gardener, Don Juan by name, with an immense black beard, a Mexican hat, and a silken sash of military crimson, will offer you orangeade; he sends to the house for sugar and tumblers, pulls the oranges from the trees, and draws the water from a clear tank overshadowed by blossoming branches, and cold as though it had been iced. This is the evening of the first day's journey, for Tasco is still three days' ride on mule-back over the stony mountains of the state of Guerrero.[2] Behind the *hacienda* there is a courtyard round which stand the house for boiling the sugar, wherein furnaces blaze night and day, another house with machinery for extracting the juice from the cane, the refining-

[1] The Mexican arroba contains twenty-five pounds.

[2] This state of Guerrero alone is three times greater than Wales in area.

rooms, and the place where the cane is dried. As this is a coffee plantation, here also there are the great mill for separating the beans from the chaff, and buildings in which they make brandy ; while there is lodging for the four hundred men employed, exclusive of boys, one hundred horses, and a number of mules. Outside are the fields of sugar-cane, the plains for cattle, and the plantations of coffee, this one containing upward of fifty thousand young plants, all fresh and vigorous, besides a great deal of uncultivated ground, abandoned to the deer, hares, and quails, of which there is a great abundance. The second day's ride brings you higher, on to the cold outer slope of the hills; and on the evening of the third day you arrive at Tasco, tired out and hardly able to stagger on foot up its narrow streets, that are paved in a flowing pattern of pebble mosaic, like the Italian grottos, and are too narrow and steep for even a mule's sure feet to tread them.

Our lodging was a house, as I have said, in the street of the Flamingo, and coming out of its shade the next morning at ten o'clock, the Festa of San Christoval was in full swing : grand mass was over, and the bull-fight, the *corrida de toros,* ready to begin. It was to take place in the square in front of the cathedral, this spot being the only piece of level ground for miles round. The enclosure took up nearly the whole extent of the square, and was in the form of a gigantic circular scaffold, some fifteen hundred feet in circumference, with room for about four or five thousand spectators. The whole of this huge wooden structure was built up and held together without the help of a single nail, being made of ordinary poles, standing just as they had been cut in the woods, and tied together with withes. The interior was enclosed by long poles crossing and interlacing each other, leaving only an opening for the door, and was divided by poles, in the same manner, into boxes. This made a gigantic frame of rustic lattice-work, admirably adapted for the hot Mexican sun, as it admitted a free circulation of air. The top was covered with an arbour made of the leaves of the

American palm, a suitable finish to a building of this simple nature, which every Indian could help to build, and when the *festa* was over it could be torn down and the materials used for firewood.

High above the poles and the roof of palm leaves stand the two high towers of the Church of S. Sebastian and Santa Prisca: this is indeed the finest and culminating work in Mexico.[1] The *corrida* was on the point of beginning, and the place was already thronged, all the cheaper seats being in that part which was exposed to the full blaze of the sun. Outside the door of each box stood the proprietor with a rickety little step-ladder of three or four steps, inviting customers to buy the seats inside. Everyone was scrambling for his seat, and in this general stampede and confusion the whole of the huge scaffold was trembling and swaying to and fro under the load of spectators. Above all this din, and

[1] The man who paid for it was the Marquis José de la Borda, before mentioned, and the whole building was finished by the year 1757, by which date de la Borda is supposed to have spent some 8,000,000 Mexican dollars on its construction. The material is a hard and fine-grained brown stone, and there is a most fantastic façade with two towers and four windows in each, while the balconies with which the four faces of each tower are decorated have a sardonic and leering mask to support their weight. Inside the church there are twelve altars with retables of carved wood, and gilded and polychrome sculpture. All the altar paintings are by Miguel Cabrera, and there are eight huge panels by him in the sacristy, which is filled with the most elaborate and fanciful chairs and tables that can be imagined, of such character and force that something transcendental has been arrived at in their making. Next to this is the Sala Capitular, in which there are portraits of de la Borda and other great dignitaries, and the floor was originally entirely covered with a superb India carpet imported to Tasco by way of Manila and Acapulco, of which a small fragment is still in use, as a rug, in the sacristy. Such is the church, described in the baldest and most uncompromising reality, but it would be impossible to describe in words the majesty and fantasm of its appearance. Underneath, as you look down from one of the towers, are the huddled roofs of the town, the tumbling, hilly country, and the plaza, which from above looks so small, although this is compensated for by its whiteness in the sun and by the feeling that it is the only level ground, apart from the floor of the church, for a huge distance round.

coming out louder and louder as everyone settled in his seat and the hub of all the voices calling out at once began to die down, came the noise of the bells ringing out of the two towers, with a vehemence that seemed to express the relief of this building at being left empty again for the day's heat, after the appalling crush at mass earlier in the morning. All the masks carved upon the façade and by each window in the towers wore an intensified leer, as if in preparation for the animal *auto-da-fé*; while those of them who were turned away from the direction of the bull-fight were preparing to watch it reflected in one of the little mirror-like clouds, or projected photographically on to one of the facets of the fathomless sea of space.

On ordinary days the plaza was allowed to sleep contentedly in the sun; but three or four times every year there was a bull-fight, or a market and fair, which was about the only opportunity the inhabitants of this far-away town were afforded to buy cloth, jewellery, and all the other products of the capital. A market day, then, was the occasion for as much excitement as a bull-fight. The pebble mosaic with which the square was paved had a fluttering air about it from the canvas shades of all the stalls that had been set up, as though it was a bed of flowers on which a whole tribe of butterflies had swarmed. The people who were buying and selling from these canvas windows were of, at any rate four, entirely distinct and separate colours. These were the Spaniards, the Indians, the Mestizos or half-castes (and some of these were a mixture of Spanish and Indian, while others were mixed Indian and negro), and, to finish with, there were quite a number of pure negroes, imported from the Gold Coast to perform the most arduous and unhealthy tasks on the plantations and in the mines. The Spaniards, and those half-castes who were rich enough to afford it, had the utmost magnificence of costume, with gold and silver embroidery and fringes, and jewelled rings and earrings: the peons—that is to say, the Indian labourers—the negroes and despised half-castes wore the wide, flapping, white pantaloons of the Neapolitan peasantry; and the stunted aquiline features of the Indians were of a perfect fitness for the punchinello costume, while an occasional negro in this dress looked like one of the dark spirits of the air masquerading under the sail-cloth of these bird-men. No surmise could be too fantastic for the objects they were bartering at the stalls. The immense high-crowned and broad-brimmed hats of the peons were whiter than the snow on the high mountains that ended every view, and they looked as quenching and cool as those white capes round the shoulders of the fiery Mexican volcanoes. Some of the peons who had ridden in from country villages had a blunderbuss, an enormous pistol, or a curved, cutting sword at their side, and they recalled what must have been a familiar sight in parts of Southern Italy till sixty years ago; for until the expulsion of the Bourbon Kings, in 1861, the brigands in Apulia, and more especially in the district between Brindisi and Taranto, and Lecce and Gallipoli, roamed about in their bands, armed to the teeth, and completely masked in the guise of Punchinello. It was that bird-like nose you saw peering in through the window at an hour when you should have been asleep; and it was this phantom, with wings growing weak from disuse and only capable of a little flying jump like the ostrich, or a quickened walk like the penguin, that terrified travellers on a lonely road, and took away their money and valuables. Out here in Mexico the black mask was unnecessary for a disguise, for the Indians were swarthy and difficult to tell one from another, while at times, as I have said, the mask was made really unnecessary by the fact of its wearer being a negro.

This particular week the market and fair were to be held for three successive days after the bull-fight, and the dry wood with which the ring was built could be pulled to pieces with an hour or two's work after the *corrida* was over, so as to give torches and bonfires to light them at their second task of putting up the stalls for the traders, and the platforms for charlatans and mountebanks. But before this could come about there was another whole day to be lived through, and the *corrida* was just about to begin, punctual to its appointed starting time of ten o'clock.

High up, on the top of the scaffold, and above the gate through which the bulls would charge into the ring, was a big band of music, the conductor of which wore a shining black mask to caricature a negro. This orchestra was continually playing, but its notes sounded soft and far away against the background of shouting and laughing voices. They seemed far removed from the purpose of this gathering, aloof and independent, like the orchestra you can hear playing, during a silent moment, in the theatre next door, through the flimsy walls. But all of a sudden there came the sound of a squawking trumpet, dying away almost before it had begun, and the whole audience became silent and attentive in a single breath. The gates were flung open and the band came nearer, and rang out loud all at once in the strains of an heroic march to which the toreadors came in, headed by the president of the fight on horseback. The burlesque negro who conducted the music gave it a specially exaggerated air, as though he, at any rate, knew the weak side of this mercenary warfare. They marched in procession right across the arena to the president's box opposite the entrance; the matadors first, and then the toreadors, the mounted picadors and their attendants, and, last of all, the most menial of the gladiators, those whose duty it was to kill with their stilettos the horses that were too badly gored by the bull to be of any further use, and had to be finished with a knife thrust into their spinal marrow; these men wore plain red pantaloons and shirts, in contrast to the other gorgeous uniforms, and their other duty was to drag out, with a team of mules, the dead body of the bull, after the matador had drawn his smoking sword out of its body.

There was now silence for a little, while the bull-fighters took up their different positions; and they were hardly in their places before a general murmur ran round, and everyone looked attentively towards the gate. The manner of introduction for the first bull was brutal in the extreme. It was by a rope two or three hundred feet long, passed through the fleshy part of the bull's nose and secured at both ends to the saddle of the vaquero, one of a band of cattle-tenders, hard riders, and brought up to deal with cattle that run wild in the woods, who came in for these fights from the neighbouring *haciendas*. In this way the bull was hauled through the streets and into the ring. Another vaquero followed close behind, with a lasso over the animal's horns, to hold him back and prevent him rushing upon his leader. When this pair appeared, hauling and beating the bull between them, there was a hurricane of laughter, and everyone all round the ring waved their handkerchiefs, making an indescribable effect: it was as though every law of nature had been contradicted and there were two huge waterfalls dashing at each other with equal force, one from above and the other from below, so that when they met, and as they passed each other, you could see the little detached heads of foam falling in either direction so quickly that you could only distinguish their mass, and were not able to follow each one separately up or down. These were the waving handkerchiefs. At the same time, through their flutter, a fanfare of trumpets could be heard announcing the animal's torture. In the centre of the ring the leader loosed one end of the rope and, riding on, dragged it trailing on the ground its whole length, perhaps a hundred yards, through the bull's nose, leaving a crust of dirt on one side as the rope came out bloody on the other. The bull, held back by the rope over his horns, stood with his neck outstretched, and when the end of the rope passed through, he licked his gory nose, pawed the ground, and bellowed.

The vaqueros, who were dressed in pink shirts and trousers, and wore small hats of thick plaited straw with low round crowns and narrow brims turned up at the sides, settled into their huge saddles, the flaps of which covered half the body of each horse, and dug their iron spurs, which were six inches long and must have weighed some two or three pounds, into their horses' flanks. One of them rode up and started the bull, and, chasing him round the ring, with a few throws of the lasso caught him by the horns and dragged him to a post at one side of the ring, where, riding off with the rope, he hauled his head down to the ground close against the post. Keeping it down in that position, some of the others passed a rope twice round his body just behind the forelegs, and securing it on the back passed it under his tail and, returning it, crossed it with the coils around his body. Two or three men on each side then hauled upon the rope, which cut into and compressed the bull's chest, and by its tightness under the tail almost lifted his hind legs from off the ground. The animal bellowed, threw himself on the sand, and kicked and struggled.

After this he was charged upon and goaded by the undaunted picadors with their lances until the blood streamed from his shoulders, and he stood quite still, desperately pawing the ground and not knowing in which direction to turn and face his enemies. At this moment the toreadors ran towards him and threw their sharp barbed banderillas into the sore wounds on his shoulders, and then, when his neck and shoulders were quivering under a whole sheaf of these darts, they would twist their ropes or throw their red cloaks round one of the darts so as to pull and tear the wound still further. This particular bull was to be killed by the picadors: they formed in front of him, each with a black or yellow poncho in his left hand, and with a spear poised in the right. They stood with legs extended and knees bent, so as to keep a firm foothold, changing position by a spring forward or backward, on one side or the other, to meet the movement of the bull's head. The death-blow had to be between the horns into the back of the neck. Two or three struck him fairly with a cutting, heavy sound, and drew out their spears reeking with blood. One man misdirected his blow: the bull threw up his neck with the long handle of the spear standing upright in it, and rushing upon the picador, hurled him to the ground and passed over his body, seeming to strike him with all four hoofs. The man never moved, but lay on his back with arms outstretched, as if dead. The bull moved on, with the handle of the spear still standing up in his neck. The vaqueros went in pursuit of him with their lassos, and chasing him round, the spear fell out and they caught him. The bull was again assaulted, worried out, and dragged away, while the wounded man was carried off, doubled up, and apparently gravely wounded. Other bulls followed, making eight in all. At twelve o'clock the church bells rang out and the fight ended; but it was only a truce, for another was timed to begin at four o'clock in the afternoon.

This later fight was the last *corrida* of the season, and some of the best bulls had been kept in reserve for it. The first that was dragged on was received with acclamations by the crowd, for he had distinguished himself by his bravery in a former fight; but he bore an ugly mark of favour, having been dragged by the nose till the cartilage was completely torn out.

The victim was then let in, lassoed, dragged up to the post, girt with the rope round his body like the other, and then again let loose, amid bursts of music, rockets, and loud shouts. The *chulos*, fighters on foot, went at him, flaring before him with the left hand red and yellow ponchos, and holding in the right darts containing fireworks and ornamented with streamers of yellow paper. These they thrust into his neck and flanks. The current of air quickened the ignition of the fire, and when the fireworks exploded the paper still rattled about his ears. The picadors then mounted their horses; but after a few thrusts of the spear the bull flinched, and the spectators, indignant that he did not show more fight, cried out for him to be taken away.

The next bull was led in by the same method, with a long rope passed through his nose, and after this preliminary torture was goaded with darts and speared fiercely by the picadors, while each time he received a blow, or one of the banderillas stuck in his shoulder, the whole crowd shouted out like one man, and laughed in great bursts like a cannonade. Each new torture was announced by a fanfare, which sounded forth like a shrill voice, and its metallic syllables held out no hope of mercy. He was then lassoed and dragged up and tortured at the post. But as even this did not goad him to enough fury, the crowd called out loudly for fire to be applied to him. Watching narrowly that the ropes around his horns did not get loose, they fixed upon his back the figure of a soldier in a cocked hat, seated in a saddle. Both the saddle and the figure of the soldier were made of wood, paper and gunpowder, making a formidable and dreadful firework. When this was fairly secured to his back they all fell back, and the picadors, mounted, and with their spears poised, took their places in the ring. A vaquero with a pointed and sardonic chin set off large and furiously whizzing rockets within a few feet of the bull; another fired in the heel the figure of the soldier on his back; the spectators shouted, the rope was slipped, and the bull let loose. His first dash was furious. Maddened by the shouts and laughter of the crowd, and by the fire, the smoke, the explosion and the awful whizzing of the engine of torture on his back, he went for the first picador, and ran his horns into the horse's belly, lifting it up and nearly tossing it over the barrier on to the crowd behind. The laughter was louder than ever, and the bull dragged out his blood-stained horns with a horrible slipping sound. The horse's entrails came out, splaying themselves into a horrible resemblance to some sea-animal, with their red pipes and smoking, seething mass. After its wound was stuffed with straw, the animal was quickly stitched up, beaten on to its feet again, and led out, blindfolded, once again towards the bull. Meanwhile he had charged another horse, and received a second awful thrust of the picador's spear in his flank. The first horse gave a moaning, pitiful cry as the horns opened its wound once more, and the bull, rejoicing in its revenge, stood over the prostrate body, digging its horns again and again into the stomach, trying to enlarge and make fatal his first stab. He was at last tempted away with a red cloak and a furious rocket, and fixed his attention on to the second horse, which was being beaten towards him with a timid but brutal-looking picador on its back. The animal could hardly stand, and was dropping great gouts of blood on to the sand from the terrible grape-like bunch of entrails that was hanging out from below its belly. The picador's lance went right into the bull's shoulder with a clenching, grating violence, while the horns dug themselves savagely into a fresh place on the horse's neck. The bull all this time was bleeding from scores of wounds, his neck and back were a fluttering mass of darts, the firework was burning furiously into his flesh, and he was fighting with fictitious strength.

He made a ferocious advance towards a third horse, lifted it high up on his horns, while both of them bled together and made the sands dark with blood. He was thrust at by four picadors, had fresh darts thrown at him, and his burnt fat was sizzling and scenting the air. In the corner, a few yards away, knelt some half-dozen chulos, two or three of them holding the head and tail of each of the two dying horses, while the most experienced pair of them drew a little stiletto from their belts, and seemed to be gently stroking the necks of the horses as they felt for the right spot to plunge their daggers in.

The powder was now burned out, and the bull, with gaping wounds and charred, smouldering flesh, turned and ran, bellowing for escape at the gate of entrance, and then crawled round the wall of the ring, looking up at the spectators, and pleading to the mild faces of the women with imploring eyes. A matador stepped up, motioned with his left hand, and thrust a straight long sword into his back up to the hilt. The bull sank on to his knees and then stumbled up again, peaceful and calm, while the matador went over to him, drew out the sword, and then pressed it back again in a new place: the knees gave way, he gave one moan, rolled his eyes and lolled his stained tongue. A moment later, when they had all stood at his death-bed, he was dragged out by a jangling mule team, which drew out the three horses that were his victims with him.

It was almost dark, and the last bull was dragged in. He was stabbed, fringed with darts, tortured with the rope, and burnt with fire. But the vesper bell rang out suddenly, and with this the ring was opened to the boys, who, amid roars of laughter, pulled, hauled and hustled him till he could hardly stand. No one moved from his place yet. The bells rang out louder and louder as their metal seemed to grow molten with the heat of the blows rained upon them, and the conductor of the band, in his shining black mask, directed and sounded forth a fine burlesque march, to which the toreadors filed away, grumbling at their pay, but resolved to gamble it away that evening. They were shabby, with wet and ruffled plumes, torn shirts, and brown stains on each arm and leg—blackened hands from the smoke, singed, even, with the fire, and still slippery and wet with the promiscuous blood. The most heroic of the company carried a bull's head with glassy eyes and lolling tongue, the blood still hanging congealed, like a rich and fantastic lace, round the jagged skin edge of the neck. They limped, stumbled, and some of them were so tired that they seemed to walk on air, with their legs cut off at the knee; but the music got the lot of them safely over its tight-rope to the benches and the brandy behind.

Biographical Index and Bibliography

Prefatory Note to Biographical Index

A few words of explanation are necessary as to the scope and method of this Index. Its purpose is to give the few most salient details in the lives of the various painters, musicians, architects, and rulers mentioned in the course of the book. In order to complete this repository I have added notes on Caserta, Mafra, the Escurial, and one or two other of the chief buildings mentioned, while as regards Italy, that one of the countries dealt with of which I am most qualified to speak, I have brought out all the information I can by dealing in considerable detail with a few places that have actually hardly been mentioned in the course of the book. Thus Lecce, Noto, Catania, and Syracuse are all discussed, and remarks on each of them may be found in their respective alphabetical order. The sources of my remarks are those to be expected. For biography I have consulted the *Encyclopædia Britannica*, Grove's and Baker's *Musical Dictionaries*, and Wornum's and Bryan's *Dictionaries of Painters*. For details of places I have relied upon guide-books, chiefly early editions of Murray's *Handbooks*, and various eighteenth-century books of travel. I have, however, in all these cases reduced the information where dealing with some one person or object well known to all, while expanding it where the person or thing is little known. Thus the Escurial is given only a small space, while much is devoted to Mafra or to Caserta; and the same remark applies to Tiepolo, contrasted with, for example, Solimena or Sebastiano Conca. Mexican architects and painters are not included in the Index, for I have put all the available information about them into the body of the book; while the painters and architects of Messina I have neglected, because there is nothing now left of their handiwork by which to judge them.

Biographical Index

ALBERONI, CARDINAL: *b.* Piacenza, 1664, *d.* Piacenza, 1752. He became Consular Agent for the Duchy of Parma at Madrid and arranged the marriage of Philip V. with Elizabeth Farnese in 1714. The Queen interested herself actively in Alberoni and, in 1717, he became a Cardinal. He planned with Philip V. and Elizabeth a second Spanish Armada against England, and his warlike policy brought down upon Spain the combined forces of England, France, Holland and the Empire. In 1719 he was banished from Spain. His political power was now ended and Alberoni, after filling several minor diplomatic appointments, retired to his birthplace, where he founded the still existing Collegio Alberoni.

AMIGONI, JACOPO: *b.* Venice, 1675, *d.* Madrid, 1752. He visited London in 1729 and practised history and portrait painting in England for ten years. He was afterwards, on his friend Farinelli's recommendation, Court painter to Ferdinand VI. of Spain. Doctor Burney, in his *Musical Tour,* mentions four pictures of the principal scenes out of the opera of *Didone and Nitelli,* and also a portrait group of Farinelli, Metastasio and Porpora, which hung in Farinelli's villa near Bologna. Amigoni also painted a large portrait of the singer, which is in the Accademia Filarmonica of Bologna, and a fine group of Philip V. of Spain and his family.

ARANJUEZ. The palace, some thirty miles from Madrid, built by Philip V. in 1727, and enlarged and restored after a fire by Charles III. in 1775-1778. The palace contains pictures and frescoes by Luca Giordano, Bayeu, Amigoni and Raphael Mengs, and the celebrated Sala Japonesa designed by Gius. Gricci of Naples in 1763 for Charles III., and executed in the Buen Retiro porcelain factory. There are famous and beautiful gardens attached to the palace, in which stands the Casa del Labrador, a pavilion built by Charles IV. in 1803, where the walls are panelled like tapestry with an inlay of platinum, gold and bronze.

Cf. *Travels through Spain*, by John Talbot Dillon, Knight and Baron of the Sacred Roman Empire, London, 1780 (with a fine frontispiece of Charles III. in the robes of his new Order of Carlos Tercero, by Antonio Velasquez), p. 81 *et seq.*, "Aranjuez":

"On one side fine avenues of stately oaks and lofty elms convey the truest idea of magnificence, while they afford the most reviving shade; on the other the sudden transition to lawns and wildernesses, the cascades of water breaking through the thickets, the tuneful songs of numberless birds sheltered in these cool recesses, the occasional appearance and passage of the monarch, attended by the grandees of his kingdom—all these objects united and concentrated in one point fill the imagination with pleasing ideas and impress the mind of the traveller with a thousand agreeable sensations, particularly in the spring, when everything is in high bloom and perfection, and engage him to look at Aranjuez as one of the most beautiful places in Europe."

Augustus II., King of Poland and Elector of Saxony: *b.* 1670, *d.* 1733. In 1694 he became Elector of Saxony, and in 1696 he turned Papist in order to secure his election as King of Poland. Very extravagant, very luxurious, immensely strong, and the father of some three hundred children, only one of whom, Augustus III., was legitimate.

Bibbiena. This family, surnamed Galli, were the leading perspectivists and theatrical artists of Europe. They were at work all over Europe from 1650 down till the death of Antonio Galli at Milan in 1774. Most famous of the family was Ferdinando, born Bologna, 1657, who worked chiefly in Vienna for the Emperor Charles VI. He died at Bologna in 1743. Other members of this family were Alessandro, Antonio, Carlo, Ferdinando II., Francesco, Giuseppe and

Giovanni Maria. They worked all over Italy and in Spain, Portugal, Poland, Russia, Denmark and the Empire. There are theatres built by them still in existence at Bologna, Verona and Bayreuth.

Buen Retiro. A palace of the Spanish kings in the environs of Madrid. I quote from *A Journey through Spain in the Years 1786 and 1787*, by Joseph Townshend, vol. i., p. 256:

"The palace of Buen Retiro is a vast pile of buildings, very ancient, long deserted and, when I saw it, verging to decay. The theatre is vast and opens into the gardens so as to make them, upon occasion, a continuation of the scene. Here Ferdinand VI. frequently amused the public with operas, of which his Queen, Barbara of Portugal, was extravagantly fond. The great saloon, called 'El Cason,' with its antechamber painted by Luca Giordano, remains a monument of his taste, invention, judgment and imitative powers. In the principal compartment of the roof is represented Hercules giving the Golden Fleece to Philip the Good, Duke of Burgundy. In a subordinate compartment Pallas and the Gods are seen subduing the Titans, answering to which the majesty of Spain appears ruling the terrestrial globe. The rest is filled up with allegorical figures, finely expressed. The antechamber contains the Conquest of Granada. From the great saloon we go to the garden by a little oval cabinet, covered entirely with looking-glass, in the ceiling of which is represented the Birth of the Sun, with people of all nations worshipping the rising deity, whilst the priests are engaged in offering sacrifices. This likewise is by Giordano.

Cafarelli, Gaetano: *b.* Bari, 1703, *d.* Naples, 1783. Porpora kept him on one exercise for five or six years and then dismissed him with the words: "Go, my son! I have nothing more to teach you. You are the greatest singer in Europe." In 1724 he made his début in Rome in a female character, as was usual with the *castrati* singers. Many stories are current of his self-esteem and braggadocio. At the age of sixty-five he was still singing, and had bought the Neapolitan Dukedom of San Dorato, where he lived in great splendour. He died in 1783, leaving his great fortune and the dukedom to a nephew.

CALABRESE—*real name* MATTEO PRETI: *b.* Taverna, Calabria, 1613, *d.* Malta, 1699. Painter of the Neapolitan school; only recently recognised as one of the best Italian painters of the seventeenth century. He travelled to Paris and Madrid, and shows eclectic influence. He frescoed S. Andrea della Valle in Rome and S. Pietro a Majella (now destroyed) in Naples, while his chief work was in Malta, of which state he was made a Cavalier. Dominici mentions a large number of his pictures which he executed for various churches in Taverna, his Calabrian birthplace. As far as I know these have never been visited by a modern authority, and they should make an interesting study.

CAMBIASO, LUCA: *b.* Moneglia, 1527, *d.* Escurial, 1585. He went to Spain in 1583, at the invitation of Philip II., and executed large works at the Escurial, being paid 12,000 ducats for a fresco of Paradise on the ceiling of the choir of the Escurial Church, the largest sum paid up to that time to any artist in the history of modern art. He is a weak artist, whose drawings are preferable to his paintings.

CARACCIOLO, GIAMBATTISTA: *b.* Naples, 1580, *d.* 1641. Neapolitan painter who followed Caravaggio. There are many paintings of his in various Neapolitan churches.

CARAVAGGIO, MICHELANGELO—*real name* AMERIGHI: *b.* Caravaggio, 1569, *d.* Porto Ercole, 1609. The head of the naturalist painters and the most influential artist of his age. Worked at Rome, Naples, Messina, Syracuse and Malta. The tumultuous sordidness of Caravaggio's life was in keeping with the violent realism of his work.

CASERTA. The palace built by Charles III., some twenty miles from Naples, near the ancient Capua. The architect was Luigi Vanvitelli (*q.v.*). The palace was, in its day, held to be the greatest work in building since the time of the Romans. The dimensions are enormous, the length of the south front being 830 feet and the height of the whole building 135 feet. There are four immense courts, through the connecting sides of which runs a vestibule with rich marble columns, and down this corridor, as through the wrong end of a telescope, you can see the gardens and the great cascade stretching two miles away into the mists. Over this vestibule there is a large marble hall, into which the marble staircase, the chapel and the principal State apartments lead. The chapel, full of lapis and rich marbles, contains five pictures by Conca, and altar-pieces by Bonito and Raphael Mengs. The theatre has forty boxes in five tiers with many alabaster columns, and the Royal box, with twelve Corinthian columns of giallo antico from the Temple of Serapis at Pozzuoli. Behind the palace stretch the gardens, with one long cascade arranged to form a combination of fountains as it flows down to the palace, near which the waters disappear below ground and join the waters from Carmignano through a covered passage in order to supply the capital. The chief basin of the cascade represents the story of Diana and Actæon. Behind the hill at the top of the cascade can be seen the aqueduct by which the water is carried from Monte Taburno, twenty-one miles away. In one place, where it traverses a valley, the aqueduct rises in three tiers of arches to the height of 190 feet. All of these huge labours—the palace, the gardens and the aqueduct—were principally the work of slave gangs, composed of Moorish and African captives and of criminals from the bagnios, and it may be said with truth, therefore, that Caserta was the last work of slave labour in Europe. The palace was unfinished when Charles III. left Naples and took up the throne of Spain, but it was slowly finished and worked upon by his son, Ferdinand I., though it was left to Murat, during the few years he reigned in Naples, to finish the decoration of the State rooms. Ferdinand had proposed a model town of Caserta to be laid out as a residence for the silk-weavers whom he established there, the name of which was to be Ferdinandopolis, but this, with many other schemes, was discontinued through economy or laziness. The palace was the summer residence of the Neapolitan Court down till 1860, in the year previous to which Bomba died there after his death journey from Lecce. At present only one set of rooms, those facing Naples, may be visited, and no one is allowed over the rooms looking out on the garden. Vanvitelli published a large and magnificent work on Caserta, with many plans and plates, in which the palace can be studied in the finished state to which it never attained, except on paper.

CATANIA. A seaport town of 150,000 inhabitants on the slopes of Etna. I mention it here because it contains the convent of S. Nicolo or, as it is sometimes called, S. Benedetto, and this building shows very distinct Leccese influence. It was rebuilt in 1693-1735, after the earthquake, and is more than half unfinished. The church, with an incompleted façade, has on its left the monastery, with two enormous arcaded, double-floor cloisters, with a pavilion-like fountain of a strange Mudejar-like architecture in the middle. A similar building with two courts, on the other side of the church, was hardly begun and has never been continued. The finished portion has a many-balconied front in the peculiar Catanian style, with grotesque masks as brackets for the balconies. In old guide-books this convent is described as a wonder of the world and, had it been completed, it would have eclipsed Mafra, in Portugal, for size. It was famed for its good food and was for this reason a favourite stopping-place with the Bourbon kings, on which occasions the band from the San Carlo at Naples used to arrive at Catania, and there were great and costly festivities. There are other buildings of like style—the palace of Prince Biscari (best seen from the Syracuse train window) and the Municipio—while in the district, at Acireale and Nicolosi, there are fine churches and palaces, and at Aci Sant' Antonio the house and garden of Prince Carcaci are worth a visit.

Biographical Index

CHARLES II. of Spain : *b.* 1661, *d.* 1700. The son of Philip IV. and his second wife and niece, Maria, daughter of Emperor Ferdinand III. Charles was so delicate that he had to be fed at the breast till five or six years old, and for many years after that was never allowed to walk. He was left entirely uneducated because his health could not stand the strain. He married Maria Louisa of Orleans, who died in 1690, and whose catafalque was designed by Churriguerra and is illustrated in Don Juan de Vera Tassis y Villaroel: '*Noticias Historiales de la enfermedad, muerte, y exequias de Donna Maria Luisa de Borbon*, Madrid, 1690, engraved by Ruiz de la Iglesia from Churriguerra's drawing, the original of which exists in the possession of Don Felix Boix, the famous Catalan engineer. Charles married, the next year, Maria Anna of Neuburg, who survived him. Charles, the last male Hapsburg of the Spanish branch, had all the Hapsburg peculiarities developed to their fullest extent. He was melancholy, superstitious, bigoted, inordinately fond of shooting, terrified of witchcraft, and so handicapped by his Austrian jaw that, with increasing age, it became impossible for him to eat solid food. He died in November 1700, and the wars of the Spanish Succession at once ensued.

CHARLES III. : *b.* 1716, *d.* 1788. The most enlightened of the Kings of Spain of the Bourbon dynasty. He was the eldest son of Philip V. and Elizabeth Farnese. He left Spain when sixteen years old to become Duke of Parma, and he left Parma, taking with him most of its art treasures, in 1734 for Palermo, where he was crowned King, and in a victorious campaign defeated the Austrians at Velletri in 1744, and was recognised King of Naples by the Treaty of Aix-la-Chapelle in 1748. In 1759 he was proclaimed King of Spain and resigned Naples and Sicily to his third son, Ferdinand. He married Maria Amalia of Saxony. He was a very great patron of art, besides being a builder on an immense scale; and it is much to his credit that he employed Tiepolo in the palace at

Madrid, and discovered Goya, whom he set to work on the tapestry cartoons. Charles was of a very melancholy disposition and indulged his family enthusiasm for shooting to an exaggerated degree as an antidote to his depression. His appearance was very peculiar—very thin, very gaunt, very untidy and badly dressed, and with a perfectly enormous nose. He had no military tastes—would never wear uniform and hated reviewing. The study of insanity and melancholy in his family is deeply interesting. Philip V., his father, and Ferdinand VI., his stepbrother, were both melancholic to the verge of lunacy. Charles's eldest son had to be set aside from the succession because he was epileptic and an idiot from childhood, while Ferdinand, his third son, whom he left as King of Naples, was designedly never educated, for it was supposed that his mind could never stand the strain. Charles's daughter, Maria Luisa, married the Emperor Leopold II., the brother of Joseph II. and Marie Antoinette. They had sixteen children—among them Francis II., the last Holy Roman Emperor; Ferdinand III. of Tuscany, a very enlightened ruler; the Archduke Charles, a famous soldier; Joseph, the Palatine of Hungary; and the Archduke John, another soldier and a famous philanthropist. Francis II. married, in 1790, his cousin, Maria Theresa, daughter of Ferdinand of Naples. Their children were Marie Louise, wife of Napoleon, and the Emperor Ferdinand I. (1793-1875), an imbecile, who resigned the throne to Franz Josef in 1848 and lived the rest of his life in retirement at Prague. We have therefore many instances of the inheritance of the good and the bad strains in Charles III.; for while imbecility was introduced into the Hapsburgs, and such princes as Charles IV. and Ferdinand VII. of Spain, and Ferdinand I. and Ferdinand II. (Bomba) of Naples were the scandal of their different generations, we have, on the other hand, the good qualities in Charles III. transmitted to such men as the Archdukes Charles and John, the Emperor Francis II., a very able diplomat, and the benevolent and enlightened Grand Dukes of Tuscany.

CHARLES V. : *b.* 1500, *d.* 1558. The most powerful prince since the time of Charlemagne, whose kingdom, won by inheritance and not by conquest, included Spain, the Netherlands, Germany and the Empire, Poland, Milan, Naples and Sicily, Burgundy, and the huge Spanish possessions overseas. We are only concerned here with his last years, and merely state, therefore, that at Brussels on 25th October 1555, in the Hall of the Golden Fleece, he resigned the Netherlands to his son Philip. On 16th January 1556 he resigned the Imperial throne, Spain, Sicily and Burgundy, and on 17th September 1556 he set sail from Flushing, an English fleet from Portland bearing him company down the Channel. On 3rd February 1557 he was installed in his monastic retreat at Yuste in Estremadura, where he lived among the monks, but not as one of them, for, as the *Encyclopædia Britannica* points out : "Gastronomic indiscretions still entailed their inevitable penalties." He died at Yuste, 21st September 1558. This was the period at which Europe was threatened with absolute Hapsburg supremacy. Philip II. was King-Consort of England, and soon after, in 1580, obtained Portugal and all her colonies. Only France and the Venetian Republic were safe from the matrimonial aggrandisements of the Hapsburgs. Their power was broken, however, by the division of their inheritance into two portions, Charles's brother, Ferdinand I., retaining the Empire, and Philip inheriting all the remainder of the Hapsburg possessions.

CHARLES VI. : *b.* 1685, *d.* 1740. The last male Hapsburg Emperor, second son of Leopold I. by his third wife, Eleanora, daughter of Philip William of Neuburg, Elector Palatine of the Rhine. In 1700 he went to Spain to take up the succession which he claimed on the death of Charles II. of Spain, as the senior male Hapsburg. In 1708, at Barcelona, he married Christina of Brunswick-Wolfenbüttel (1691-1750), and in 1711 left Spain and took up the throne of the Roman Empire on the death of his brother, Joseph I. He would never recognise, and neither would the Catalans who supported him, Philip V. as King of Spain. He was the father of the Empress Maria Theresa, and the patron of the architect, Fischer von Erlach.

CHURRIGUERRA, JOSÉ: *b.* Salamanca, 1650, *d.* 1723. The scapegoat of architecture, whose fine Ayuntamiento and Plaza Mayor of Salamanca everybody admires, till they find it is the work of Churriguerra. He was a mild but fluent architect, on whose head has been heaped the blame for the excesses of such men as Pedro Ribera. Besides his work at Salamanca, Churriguerra built several churches and church portals in Madrid, and some twenty miles from that city, for Don Juan de Goyeneche, he built the small palace and the church and entire village of Nuevo Bastan, now the property of the Conde de Saceda. The village has six streets, four squares, a town hall and a prison. Geronimo and Nicolo Churriguerra, the sons of José, completed many of the works begun by their father. The term Churriguerresque, as applied to the wilder and most undisciplined examples of Spanish baroque, is more strictly applicable to architects posterior to, but influenced by, Churriguerra, among whom one can enumerate the family of Garcia de Quinones, Don Pedro de Ribera (the wildest of them all), Tomé Gabilan, Tomas de Jauregui, Jaime Bort, Galuci and Sani (both Italians), Manuel Garcia, Antonio Marcelo Valenciano, Roldan, Narciso Tomés, Lucas and José Blanco, and Alonzo Aleman. As specimens of the style I may mention the façade of S. Cayetano in Zaragoza, the Cathedral of Jaen, Santo Tomas in Madrid, the sacristy of Salamanca Cathedral, the façade of San Marcos in Leon, the Jesuit College and cloister in Salamanca, the great door of the Provincial Hospital in Madrid, the Church of San Martin Pinario in Santiago da Compostella; and, in the way of palaces, the palace of the Marques de Miraflores in Madrid (the work of Don Pedro de Ribera) and the palace of the Marques de Dos Aguas, in Valencia, with its portal by Vergara. There are also buildings in this same manner in Sicily, at Catania (the palace of Prince

Biscari and the monastery of S. Benedetto), and at Messina (before the earthquake destroyed them); at this latter place, more particularly, the Church of S. Gregorio, with the spiral campanile by Calamech, and many buildings, never properly studied yet by any architect, at the towns of Noto, Modica and Ragusa. In addition to these there are the churches and palaces in Apulia, notably at Lecce; and in the island of Malta several churches and palaces and the Auberge de Castile, the architect of which must have known either the convent of S. Benedetto at Catania or the Municipio or Prefettura of Lecce. In Portugal, also, there are buildings of this type, while the style reached to its utmost expression in Mexico, as detailed in Part IV. of this essay.

CIMAROSA, DOMENICO: *b.* Aversa, 1749, *d.* Venice, 1801. He wrote eighty operas in twenty-nine years. In 1781, as a *tour de force*, he brought out two operas in Naples, one in Rome and two in Turin. In 1789 he went to Russia for three years, and whilst there wrote three operas and five hundred several pieces of music. He proceeded thence to Vienna, where he produced his masterpiece, *Il Matrimonio Segreto*, in 1792.

CLOVIO, GIULIO: *b.* Grisone in Croatia, 1498, *d.* Rome, 1578. The most famous—and the last—of illuminators. It was he who, perhaps as a fellow-colonial (for they were both colonial subjects of Venice), sent El Greco to Rome with an introduction to Cardinal Farnese. His most famous work, *The Virgin of the Uffizio*, painted in nine years for Cardinal Alessandro Farnese, in the Royal Library at Naples, disappeared in 1860, but there are works by him in the British Museum, in Paris, in Rome, and in Ravenna.

CONCA, SEBASTIANO: *b.* Gaeta, 1676, *d.* Naples, 1764. The pupil of Solimena, and next to Solimena and di Mura the best Neapolitan painter of the eighteenth century. He painted at Rome, S. Martina and S. Giovanni in Laterano, and at Subiaco. There is a good work by him in Siena, *The*

Probatica, or *Sacred Pool of Siloam*, in the chapel of the Hospital of S. Maria della Scala, and he worked for the chapel at Caserta, and for the Church of S. Chiara at Naples, where there is his best work, the ceiling fresco of David dancing before the Ark.

CORENZIO, BELISARIO : *b.* 1558, *d.* Naples, 1643. A painter of Greek origin. Worked at Naples, plotted with Ribera and Caracciolo against all competition, and was killed by a fall from a scaffolding in the Church of SS. Severino e Sosio at Naples. An able frescoist.

CRESPI, G. M.—"LO SPAGNUOLO": *b.* Bologna, 1665, *d.* 1747. A painter of the late Bolognese school, of the same generation as Guercino and Magnasco. He painted altar-pieces—a very good one is at Ferrara, the Swoon of S. Stanislaus, in the Gesu—and he excelled in caricature.

DINTZENHOFER, KILIAN IGNAZ : *b.* Prague, 1690, *d.* 1752. The foremost member of a famous family of Bohemian architects to whom Prague owes its present appearance, as Vienna does to the work of Hildebrand and Fischer von Erlach. The Dintzenhofer family filled Prague and the lesser Bohemian towns with churches, convents and palaces. Pommersfelden, the seat of the Schönborn family, twelve miles from Bamberg, is the work of Kilian Dintzenhofer.

DOMENICHINO—*real name* ZAMPIERI : *b.* Bologna, 1581, *d.* Naples, 1641. A mild and agreeable Bolognese painter, held by Rubens to be the best painter of his day in Rome. He frescoed the dome of the chapel of the Tesoro in S. Gennaro at Naples, and was poisoned, or worried to death, by the machinations of Ribera, Caracciolo and Belisario Corenzio.

EGIZIELLO—*real name* GIOACCHINO CONTI : *b.* Arpino, 1714, *d.* Rome, 1761. A celebrated soprano. He was called Egiziello after his master, Domenico Gizzi. His début was at Rome in 1729, after seven years' study. He sang in Madrid, Lisbon and London, and retired in 1757. When he first heard Farinelli, in Dr Burney's words, "he was so modest and diffident that he burst into tears and fainted away in despondency." In 1743 he sang in Lisbon, and two years later Charles III. of Spain engaged him and Cafarelli to sing at Madrid in the *Achille in Sciro* of Pergolesi. Cafarelli came to Madrid for this purpose from Poland, and Egiziello from Portugal.

ESCURIAL, THE. Thirty miles from Madrid; built by Philip II. of Spain. The first architect, J. B. de Toledo, died soon after laying the foundation stone, and the work was carried out by Juan de Herrera (1530-1597), but everything was criticised and ordered in detail by Philip himself. By 1584 the building was practically finished, except for the Pantheon, completed in 1654, and some apartments added on and altered by Charles III. The Escurial well merits its appellation of "The Eighth Wonder of the World."

FANSAGA, COSIMO, of Bergamo (1591-1678). Practised as an architect at Naples. He built the half-finished Palazzo Donna Anna on the Mergellina overlooking the sea, the Church of S. Teresa on the Chiaja, the doorway and staircase of the magnificent Palazzo Maddaloni in the Toledo, the Palazzo Stigliano for the Duke of Ossuna, the Porta and Fonta Medina, the Chapel of S. Ignazio in the Gesu Nuovo and, last and most important, he re-designed and carried out the Certosa of San Martino overlooking the city. He also designed the *guglia* of S. Domenico. Fansaga was the chief seventeenth-century Neapolitan architect, as Sanfelice was that of the eighteenth century.

FARNESE, ELIZABETH: *b.* Parma, 1692, *d.* Spain, 1766. She was the daughter and heiress of Odoardo II., Farnese, Duke of Parma. In 1714 she married Philip V. of Spain, as his second wife. Before long she had attained complete mastery over her husband (*vide* CARDINAL ALBERONI). One of her keenest objects was to maintain the Duchy of Parma in her family, and she had the satisfaction of handing this to her son, Charles III., in 1734, and when Charles moved on to Sicily and Naples, to her second son Philip, in whose family the duchy remained down till 1859. After her husband's death, in 1746, she built the palace of Rio Frío, fourteen miles from La Granja, and, surviving him twenty years, was buried with him in the Panteón in the Colegiata of La Granja.

FARINELLI—*real name* CARLO BROSCHI: *b.* Naples, 1705, *d.* Bologna, 1782. Farinelli, the hero of the third part of this book, was the greatest of the *castrati*, and probably the most skilled and beautiful singer who has ever lived. He was taught by the great Porpora, and made his début at Rome in 1722, in Porpora's opera, *Eumene*. He visited Vienna in 1724, 1728 and 1731. It was at Vienna that the Emperor, Charles VI., persuaded him to drop his virtuosity and acquire lyrical perfection. He came to London in 1734, and his success in Porpora's operas caused Handel to leave the stage and concentrate on oratorio. In 1736 he went to Madrid, and his singing cured Philip V. of melancholia. For twenty years he remained in Philip's confidence: he acted as unofficial Prime Minister, was given a salary of 50,000 francs, and was made a Knight of Calatrava, one of the highest Orders of Spanish chivalry. During this time he sang the same four songs every night to the King. Philip's son, Ferdinand VI., was as enthusiastic about Farinelli's art as his father, and retained him in his official appointments; but on the accession of Charles III. Farinelli was pensioned off and withdrew to Bologna, near which town he built a handsome villa. Dr Burney visited him there in the year 1772, and gives a detailed account of his interview in the *Musical Tour*.

FERDINAND IV.: *b.* Portici, 1751, *d.* Naples, 1825. He was the third son of Charles III. and Maria Amalia of Saxony. In 1759, when Charles withdrew from Naples to become King of Spain, he left Ferdinand, a boy of five, as King of Naples under the regency of the Tuscan Minister, Tanucci. Ferdinand was left completely uneducated, and he grew up very slow and stupid, and very lazy. He had the enormous physical strength of the Saxon family, which he inherited from his mother, and he spoke Neapolitan dialect better than Italian or Spanish. He married Maria Carolina, the daughter of the Empress Maria Theresa, a capricious and wicked woman. From 1806 till 1815 Ferdinand retired to Sicily, and when he came back, after Napoleon's fall, he dropped the title of Ferdinand IV. and called himself Ferdinand I. of the Two Sicilies. Charles IV. of Spain (1748-1819) was his elder brother, and they never met from 1759 till 1817, when Charles was in exile, but the dying wish to see his brother expressed by Charles could not cut short Ferdinand's day of shooting. Ferdinand remains one of the favourite tyrants of historians; but it is only fair to add that every English traveller who met him commented on the charm of his manner and on his fine presence. His physical appearance is very closely paralleled in Goya's portraits of his brother, Charles IV., and this is particularly to be observed at Capodimonte, near Naples, where a portrait of Charles by Goya hangs, not far from the big group of Ferdinand and his children, by Angelica Kauffmann, a feeble painter, but even she was unable to avoid the proportion of his Bourbon nose.

FERDINAND VI.: 1713-1759. Second son of Philip V. of Spain by his first wife, Maria Louisa of Savoy. He married, in 1729, Maria Magdalena Barbara, Infanta of Portugal. Her homely looks, on their first meeting, caused him a visible shock. When complimented on his shooting, Ferdinand replied: "It would be hard if there were not something I could do." Shooting and music were his only pleasures, and he was the most fervent patron of the art of Farinelli. In the course of years he became devoted to his wife, and when she died, in 1758, he was distracted with grief, would not even dress, but wandered unshaven and unwashed, in a night-gown, about his park. He became King of Spain in 1746 on the death of his father, Philip V.

Giordano, Luca: *b.* Naples, 1632, *d.* Naples, 1705. The greatest frescoist and extempore painter of the school of Naples. Works by him are in every gallery in Europe. He went to Spain in 1690, and returned to Naples in 1702 in possession of a great fortune. Full details of his career are given in the body of the book.

Granja, La. A palace seven miles from Segovia, built for Philip V. in 1721-1723 by C. Ardemans from the designs of Juvara and Sacchetti. The Colegiata, or palace-chapel, has a marble altar designed and sculptured by Solimena, with the Panteón, or chapel, in which are buried Philip V. and Elizabeth Farnese. The famous gardens of La Granja have fountains more powerful than those of Versailles, by the Frenchmen Thierry and Frémin. The whole of the site of three hundred and fifty acres for these gardens had to be levelled down or built up on the precipitous hillside 3800 feet above the sea, which Philip chose for this luxurious retreat. The palace here, now unfortunately nearly destroyed by a fire, was finer in its decoration than Aranjuez, as it was less spoilt by additions of the Empire period.

Greco, El, Domenico Theotocopuli: *b.* Candia, Crete, about 1547, *d.* Toledo, 1614. By 1570 Greco was in Venice, where he is said to have worked in Titian's studio, and in the same year Giulio Clovio (*q.v.*) sent him with a letter of introduction to Cardinal Farnese at Rome. About 1575 Greco left Rome and proceeded to Spain, hoping, no doubt, to make his fortune there, as many other Italian painters were doing. By 1577 he was painting eight pictures for the Church of S. Domingo el Antiguo at Toledo, and in the same year he painted the famous picture of the *Expolio* for the cathedral there. In 1580 Greco painted the *S. Maurice* for the Escurial, but it did not meet with the approval of Philip II., and he obtained no more commissions for the Escurial. *The Burial of Count Orgaz* belongs to the same years as the *S. Maurice*. Greco's most effective work belongs to his last years, from about 1600 onwards, to which period belong the *Laocoön*, the two landscapes of Toledo, and *The Opening of the Seven Seals*. Greco executed a few works of sculpture, but there is nothing of great importance left by him, for his largest work, the two tombs, with life-size statues, of Don Gedeón de Hinojosa, Minister of the Council of the Chamber of Castile and of the Council of the Chamber of the Indies, who died in 1595, and his wife, Catalina Velasco, both of which were in the convent of the Discalced Franciscans at Illescas, perished when the convent was destroyed. His son, Jorge Manuel, an architect and an indifferent painter in his father's manner, died in 1631. The poets Paravicino and Gongora both addressed sonnets to Greco — a fact which proves that he had the sympathy of the men of culture of his day.

GUARINO GUARINI: *b.* Modena, 1624, *d.* Milan, 1683. Guarini, with Juvara, are the two most successful followers of the style of Borromini. Like Juvara, Guarini worked chiefly at Turin for the House of Savoy. He had previously studied his art in Rome, where he had been made a Theatine monk in 1641. At Turin his best works were the Chapel of the Sudario at the Duomo, the Theatine Church of S. Lorenzo, San Filippo Neri, the palace of Prince Philibert of Savoy, and the Palazzo Carignano. He also built two churches, and stayed for a considerable period, in Paris. His drawings were published at Turin in 1737, long after his death, by the Theatine monks.

HILDEBRAND, JOHANN LUCAS: *b.* Genoa, 1660, *d.* 1750. One of the leading baroque architects of the Empire. He built in Vienna the palace of Prince Eugene of Savoy, and also that of Prince Wenceslaus Kaunitz, and he worked a great deal for the Emperor Charles VI.

JUVARA, FILIPPO: *b.* Messina, 1685, *d.* Madrid, 1736. Juvara and Guarini (*q.v.*) were the most competent architects who followed the manner of Borromini. Juvara became a priest and studied in Rome under Carlo Fontana (the designer of the palace on Isola Bella in Lake Maggiore, and of the Liechstenstein palace at Vienna). He worked chiefly at Turin for Vittorio Amadeo II. of Savoy, for whom he built the palaces of Veneria Reale and Stupinigi, and the huge mass of the Superga that overlooks Turin. He visited Portugal, but, although loaded with presents, his plan for the palace-convent of Mafra was not accepted by João V. His last work was a model for the new palace at Madrid, to be 1700 feet square, 100 feet high, with a courtyard 700 × 400 feet. He died at Madrid in 1736, having recommended his pupil, Sacchetti, to Philip V., as the best living architect to complete the new palace. Juvara's palace at Madrid, had it been proceeded with, would have been the most magnificent in Europe, with its chapels, gardens, theatre and dependencies. His wooden model for it is still preserved at Madrid.

Lanfranco, Giovanni: *b.* Parma, 1581, *d.* Rome, 1647. Painter of the Bolognese school. Worked in Naples at the Certosa di S. Martino, at the SS. Apostoli, at the Gesu, and at the Cathedral of S. Gennaro.

Lecce. Of Lecce, that is so fully and ably described in Mr Martin Shaw Briggs' book, *In the Heel of Italy* (Andrew Melrose, 1910), it is very difficult to know what to say in the space of a few lines; so let me dive into the matter at once and say that for sheer beauty and gaiety there are few buildings of any period that can compare with the Prefettura and the Seminario. This first building, formerly a Celestine convent, is the work of the architect Zimbalo, who also put up the statue of S. Oronzo, and built the great church of the Rosario. Cino, the pupil of Zimbalo, built the Seminario (1694-1709), the Sacramento and the Carmine, and probably the façade of the Church of S. Nicolo e Cataldo, just outside the walls. M. S. Briggs divides the late buildings into three groups: those commenced by Charles V. (1539-1549), the churches built from 1575 to 1600, and the fully fledged art of 1660-1720. A visit to the interior of one church is enough; their interiors are all the same—huge altars with twisted pillars, the coils of which are swarming with *amorini* all carved in a friable white pumice-like stone, and no pictures to speak of. It is entirely an art of façade at Lecce, and every effect their architects got was made more telling by the stone—the local Leccese stone—of a lovely golden colour, that is as soft as clay when it is quarried, so that it may be carved into any shape, and then in the space of a few days the stone hardens and age gives it gradually the yellow tone that one must ever afterwards associate in one's mind with Lecce.

It is difficult to choose between buildings that are so good each in their own and yet in a similar way as the Prefettura and the Seminario: yet of these two I would single out the Prefettura for preference, and my choice is decided by the dazzling beauty of the Church of Santa Croce, to which the Prefettura is tacked straight on. This church was begun in 1549 and never finished till 1697, and the chief feature in its façade is a really magnificent rose-window. I can attempt no description of the façade, but the photograph in these pages gives some idea of its appearance. The moment when one first comes into this piazza and sees the church and the Prefettura in front of one is unforgettable; it is such a harmony as one would never think possible of achievement except in music. The Seminario, on the other hand, is almost as superb in its way with the square it stands in, composed of the cathedral, the campanile and the bishop's palace, or Vescovado. Any town in the world would be exceptional in the possession of two buildings of this nature, but there is yet another, the Municipio, another ex-convent, which is nearly as good, except that it is marred by bad position, being on a kind of island site where it is difficult to get a good view of it.

Palaces, mostly rather on the small side, are innumerable, and there is no space here to mention them by name. Other churches, to the number of twenty or twenty-five, deserve a visit, but I can only name here the Carmine, the Gesu and the Rosario, which has a great cloister by Cino, and on the façade of the church huge stone bowls of flowers and fruit at which great stone birds are pecking, while just outside the town is the Church of S. Nicola e Cataldo, standing in the middle of a beautiful garden.

Near Lecce there are small towns full of the same architectural character. There are, for example, Galatina and Soleto, which stand two miles apart and about twelve miles from Lecce, both of which towns I have visited. Soleto has a really fine campanile built about 1400, with a cupola of glazed tiles added in later days, and both Soleto and Galatina have that extraordinary and blinding whiteness which seems to be the note of all the towns, save Lecce itself, in Apulia. Gallipoli, like a smaller Syracuse, is on an island, and has a cathedral with a good front, difficult to see because of the narrow street, with large pictures by Malinconico and the Verrio family inside. Copertino, Sternatia, and especially Nardo, are other places full of churches, three or four in each of them, and a piazza complete with the *guglia* of some saint, at the latter. But over and above these villages, and not including Otranto and Taranto (yet another Syracuse), there are places in Apulia not mentioned even by M. S. Briggs and, so far as I know, never yet visited by anyone competent to draw or describe them. Oria, for example, the legendary place of origin of the world-famous Doria family, and Francavilla, Gravina, Ostuni and Manduria, all these four considerable towns are known to contain palaces and churches innumerable. Lecce is, in itself, fuller of beauty than any place I have ever reached, except Venice, and round it in such towns as those mentioned there must be a whole gold-mine for eyes that appreciate the subtle beauty of this southern architecture. It can never be stressed too much that in this part of Italy, some two hundred and fifty miles from Naples, you are, as it were, in another country from Naples or from Rome. It is as different as Portugal is from Spain. The Leccese nobles, many of them rich families, with motor cars waiting in the courtyards of their palaces, never go to Naples as the capital of their country. They all must have visited Rome some time in their lives, but it is to Bari and to Foggia that they look for the opera season and the balls at which they present their daughters. To many people, and more especially to classical scholars, Apulia and the Gulf of Taranto have been dead since the days of Horace; to enthusiasts of a later date these regions became a desert at the death of Cassiodorus or, at latest, with the fall of the Hohenstaufen. But although it is true that from Taranto, for the two hundred and ninety miles' journey to Reggio, opposite Messina, there is a frightful and appalling waste, with but few signs of the local and very malarious inhabitants, yet Apulia, and indeed the whole country between Bari and Taranto, is full of the traces of a civilisation that has not yet been dead a century and a half. The architecture of these towns forms a link between the Italian and the late Spanish buildings, but has yet a character distinct from either, being more cheerful than the Roman and less delirious than the Spanish. Only at two places outside Apulia is the like to be seen—at Catania, in the convent of S. Benedetto, and at Malta, in the Auberge de Castile, for both these buildings show that their architects must have visited Lecce and set eyes on the Prefettura and the Seminario. Particularly remarkable, as I have said, are the country towns round Lecce, with their dazzling white walls and shrill green spring vegetables (a spring which arrives three times over, for they have three crops a year), and it is in this country that Pulcinella was a familiar and overbearing figure down to modern times, for up till 1860 the Apulian brigands always went about their business masked and beaked in this disguise. The music in this country must have been wonderful in the seventeenth and eighteenth centuries; and Dr Burney, in his *Musical Tour*, mentions the excellence of the Leccese folk-songs that he heard sung at Naples, and also comments on the fact that most of the *castrati* were obtained from Apulia, presumably because there were numerous good singers there, and because the manufacture of these *virtuosi*—a practice stringently forbidden by law—was carried out more easily so far away from the capital of the kingdom. I can only say of Lecce in conclusion that no lover of Renaissance architecture can satisfy his curiosity after perfection until he has visited this small town and become dazed by its bewildering plethora of beauty ; for Apulia is like a newly discovered appendix to Italy and Spain, and no journey can be too long that leads one to such a display of the art of the Latins.

MAFRA. The palace-monastery of the Portuguese kings, some twelve miles from Cintra. A full account may be found in Walter Crum Watson's *Portuguese Architecture* (Constable, 1908), and in Fra João di S. Joseph do Prado's *Monumento Sacro di Mafra* (Lisboa, 1751). João V., the spendthrift, vowed, if a son was born to him, to build the largest and richest monastery in the country on the site of the poorest. The foundation stone was laid on 17th November 1717, this ceremony alone costing upwards of £40,000. As a rule 14,700 workmen were employed, but when the works were hurried on to completion between June and October of 1730, 45,000 men worked on the building and 1266 oxen were bought to haul the heavy stones. The architect chosen, after Juvara's plan had been rejected, was Frederic Ludovici or Ludwig, a German from Ratisbon. The church was dedicated in 1730, and the hospital, built to accommodate the sick workmen, cost 92,000,000 reis—about £20,000. The works of the clock, chimes and bells were ordered in Holland, but the manufacturers refused to supply them, fearing that the kingdom of Portugal could not bear the expense. João V. wrote back saying that he had made a mistake in the order and that he wished twice the expense to be incurred, and with this letter he prepaid all expenses. On the day of dedication, the King's birthday, and for a week after, all comers were entertained by the King, there being nine thousand guests on the first day alone (Murray's *Handbook*, 1887).

The palace may be divided, says Mr Crum Watson, into two main parts: one to the east (560 × 350 feet) built round a large square court and devoted to the monks, containing the refectory, chapter-house, kitchen, a huge library and cells for two hundred and eighty brothers. The other and more extensive part to the west comprises the King's apartments to the south, the Queen's to the north, and between them the church. The dimensions of the whole, 290,000 square feet, rival the 300,000 square feet of the Escurial. The refectory, 160 feet long, has beautiful hanging brass lamps, and, for tables, splendid slabs of Brazil wood. The library, 200 feet long, is one side secular and one side religious, with a separate space for the books of each different country. The inside of the church is of white marble, with pilasters of pink marble, and the altar-pieces are by Trevisani (1656-1746). Finally, there are two towers 350 feet high, and a flat roof on which 10,000 men could be reviewed, presumably as a warning to the Martians. The clocks in the towers are set in motion by immense cylinders covered with spikes, there being upwards of 200 tons of metal in each tower. The palace is now deserted, only one hall, the *camera de audiencia*, being preserved as it was in the time of Don João; but Beckford in his letters gives a magnificent description of the place when it was still swarming with courtiers and ecclesiastics. The architect Ludovici built only one other edifice of importance, the Capella Mor, at Evora, 1717-1746.

MENGS, RAPHAEL: *b.* Aussig, Bohemia, 1728, *d.* Rome, 1779. He studied first at Dresden and then at Rome under Conca. In 1757 he painted his famous fresco of Mount Parnassus in the Villa Albani at Rome, and in 1761 he went to Spain for Charles III. and painted the fresco of the Graces in the King's ante-chamber, and Aurora in the Queen's apartment, in the palace at Madrid. He then returned to Rome for three years, but went back once more to Madrid in 1773, when he painted the Apotheosis of Trajan on the ceiling of the great saloon of the palace. The art of Mengs typifies the classical reaction of Winckelmann and Lessing which was to produce Canova and, perhaps, Alfieri; he was the determined opponent of Tiepolo and tried to influence, unsuccessfully, the King's mind against the Venetian painter.

It is said of Mengs that his frescoes are better than his paintings; yet his pastels at Dresden are as good as Rosalba's, and his portraits of the Bourbons at the Prado are certainly no worse than those to be seen in Italian galleries by Batoni or Alessandro Longhi.

MURA, FRANCESCO DI: *b.* (?), *d.* 1743. Known as Franceschiello. He was the chief pupil of Solimena and worked, in fresco, in the churches of S. Chiara, S. Maria Annunziata and the Carmine, at Naples. His best works are the frescoes at S. Severino e Sosio at Naples and the rooms which he painted at the Royal palace at Turin, about 1730, with the Olympic games and the achievements of Achilles. A most prolific and successful frescoist, who, had he worked more in private houses and less in churches, would not be far behind Tiepolo in the popular estimation. Townshend, in *A Tour through Spain* (London, 1788, p. 254), says there are some tolerable paintings by di Mura in the Church of S. Francisco de Sales at Madrid, and it is this same church that contains the monuments by the Italian Sabatini, to Ferdinand VI. and his wife, Barbara of Portugal; for Ferdinand, and his father, Philip V., who is buried in the Colegiata at La Granja, are the only kings of Spain not interred in the Pantheon at the Escurial. There are paintings, or frescoes, by di Mura to be seen in nearly every church in Naples, and the traveller soon learns to distinguish his peculiar style, which is very pleasing, with its rapidity and fullness. A peculiarity in his work is the amount of green that he uses, chiefly in the costumes of his characters. There is an excellent picture by di Mura over the door in the sacristy of the Certosa di S. Martino at Naples, and a fine sketch for his chief picture over the organ in the Church of S. Chiara at Naples is to be seen in the picture gallery at the monastery of La Cava, near Salerno.

NOTO is a town of some twenty-five thousand inhabitants, which is twenty-one miles, by rail, south of Syracuse, in Sicily. This town is of peculiar interest in the study of late southern architecture, as it was refounded and almost entirely rebuilt in 1703, after the great and appalling earthquake of 1693. I can only describe the town as it appeared in the course of a day's visit from Syracuse. Coming up from the station, about a mile from the town, you enter a long straggling street and come through an archway of about 1820 into the town. Just at this point the fine buildings begin. There is a convent on the right of the road, with magnificent carved windows, the top series of which have no rooms behind them, but give direct on to the blue sky, and there must be some kind of a roof garden just below them. Across the road there is another fine convent of the same type, and all the windows in these two buildings have splendid iron grilles. The street now leads straight on into the piazza, where the Duomo stands at the top of a fine flight of steps. This piazza is laid out with clipped trees, and on the lower side of the square there stands the Municipio, a good building of slightly later date, with arcades and much balustrading. Next door to the cathedral is one of the chief palaces of Noto, and it was here that the Bourbon kings were lodged when they visited this town. Noto, indeed, was popular with them, and in 1837, after some disturbances, they made Noto capital of the province instead of Syracuse, while the title Count of Noto still remains in the family of the Neapolitan Bourbons. The main street leads straight on past the cathedral and past more palaces to the huge church of the Benedictines. But in a narrow steep lane leading uphill from this main street, and running past the corner of the palace where Ferdinand and Bomba used to lodge, is the best building in Noto and one of the most extraordinary in Sicily or Southern Italy. This is a palace in the golden stone of which everything in Noto is built; its balconies are carved with such detail and such deep cutting that they have the crumbling gold appearance you only get on a *cassone* or a *torciere*. There is a central doorway and on each side of this are four sets of windows. The first that you come to has five supports, like all the others, and each one of these represents a galloping and winged horse, while the next window shows five Chinamen, the one after that five saints, and the last before the doorway five sea-monsters, and all of these are repeated over again in the same order on the other side of the doorway. Above the stone-work each window has beaten-iron balconies ending with a carnation or a passion flower at each corner, like those to be seen in Syracuse. At the top of this lane there is another street parallel to the main one, and on each side of this there are more palaces, to the number of six or eight, all of which have truly magnificent balconies with the boldest ironwork imaginable.

Such is the town of Noto, in a bald and necessarily un-detailed description, but there are two more towns to the south where the characteristics of Noto are still further improved upon by a larger and more wealthy population. These two towns are Modica, thirty-five miles away, with sixty thousand inhabitants, and the double town of Ragusa, with a like population, some fifteen miles beyond Modica. These I have not visited, but they are described in Mr Douglas Sladen's *Sicily—the New Winter Resort* (Methuen, 1905). According to Mr Sladen, Modica has three splendid churches—S. Giorgio Grande, S. Giovanni and S. Pietro—all of which are at the heads of huge flights of stone stairs. Ragusa Superiore has the Duomo of S. Giovanni on a terrace above the town, while the Church of S. Giorgio, in Ragusa Inferiore, is another of these churches at the top of a staircase. From the little that I saw of Noto I can express my conviction that Modica and Ragusa must be worth an arduous journey to see, for they should contain as much architectural character as Lecce. Mr Sladen does not mention any palaces in these two towns, but they are certain to be there, and in greater profusion than at Noto, while the characteristic points of Noto architecture, the blank windows in masking screen walls, the superb balconies, and the huge flights of steps leading up to the terraces on which the churches are built, all these features would be improved upon and carried to their highest perfection. Except for Mr Sladen's book there is no other I know of, old or new, that even mentions these three towns, but it is obvious that they would repay investigation, like the buildings of Apulia that Mr Martin Shaw Briggs has written upon. At Ragusa and Modica it is not only the late buildings that are of interest; in both towns there is a great deal of Gothic, in a manner peculiar to these two places. At Noto and, doubtless, at Ragusa and Modica, the churches are, like those in Apulia, singularly disappointing and uninteresting inside, and the same applies, no doubt, to the palaces, which will have been redecorated when each generation married. In this part of the world it is the exterior beauty that is aimed at; it is upon the sun and the strong blue air that they rely for their effects. On a wet day all the beauty goes, but so it would do in a theatre if the rain came in through a broken roof and all the lighting went wrong. On a fine day, however—and there must be at least three hundred of such days in every year—Noto is one of the most beautifully built towns in Europe, and this remote little place on the confines of civilisation comes out in the memory, like Würzburg and Nymphenburg, as one of the finest achievements of an age which produced Mozart and Tiepolo.

PAISIELLO, GIOVANNI: *b.* Taranto, 1741, *d.* Naples, 1816. He wrote fifty operas in twelve years. From 1776 he lived eight years in Russia on a huge salary from the Empress Catherine. He produced *The Barber of Seville* there in 1776. Paisiello was the last of the old Neapolitan *opera buffa* composers before the advent of a fresh kind of genius, Rossini.

PHILIP II. OF SPAIN: *b.* 1527, *d.* 1599. The son of the Emperor Charles V. and Isabella, daughter of Emanuel the Great of Portugal, by his wife the Infanta Maria, daughter of Ferdinand and Isabella the Catholic. In 1556-1557 Charles V. renounced the throne and divided the Hapsburg dominions between his son Philip and his own brother, Ferdinand I. Unfortunately he allowed the Netherlands to go, with Spain, to Philip—a fatal piece of policy, as it concentrated all the energy of the Spaniards into the Netherlands, so far away and difficult of access. But for this, Philip's policy would have been the pacification of the Mediterranean and the defeat of the Turks, with probably a continuation of his father's policy of subduing Tunis and North Africa. In 1565 Philip began building the Escurial, a process over which he exercised the most careful supervision, and it was within the walls of the Escurial that he passed most of the latter part of his life.

PHILIP V. OF SPAIN : *b.* Versailles, 1683, *d.* La Granja, 1746. He was the son of the Dauphin Louis of France and his wife, Maria Anna, daughter of Ferdinand Maria, Elector of Bavaria. He was brought up at the Court of his grandfather, Louis XIV., under the title of Duc D'Anjou. In 1700, when Charles II. of Spain died, Louis XIV. promoted his grandson's accession to the throne, and Philip proceeded to Spain, where he fought various campaigns against his rival, Charles of Austria, and married, in 1702, Maria Louisa of Savoy. She died in 1714, and in the same year Philip married Elizabeth Farnese. Luis I. and Ferdinand VI. were the children of the first marriage, Charles III. and Philip, Duke of Parma, of the second. Philip was profoundly melancholic and in 1724 retired from the throne in favour of his son Luis I., but Luis died in seven months and Philip again became king. He had a great love of building and was a fervent collector of works of art. He built the palaces of La Granja and Aranjuez, and began the rebuilding of the palace at Madrid. Towards the end of his life Philip's melancholy became merged into madness, and it was only the soothing genius of Farinelli that was any solace to him. He died in 1746 and is buried, with Elizabeth Farnese, his second wife, in the Colegiata of La Granja.

PIAZZETTA, G. B. : *b.* Venice, 1682, *d.* 1754. Painter of the Venetian school, who was influenced mainly by Guercino and by G. M. Crespi of Bologna. He frescoed the cupola of a chapel in S. Giovanni e Paolo of Venice. His best work is the Beheading of John the Baptist in S. Giovanni at Padua. Large numbers of his drawings are preserved, and he excelled in book illustration, his chief works in this genre being drawings for the *Gerusalemme Liberata* and for the ten-volume edition of Bossuet's works. Besides these he executed many small vignettes and frontispieces—as, for example, the frontispiece to Algarotti's *Il Newtonianismo per le dame*, nearly all of which were published, with the two works mentioned, by his friend Albrizzi, the Venetian publisher.

PORPORA, NICOLO: *b.* Naples, 1686, *d.* Naples, 1766. Opened vocal school at Naples in 1712 and became the greatest singing teacher of his age. Among his pupils were Farinelli, Porporino, Cafarelli and Senesino. In 1721 he became *chamber-virtuoso* to the Prince of Hesse-Darmstadt. From 1729 he produced several operas in London in opposition to Handel. From 1745 he stayed three years in Venice, for part of which time Haydn was his pupil. From 1748-1751 he lived in Dresden, returning to Naples for the last years of his life in 1755. He wrote fifty-three operas and much chamber and church music.

RIBERA, GIUSEPPE—SPAGNOLETTO: *b.* Jativa (Valencia), 1588, *d.* Naples, 1656. The greatest of the Naturalisti painters and a disciple of Caravaggio. He worked chiefly in Naples, but his works may be seen in Spain, at Salamanca, and in the Prado.

RENI, GUIDO: *b.* near Bologna, 1575, *d.* 1645. Guido left Bologna in 1602 and lived for twenty years in Rome, when he returned and opened a school in Bologna. He worked in Naples a year or two before his death, painting three pictures for S. Filippo Neri and a large unfinished *Nativity* for the Certosa of S. Martino. There is a good picture, *Ulysses and Nausicaa*, by Guido, in the picture gallery at Naples.

SACCHETTI, G. B.: *b.* Turin, (?), *d.* Madrid, 1764. Chosen to build the palace at Madrid after the death of Juvara. This was begun on his plan in 1737 and is of granite, of nine floors, 100 to 150 feet high. He also completed the palace of San Ildefonso near Segovia, which had been begun on the plans of Juvara.

SANFELICE, FERDINANDO: *b.* Montagna, 1675, *d.* 1750? An architect who left his mark on Naples, as Fischer von Erlach did on Vienna. He excelled in designing palaces, and his especial forte was the construction of double staircases, many of which still exist at Naples, but have been neglected by architects for the last century and a half. Staircases by Sanfelice may still be seen at the Palazzo Majo and the Palazzo Serra Cassano (the finest of all). Other fine works by him are the staircase in the monastery of San Giovanni e Carbonara, with its library in the form of a star over a bastion, the Palazzo Monteleone, and the huge Palazzo Sanfelice built for his own residence, with two huge flying staircases. Outside Naples, at Pizzofalcone, he built the Palazzo Serra, with a fine stair and splendid apartments. He was painter and poet as well as architect, and was the pupil and friend of Solimena, who painted two rooms of the Sanfelice palace with frescoes, now covered over and forgotten about.

SENESINO, FRANCESCO: *b.* Siena, 1680, *d.* 1750. He sang in Dresden in 1719. Handel heard him there and engaged him for London, where for fifteen seasons he was the popular idol in all Handel's operas. In 1735 he returned to Siena. In London he was preferred to Farinelli.

SOLIMENA, FRANCESCO—called L'ABATE CICCIO: *b.* Nocera di Pagani, 1657, *d.* Naples, 1747. Solimena studied under Francesco di Maria and Giacomo del Po. After the death of Luca Giordano he was considered the ablest painter and frescoist of his day. Like Luca Giordano he was the master of many styles and would paint in the manner of Guido, Carlo Maratta, Pietro da Cortona, Lanfranco or Calabrese. He painted not only history and portraits, but still-life, landscapes, animals and architectural pieces. He had a famous school, the scholars from which were the last distinguished painters of Naples. He worked enormously at Naples, and there are other great works by him at Monte Cassino. His easel-pictures can be seen at Dresden and, best of all, in the collection of Count Harrach at Vienna. The authorities say that his " greatest performance "—and what a performance it is—is the huge fresco of the Last Supper in the refectory of the Conventuali at Assisi. To find Conca at Siena, and Solimena at Assisi, such is the continuity of Italian tradition. He died, immensely wealthy and aged ninety, at his villa near Portici.

STANZIONE, MASSIMO : *b.* Naples, 1585, *d.* Naples, 1656. Painted much in fresco, notably at the Certosa di S. Martino and in S. Gennaro at Naples.

SYRACUSE. I mention Syracuse because of its Piazza del Duomo, which is, as M. S. Briggs says, one of the best places in which to look upon baroque art. There is a superb façade to the cathedral, and the Municipio, the Palazzo Bosco, the Archivescovado and the Church of S. Lucia complete the points of interest in this square and give it superb beauty. All these buildings are in a lovely orange-gold stone. There are other fine palaces on the island, and the best features in all of them are the balconies—not for the carving of the supports, as I stressed upon in describing Noto, but for their magnificent beaten-ironwork, with hammered flowers at each corner. On the mainland there is the Church of S. Lucia al Borgo, with a sunken octagonal church near by, both with good seventeenth-century features, and the former church contains an interesting but fearfully damaged altar-piece by Caravaggio.

TIEPOLO, G. B. : *b.* Venice, 1692, *d.* Madrid, 1769 ? 1770 ? Painter and frescoist, in both of which arts he excelled every other Italian painter of his age. His best frescoes are the following :—Udine, Palazzo Vescovile ; Venice, Palazzo Labia, Palazzo Rezzonico, and Church of Gesuati ; Bergamo, Cappella Colleoni ; Milan, Palazzo Clerici ; Würzburg, Bavaria, the Bishop's Schloss ; Madrid, the Royal Palace ; and Aranjuez, some altar-pieces in the Convento di San

Pascual. Tiepolo was held in high esteem in his day; he refused, on the plea of insufficient payment, or was refused for asking too much, an offer to fresco a large hall in the King of Sweden's palace at Stockholm, but worked for a huge salary in Würzburg, and spent the last eight years of his life in Spain in the service of Charles III. He had finished the throne-room and two ante-rooms in the palace at Madrid and was about to begin his designs for work at the Orangery at Aranjuez when death overtook him. His son Domenico, mentioned in Part I. of this essay, was born in 1734 and died in 1804. There are altar-pieces by Tiepolo, his last works, still to be seen in the Conventual Church of San Pascual Baylon at Aranjuez, while, in the convent attached to this, there is reputed to be a large picture of the Last Supper, but strict *clausura* is in force and in consequence no one has been able to set eyes upon it. *Cf.* Molmenti's *Tiepolo.*

VANVITELLI, LUIGI: *b.* Naples, 1700, *d.* Caserta, 1773. Son of the painter, Gaspare van Vitel of Utrecht. He worked as an architect in Rome and Loreto, where he built the lofty campanile with a pyramid to the palace built by Benedict XIV. His chief works are at Naples—the Church of S. Maria Annunziata, and the Palazzo Casacalenda in the Largo S. Domenico; but outside Naples, for Charles III., he built the palace of Caserta (*q.v.*), the greatest building feat of its age in Europe. Vanvitelli reintroduced a sober and solid classicism, which is yet too early and too natural to be styled a classical revival. A striking instance of his ingenuity is the sunk garden in the court of the convent of S. Marcellino, at Naples. Vanvitelli's sons were also architects and painters, and one of them painted the existing ceiling in the opera house of S. Carlo at Naples.

VERRIO, ANTONIO: *b.* Lecce, 1639, *d.* Hampton Court, 1707. He painted frescoes at Windsor between 1676 and 1681 for Charles II., and others at Hampton Court and Burleigh. His best works are at Chatsworth. Verrio accumulated a large fortune and died a very rich man.

Bibliography

No attempt is made in these brief notes at a complete bibliography of every book consulted in the making of these pages. I give only the few most important modern authorities, and those books of the seventeenth and eighteenth centuries most likely to interest students of the period under discussion. Owing to the small scope of this bibliography no alphabetical order is attempted.

Modern Authorities

Martin Shaw Briggs : *In the Heel of Italy.* London, 1910.

F. Sylvester Baxter : *Spanish Colonial Architecture.* Boston, U.S.A., 1901.

(*Cf.* Introduction.)

F. Dies Barroso : *El Arte en la Nueva España.* Campania de Artes Graficas. Mexico, 1922.

(*Cf.* Introduction.)

Constantin Uhde : *Baudenkmaler in Spanien und Portugal.* Ernst Wasmuth Verlag. Berlin.

August L. Mayer : *Alt-Spanien.* Delphin Verlag. Munich, 1921.

Otto Schubert : *Geschichte des Barock en Spanien.* Paul Neff Verlag. Esslingen, 1908.

H. Baerlein : Preface to Calderon de la Barca's *Life in Mexico* in " Everyman " edition. London.

François Rousseau : *Régne de Charles III. d'Espagne.*

(An excellent history of Charles III.)

Louis La Baume and William Booth Papin : *Picturesque Architecture of Mexico.* Boston.

Bibliography

MANUEL G. REVILLA: *El Arte en Mexico.* Mexico, 1893. *The Architectural Record,* vol. xxxvii., January to June, 1915, p. 534.
(Article on Mexican Architecture.)

MADAME CALDERON DE LA BARCA: *Life in Mexico.* "Everyman" series.

W. LÜBKE and M. SEMRAU: *Der Kunst der Barockzeit.* Stuttgart, 1905.

ANDRÉ MICHEL: *Histoire de l'Art,* vol. iv., part ii., pp. 855-869.
(For illustrations of the "Manoeline" buildings in Portugal.)

JOSE N. DA FONSECA: *An Historical Sketch of the City of Goa.* Bombay, 1878.
(The only competent history and guide to Goa.)

C. A. MONTALTO DE JESUS: *Historic Macao.* Hong-Kong, 1902.
(The only history of Macao.)

A. DANVILA JALDERO: *La Architettura Churrigueresqua in Historia y Arte.* Madrid, April 1896.
(Contains interesting information of the architects in question.)

R. M. JOHNSTON: *The Napoleonic Empire in Southern Italy and the Rise of the Secret Societies.* London, 1904.
(Page 12 *et seq.* for an account of the condition and numbers of the clergy in this kingdom at the close of the eighteenth century.)

KARL EUGEN SCHMIDT: *Das Spanischen Versailles in Weite Welt,* vol. xxii., pp. 950-956. Leipzig, 1902.

R. CUNNINGHAME GRAHAM: *A Vanished Arcadia—The Jesuits in Paraguay, 1607-1767.* London, 1901.
(The best authority on this subject.)

W. H. KOEBEL: *In Jesuit Land.* With an Introduction by R. Cunninghame Graham. London, 1912.

T. P. TERRY: *Terry's Guide to Mexico.* Ed. 1923.
(Excellent and comprehensive, with special notes on Mexican architecture.)

Bibliography

GENARO GARCIA and ANTONIO CORTES: *La Architectura en Mexico.* Museo National de Arquælogia. Mexico, 1914.

(Contains fine photographs of Mexican churches.)

BOOKS PUBLISHED BEFORE 1860

L. VANVITELLI: *Dichiarazione dei Disegni del Reale Palazzo di Caserta.* Napoli, 1756.

(With numerous fine plans and engravings from the designs of Vanvitelli.)

BIBBIENA: *Archittettura i Prospettive.* Augsburg, 1740.

(With dedication to, and portrait of, the Emperor Charles VI., patron of Farinelli.)

FRA FRANCISCO DE LOS SANTOS: *Descripcion breve del Monasterio di S. Lorenzo del Escorial.* Madrid, 1657.

(A panegyric—if ever there was one—in Gongoristic prose.)

Also *Descripcion de las pinturas al fresco del R. Mon. del Escor*: for Luca Giordano's frescoes. Madrid, 1695.

(A description very much at one with Giordano's frescoes.)

(*Cf.* the English translation of the former by G. Thompson. London, 1760.)

FRA JOÃO DI S. JOSEPH DO PRADO: *Monumento Sacro di Mafra.* Lisboa, 1751.

(Another panegyric, but this belongs to a more sober age.)

MARC ANTONIO DEL RE: *Ville di Delizia, o siano campareccі nello stato di Milano, divise in sei tomi con espressive le piante, é diverse vedute nelle medesime*; vol. i., Milano, 1727; vols. ii. and iii., Milano, 1743.

(The best contemporary book on Italian seventeenth- and eighteenth-century villas.)

ESTERHAZA: *Excursion á Esterhaz en Hongrie.* Vienna, 1784.

(A very entertaining book.)

MATTHAEUS DANIEL POEPPELMANN: *Vorstellung und Beschreiburg des—so genannten Zwinger Gartens Gebaüden, oder der Königl: Orangerie zu Dresden, in vier und zwanzig kupffer stucken.* Dresden, 1729.

Bibliography

LA TORRE FARFAN : *Fiestas de Sevilla.* Seville, 1672.

(This book has several fine engravings by Valdes Léal (1622-1690), one of the best painters of the school of Seville.)

DON JUAN DIAZ DE TORRES : *Estado y forma que al presente tiene el real nuevo sitio de San Ildefonso.*

DE SOLIS : *La Conquista de Mexico.* Madrid, 1783.

FR. MANOEL DOS SANTOS : *Alcobaca illustrada.* Coimbra, 1710.

DON JUAN DE VERA TASSIS Y VILLAROEL : *Noticias de la enfermedad de Donna Maria Luisa de Borbon.* Madrid, 1690.

(With a plate of the Queen's catafalque designed by Churriguerra and engraved by Ruiz de la Iglesia.)

FRANCISCO XAVIER DE CASTAÑEDA : *Il Trasparente.* Toledo, 1732.

(A poem to the Churriguerresque "Trasparente" in the Cathedral of Toledo.)

P. M. FR. ENRIQUE FLOREZ : *Espana Sagrada.* Madrid, 1750.

JOSEPH TOWNSHEND : *A Journey through Spain in the Years 1786 and 1787.*

ABBÉ DE SAINT-NON : *Voyage Pittoresque au royaume des deux-siciles.* Paris, 1786.

(Excellently written, with vignettes by Fragonard and Hubert Robert.)

BRYDONE : *Travels in Sicily.*

KEPPEL CRAVEN : *Travels in Southern Italy and Calabria.* London, 1827.

Letters from Naples and the Campagna Felice. London, 1815.

(With superb aquatint illustrations by Thomas Rowlandson.)

DANVERS : *The Portuguese Empire in India: its Rise and Decline.* London.

PADRE PEDRO LOZANO : *La Descripcion Geografica del Gran Chaco.* Cordoba, 1733.

(One of the few contemporary Spanish authorities on Jesuit Paraguay.)

Bibliography

GUARINO GUARINI: *Architectura Civile. Opera postuma.* Torino, 1737.

WILLIAM BULLOCK: *Six Months' Residence in Mexico.* London, 1824.

H. G. WARD: *Mexico in 1827.* London, 1828.

Biblioteca de Autores Espanoles, vol. xlvi. Madrid, 1858.

(The funeral discourse on the architect Ventura Rodriguez, by Jovellanos, contains most interesting comments on the Churriguerresque architecture that Rodriguez succeeded in expelling from Spain.)

Printed in the United States
40704LVS00011B/34-45

9 781417 925636